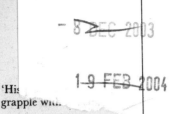

D1388792

'His
grapple with

A Lie of the Mind: 'Strange and hau...
about Oedipal myths, the bizarre nature of r...
America. But its meaning emerges more through its mood than through any
direct statement . . . Sam Shepard's most striking qualities are his charity
and humour. He writes uncensoriously about the weirdest people and
reveals the absurdity of the everyday.' *Guardian*
'Exhilarating . . . a play of penetrating originality.' *New York Times*

States of Shock: 'All Shepard is doing is to connect usually separated
experiences. But such is his theatrical gift that the event develops beyond
derisive comedy and acquires a life of its own in which desert crossfire and
dinner-table bickering coalesce in portraying America.' *Independent on Sunday*
'By turns violent, vulgar, posed, stunningly theatrical . . . *States of Shock* is
also often very funny.' *Independent*

Simpatico: 'Splendid . . . a beautifully developed psychological thriller . . .
like Mamet, Shepard has a gift for spare, edgy speech that combines the
menacing and the comic.' *Daily Telegraph*
'As in any Ibsen play, the past constantly shadows the present. But Shepard
is not primarily concerned with the mechanics of blackmail. What give his
play the status of poetic myth is his concern with lost American values.'
Guardian

Sam Shepard was born in 1943 in Fort Sheridan, Illinois. He moved to
New York from California just as the off-off Broadway theatre scene was
emerging. His first short plays were staged in 1963. He came to London in
1971 (*La Turista* had already been seen at the Theatre Upstairs, 1969), and
his subsequent UK productions include: *The Unseen Hand* (also Theatre
Upstairs, 1973); *Tooth of Crime* (Open Space 1972; Royal Court, 1974);
Geography of a Horsedreamer, directed by Shepard, and *Action* both at the
Theatre Upstairs, 1974); *Curse of the Starving Class* (Royal Court, 1977);
Suicide in B Flat (Open Space, 1977); *Seduced* (Theatre Upstairs, 1980); *Buried
Child* (Hampstead, 1980); *True West* (National Theatre, 1981); *Fool for Love*
(National Theatre, 1985, which he had directed himself in New York); *A Lie
of the Mind* (Royal Court, 1987); *States of Shock* (off-Broadway, 1991;
Salisbury Playhouse, as part of the Royal National Theatre's 'Springboards'
season, 1993); and *Simpatico* (Royal Court, 1995). Eleven of his plays have
won 'Obie' awards. His screenplay for Wim Wenders' *Paris, Texas* won the
Golden Palm Award at the 1984 Cannes Film Festival and he directed his
own screenplay, *Far North*, in 1988. In the spring of 1986, he was admitted to
the American Academy of Arts and Letters. A collection of short stories,
Cruising Paradise, was published in 1996.

SAM SHEPARD

Plays: 3

A Lie of the Mind
States of Shock
Simpatico

Methuen Drama

METHUEN CONTEMPORARY DRAMATISTS

This collection first published in Great Britain in 1996
by Methuen Drama

Methuen Publishing Ltd
215 Vauxhall Bridge Road
London SW1V 1EJ

10 9 8 7 6 5 4 3 2

www.methuen.co.uk

Methuen Publishing Ltd reg. number 3543167

A Lie of the Mind first published in Great Britain by Methuen London in
1987. Copyright © 1986 by Sam Shepard
States of Shock first published in Great Britain by Methuen Drama in 1993
in a volume with *Far North* and *Silent Tongue*. Copyright © 1992, 1993
by Sam Shepard
Simpatico first published in Great Britain by Methuen Drama in 1995 in the Royal
Court Writers series. Copyright © 1995 by Sam Shepard
Collection copyright © 1996 by Sam Shepard

The author has asserted his moral rights

ISBN 0 413 70840 3

A CIP catalogue record for this book is available from the British Library

Grateful acknowledgments are made to the following for permission to reprint previously
published material: *Ludlow Music, Inc.:* 'Goodnight Irene' words
and music by Huddie Ledbetter and John A. Lomax. TRO-© Copyright
1936 (renewed), 1950 (renewed) Ludlow Music, Inc., New York, New York.
Used by permission. *Fisher Music Corporation* and *Lindabet Music*: Excerpt
from 'Good Morning Heartache' by Dan Fisher, Irene Higginbotham, and
Ervin Drake. Reprinted by permission of Fisher Music Corporation and Lindabet
Music, care of Songwriters Guild of America on behalf of Lindabet Music

CONTENTS

CHRONOLOGY
of first performances

	USA	UK
Cowboys	1964	
The Rock Garden	1964	
Up to Thursday	1965	
Dog	1965	
Rocking Chair	1965	
Chicago	1965	1976
Icarus's Mother	1965	1970
4-H Club	1965	
Fourteen Hundred Thousand	1966	
Red Cross	1966	1969
La Turista	1967	1969
Melodrama Play	1967	1967
Forensic & the Navigators	1967	
Cowboys #2	1967	1980
The Holy Ghostly	1969	1973
The Unseen Hand	1969	1973
Operation Sidewinder	1970	
Shaved Splits	1970	
Cowboy Mouth (*with Patti Smith*)	1971	1971
The Mad Dog Blues	1971	1978
Back Bog Beast Bait	1971	
The Tooth of Crime	1972	1972
Blue Bitch (televised 1972)	1973	1975
Nightwalk (*with Megan Terry and Jean-Claude van Itallie*)	1973	1973
Little Ocean		1974
Geography of a Horse Dreamer	1974	1974
Action	1975	1974
Killer's Head	1975	1979
Angel City	1976	1983
Suicide in B Flat	1976	1977
The Sad Lament of Pecos Bill on the Eve of Killing His Wife	1976	

A Lie of the Mind

A PLAY IN THREE ACTS

Dedicated to the memory of L.P.

Something identifies you with the one who leaves you, and it is your common power to return: thus your greatest sorrow.

Something separates you from the one who remains with you, and it is your common slavery to depart: thus your meagerest rejoicing.

—CESAR VALLEJO

. . .

Most were bankrupt small farmers or down-at-the-heel city proletarians, and the rest were mainly chronic nomads of the sort who, a century later, roved the country in caricatures of automobiles. If they started for Kentucky or Ohio, they were presently moving on to Indiana or Illinois, and after that, doggedly and irrationally, to even wilder and less hospitable regions. When they halted, it was simply because they had become exhausted.

—H. L. MENCKEN, *The American Language*

MUSIC NOTES

In the original New York production, which I directed, I had the good fortune to encounter a bluegrass group called the Red Clay Ramblers, out of Chapel Hill, North Carolina. Their musical sensibilities, musicianship, and great repertoire of traditional and original tunes fit the play like a glove. It would be stretching the limitations of this publication to include all the lyrics and music notations that were such an integral part of that production. But working intimately with these musicians, structuring bridges between scenes, underscoring certain monologues, and developing musical "themes" to open and close the acts left me no doubt that this play needs music. Live music. Music with an American backbone.

Since every director must develop his own personal sense of the material he's working on, I will leave the choice of music up to him. All I ask is that there *be* music and that the music serve to support the emotional values discovered by the actors in the course of rehearsal.

I would also like to thank the Red Clay Ramblers for their tremendous contribution to our original production of this play.

—SAM SHEPARD

SET DESCRIPTION

Proscenium oriented but with space played out in front of arch. Deep, wide, dark space with a four-foot-wide ramp extreme upstage, suspended about twelve feet high, stretching from stage right to stage left. When unlit, the ramp should disappear. Extreme downstage right (from actor's p.o.v.) is a platform, set about a foot off the floor, wide enough to accommodate the actors and furniture. The platform continues upstage to about the middle of the stage, then abruptly stops. Center stage is wide open, bare, and left at floor level. The impression should be of infinite space, going off to nowhere. Extreme stage left is another platform, slightly larger than the stage right one and elevated about three feet off floor level. This entire construction of ramp, platforms, and stage floor is fixed and dark in color. In the first act there are no walls to define locations—only furniture and props and light in the bare space. In the second and third acts walls are brought in to delineate the rooms on either side of the stage. Only two walls on each platform, with no ceilings. In the case of the stage-right platform, a wall with a window, extreme stage right. Another wall tying into it, upstage right, running perpendicular to it and with a door in the stage-left side of it. The downstage and stage-left sides of the platform are left open. On the stage-left platform, two more walls set the same way but leaving the downstage and stage-right sides of the platform wide open. An old-style swinging kitchen door is set in the stage-right side of the upstage wall. A window in the stage-left wall.

A Lie of the Mind was first performed at the Promenade Theater in New York on December 5, 1985. It was produced by Lewis Allen and Stephen Graham. The director was Sam Shepard.

The cast was as follows:

JAKE	Harvey Keitel
FRANKIE	Aidan Quinn
BETH	Amanda Plummer
MIKE	Will Patton
LORRAINE	Geraldine Page
SALLY	Karen Young
BAYLOR	James Gammon
MEG	Ann Wedgeworth

A Lie of the Mind received its UK première at the Royal Court Theatre, London, on 20 October 1987 with the following cast:

JAKE	Will Patton
FRANKIE	Paul McGann
BETH	Miranda Richardson
MIKE	Paul Jesson
LORRAINE	Geraldine McEwan
SALLY	Rudi Davies
BAYLOR	Tony Haygarth
MEG	Deborah Horton

Directed by Simon Curtis
Décor by Paul Brown
Music by Stephen Warbeck
Lighting by Christopher Toulain
Sound by Christopher Shutt

Act I

SCENE 1

FRANKIE, *behind audience holding a telephone, talking into it, walking in tight circles, kicking the cord out of his way.* JAKE, *upstage left on suspended platform, suitcase beside him, standing at a blue payphone on highway, talking into it. Pale yellow full moon extreme upstage right center. Impression of huge dark space and distance between the two characters with each one isolated in his own pool of light. Their voices are heard, first in pitch black. The moon comes up very softly as their conversation continues in the dark, then light slowly begins to reveal the two characters.*

FRANKIE: *(In dark)* Jake. Jake? Now, look—Jake? Listen. Just listen to me a second.

(Sound of JAKE *smashing receiver down on payphone.)*

Jake! Don't do that! You're gonna disconnect us again. Listen to me. Gimme the number where you are, okay? Just gimme the number.

JAKE: *(In dark)* There's no number!

FRANKIE: There must be a number.

JAKE: I can't read it!

FRANKIE: Just gimme the number so I can call you back if we get disconnected again.

JAKE: There's no number! It's dark! I can't read in the dark! Whad'ya think I am, an owl or somethin'!

FRANKIE: Okay, okay. Take it easy. Where are you then?

JAKE: Highway 2.

FRANKIE: What state?

JAKE: Some state. I don't know. They're all the same up here.

FRANKIE: Try to think.

JAKE: I don't need to think! I know! *(Pause)* You shoulda seen her face, Frankie. You shoulda seen it.

FRANKIE: Beth?

JAKE: I never even seen it comin'. I shoulda known. Why didn't I see it comin'. I been good for so long.

FRANKIE: Just try not to think about it for right now, Jake. Okay? Just try to let go of the thought of it.

JAKE: It's not a thought. Don't gimme that Zen shit.

FRANKIE: The picture then. Whatever—

JAKE: It's not a picture either! It's her. I see her. She's right here with me now!

FRANKIE: She's there?

JAKE: She's here! She's right here!

FRANKIE: Beth's there with you?

(JAKE smashes down on receiver again. Pools of light up now on BOTH of them. Moon full.)

Jake! Stop doing that, will ya! Just take it easy. Jake? You still there? (Pause) Jake! Don't hang up on me.

(Pause)

JAKE: She's not gonna pull outa this one, Frankie. She's not gonna. I saw her face. It was bad this time. Real bad.

FRANKIE: What happened?

JAKE: All red and black and blue.

FRANKIE: Oh, Jake—God. What'd you do?

JAKE: I never even saw it comin', Frankie. I never did. How come that is? How come?

FRANKIE: Where is she now?

JAKE: She's dead!

(Pause)

FRANKIE: What?

JAKE: She's dead!

(JAKE puts receiver down softly and hangs up this time.)

FRANKIE: Jake! Jake! Goddamnit!

(FRANKIE slams his receiver down. Blackout. Moon stays full.)

SCENE 2

BETH's *voice is heard in blackout almost overlapping* FRANKIE's *last line. Lights up fast on* BETH *downstage left as she sits up straight with a jerk as though awakened by a nightmare. She is in a white hospital bed covered with a sheet. She wears a blue hospital smock. Her head is wrapped in bandages. Her face badly bruised, eyes black and blue. Her brother,* MIKE, *stands behind her upstage of bed, arm around her shoulder, stroking her back. She tries to speak but no words come, just short punctuated sounds at the end of her rapid exhales.*

BETH: Saah—thah—Jaah—thuh—saah—saah—saah—saah—

   (Continues under.)

MIKE: *(Stroking her back)* Don't talk, Beth. You don't have to talk. It's all right, honey.

   *(*BETH *discovers bandage on her head and starts to rip it off. It starts to come apart in long streamers of gauze.* MIKE *tries to stop her but she continues tearing the bandage off.)*

BETH: *(As she rips off bandage)* Ghaah—ghaah—khaah— khaah—khaah—

   (Continues)

MIKE: No, leave that on. Leave it, Beth. You're supposed to leave it on for a while. Don't take that off.

BETH: *(Still pulling bandage off)* Am I a mummy now? Am I a mummy? Am I? Am I now?

MIKE: It's just a bandage.

BETH: *(Rapid speech; it gushes out of her)* You tell them, I'm not dead. You go tell them. Tell them now. Go tell them. Dig me up. Tell them dig me up now. I'm not in here. They can't wait for me now.

MIKE: Beth, it's all right.

BETH: Are they above us now? How deep are we in here? How deep?

MIKE: It's okay.

BETH: They leave you here to bring me back? Did they leave you?

MIKE: It's a hospital, Beth.

BETH: Iza toomb! Iza toomb! You tell them I'm not dead! Go tell them!

MIKE: Beth, it's okay. You got hurt but you're gonna be all right now.

BETH: Did they bury me in a tree? A tribe? Did they?

(MIKE *holds her firmly by the shoulders. Pause.* BETH *feels her head.)*

Whaaza plase where I fell? Who fell me?

MIKE: *(Holding her)* You're okay.

(Both BETH's *arms shoot straight up above her head. She holds them there stiffly.)*

BETH: *(Screams, holds her arms up)* WHO FELL ME!!!

MIKE: *(Trying to bring her arms down to her sides)* Beth. I'm with you now. I'll take care of you. Do you recognize me? You know who I am?

(BETH *stares at him, slowly relaxes her arms, brings them back down to her sides.* MIKE *strokes her back softly.)*

BETH: Yore the dog. Yore the dog they send.

MIKE: I'm Mike. I'm your brother.

BETH: Mike the dog.

(She spits in his face. Pause.)

MIKE: I'm gonna stay with you now.

BETH: You gant take in me. You gant take me back.

MIKE: I'm not going to take you anywhere. We'll stay right here until you're all better.

BETH: Who fell me here?

MIKE: Don't worry about that.

BETH: Who fell me? Iza—Iza name? Iza name to come. Itz— Itz— Inza man. Inza—name. Aall—aall—all—a love. A love.

MIKE: Don't try to talk, Beth. You just need some rest now.

BETH: *(Soft)* Heez with you?

MIKE: No.

BETH: Heez—

MIKE: He's gone now. He's not around. Don't worry about him. He's nowhere near here.

BETH: Don' leeve me.

MIKE: I won't, honey. I promise. I'll stay right here with you.

(Pause)

BETH: *(Soft, weeping)* Whaaz he gone?

MIKE: He's far away. He won't hurt you now.

BETH: Heez—

MIKE: Just try to get some sleep now, honey. Try to get some sleep.

BETH: Heez gone.

(Lights fade. Moon stays full but turns pale green.)

SCENE 3

Soft orange light up on stage-right platform, revealing small ragged motel couch with a floor lamp beside it. Main light source emanating from lamp. A wooden chair opposite couch. JAKE's *suitcase on floor with clothes spilled out of it.* JAKE *sits in middle of couch, legs apart, slouched forward, holding his head in his hands.* FRANKIE *stands behind couch with a plastic bag full of ice, trying to apply it to the back of* JAKE's *neck.* JAKE *keeps pushing the ice away.*

JAKE: *(Shoving ice away)* I don't want any goddamn ice! It's cold!

FRANKIE: I thought it might help.

JAKE: Well, it don't. It's cold.

FRANKIE: I know it's cold. It's ice. It's supposed to be cold.

(Pause)

(FRANKIE goes to chair. Sits. Silence between them for a while.)

You didn't actually kill her, did ya, Jake?

(JAKE stays seated. Starts slow, low, deliberate.)

JAKE: She was goin' to these goddamn rehearsals every day. Every day. Every single day. Hardly ever see her. I saw enough though. Believe you me. Saw enough to know somethin' was goin' on.

FRANKIE: But you didn't really kill her, did ya?

JAKE: *(Builds)* I'm no dummy. Doesn't take much to put it together. Woman starts dressin' more and more skimpy every time she goes out. Starts puttin' on more and more smells. Oils. She was always oiling herself before she went out. Every morning. Smell would wake me up. Coconut or Butterscotch or some goddamn thing. Sweet stuff. Youda thought she was an ice-cream sundae. I'd watch her oiling herself while I pretended to be asleep. She was in a dream, the way she did it. Like she was imagining someone else touching her. Not me. Never me. Someone else.

FRANKIE: Who?

JAKE: *(Stands, moves around space, gains momentum)* Some guy. I don't know. Some actor-jerk. I knew she was gettin' herself ready for him. I could tell. Got worse and worse. When I finally called her on it she denied it flat. I knew she was lying too. Could tell it right away. The way she took it so light. Tried to cast it off like it was nothin'. Then she starts tellin' me it's all in *my* head. Some imaginary deal I'd cooked up in *my* head. Had nothin' to do with her, she said. Made me try to believe I was crazy. She's all innocent and I'm crazy. So I told her—I told her—I laid it on the line to her. Square business. I says—no more high heels! No more wearin' them high spiky high heels to rehearsals. No more a' that shit. And she laughs. Right to my face. She laughs. Kept puttin' 'em on. Every mornin'. Puttin' 'em back on. She says it's right for the part. Made her feel like the character she says. Then I told her she had to wear a bra and she paid no attention to that either. You could see right through her damn blouse. Right clean through it. And she never wore underpants either. That's what really got me. No underpants. You could see everything.

FRANKIE: Well, she never wore underpants anyway, did she?

(JAKE stops, turns to FRANKIE. FRANKIE stays in chair. Pause.)

JAKE: How do you know?

FRANKIE: No, I mean—I think you told me once.

JAKE: *(Moving slowly toward FRANKIE)* I never told you that. I never woulda told you a thing like that. That's personal.

FRANKIE: *(Backing up)* No, I think you did once—when you were drunk or somethin'.

JAKE: *(Close to FRANKIE)* I never woulda told you that!

FRANKIE: All right.

(Pause)

JAKE: I never talked about her that way to anybody.

FRANKIE: Okay. Forget it. Just forget it.

JAKE: You always liked her, didn't you, Frankie? Don't think I overlooked that.

FRANKIE: Are you gonna finish tellin' me what happened? 'Cause if you're not I'm gonna take a walk right outa here.

(Pause. JAKE considers, then launches back into the story.)

JAKE: *(Returns to speed, moves)* Okay. Then she starts readin' the lines with me, at night. In bed. Readin' the lines. I'm helpin' her out, right? Helpin' her memorize the damn lines so she can run off every morning and say 'em to some other guy. Day after day. Same lines. And these lines are all about how she's bound and determined to get this guy back in the sack with her after all these years he's been ignoring her. How she still loves him even though he hates her. How she's saving her body up for him and him only.

FRANKIE: Well, it was just a play, wasn't it?

JAKE: Yeah, a play. That's right. Just a play. "Pretend." That's what she said. "Just pretend." I know what they were doing! I know damn well what they were doin'! I know what that acting shit is all about. They try to "believe" they're the person. Right? Try to believe so hard they're the person that they actually think they become the person. So you know what that means don't ya?

FRANKIE: What?

JAKE: They start doin' all the same stuff the person does!

FRANKIE: What person?

JAKE: The person! The—whad'ya call it? The—

FRANKIE: Character?

JAKE: Yeah. The character. That's right. They start acting that way in
real life. Just like the character. Walkin' around—talkin' that
way. You shoulda seen the way she started to walk and talk. I
couldn't believe it. Changed her hair and everything. Put a wig
on. Changed her clothes. Everything changed. She was un-
recognizable. I didn't even know who I was with anymore. I told
her. I told her, look—"I don't know who you think you are now
but I'd just as soon you come on back to the real world here."
And you know what she tells me?

FRANKIE: What?

JAKE: She tells me this is the real world. This acting shit is more real
than the real world to her. Can you believe that? And she was
tryin' to convince me that *I* was crazy?

(Pause)

FRANKIE: So you think she was sleeping with this guy just because she
was playing a part in a play?

JAKE: Yeah. She was real dedicated.

FRANKIE: Are you sure? I mean when would she have time to do that
in rehearsals?

JAKE: On her lunch break.

FRANKIE: *(Stands)* Oh, come on, Jake.

JAKE: Sit down! Sit back down. I got more to tell you.

FRANKIE: No! I'm not gonna sit down! I came to try to help you out
and all you're tellin' me is a bunch of bullshit about Beth
screwing around with some other guy on her lunch break?

JAKE: She was! It's easy to tell when a woman gets obsessed with somethin' else. When she moves away from you. They don't hide it as easy as men.

FRANKIE: She was just trying to do a good job.

JAKE: That's no job! I've had jobs before. I know what a job is. A job is where you work. A job is where you don't have fun. You don't dick around tryin' to pretend you're somebody else. You work. Work is work!

FRANKIE: It's a different kind of a job.

JAKE: It's an excuse to fool around! That's what it is. That's why she wanted to become an actress in the first place. So she could get away from me.

FRANKIE: You can't jump to that kind of conclusion just because she was—

JAKE: I didn't jump to nothin'! I knew what she was up to even if she didn't.

FRANKIE: So, you mean you're accusing her of somethin' she wasn't even aware of?

JAKE: She was aware all right. She was tryin' to hide it from me but she wasn't that good an actress.

(Pause)

FRANKIE: So you beat her up again. Boy, I'm tellin' you—

JAKE: I killed her.

(Pause)

FRANKIE: You killed her.

JAKE: That's right.

FRANKIE: She stopped breathing?

JAKE: Everything stopped.

FRANKIE: You checked?

JAKE: I didn't have to check.

FRANKIE: She might've just been unconscious or something.

JAKE: No.

FRANKIE: Well, what'd you do? Did you tell the police?

JAKE: Why would I do that? She`was already dead. What could they do about it?

FRANKIE: That's what you're supposed to do when somebody dies. You report it to the police.

JAKE: Even when you kill 'em?

FRANKIE: Yeah! Even when you kill them. Especially when you kill them!

JAKE: I never heard a' that.

(Pause)

FRANKIE: Well, somebody should check up on it. I mean this is pretty serious stuff, Jake.

JAKE: I done my time for her. I already done my time.

FRANKIE: She had nothin' to do with that. She never did.

JAKE: She got me in trouble more'n once. She did it on purpose too. Always flirtin' around. Always carryin' on.

FRANKIE: She had nothin' to do with it! You lost your temper.

JAKE: She provoked it!

FRANKIE: You've always lost your temper and blamed it on some-body else. Even when you were a kid you blamed it on somebody else. One time you even blamed it on a goat. I remember that.

(Pause. JAKE stops.)

JAKE: What goat?

FRANKIE: That milk goat we had.

JAKE: What was her name?

FRANKIE: I forget.

JAKE: What was that goat's name?

FRANKIE: You remember that goat?

JAKE: Yeah, I remember that goat. I loved that goat.

FRANKIE: Well you kicked the shit out of that goat you loved so much when she stepped on your bare feet while you were tryin' to milk her. You remember that? Broke her ribs.

JAKE: I never kicked that goat!

FRANKIE: Oh, you don't remember that huh? You broke your damn foot you kicked her so hard.

JAKE: What was that goat's name?

(JAKE *suddenly falls to the floor, collapses.* FRANKIE *goes to him. Tries to help him.*)

Get away from me!

FRANKIE: What happened?

JAKE: Just get away!

FRANKIE: You all right?

JAKE: Somethin's wrong. My head's funny.

FRANKIE: *(Trying to help* JAKE *up)* Come on, let's get you back on the couch.

JAKE: *(Pushing* FRANKIE *away, crawls on knees toward couch)* I don't need any help!

FRANKIE: You feel dizzy or something?

JAKE: *(Crawling to couch)* Yeah. All of a sudden. Everything's—

FRANKIE: You want me to get you something?

JAKE: *(Climbing up on couch and lying on his belly)* No. I don't need nothin'.

FRANKIE: You want me to get a doctor for you?

JAKE: I'm gonna die without her. I know I'm gonna die.

(Pause)

FRANKIE: I could go to her folks' place. They'd know what happened to her.

JAKE: No! You stay away from there! Don't go anywhere near there. I'm through chasin' after her.

FRANKIE: Somebody's gotta find out, Jake. Sooner or later.

(Pause. JAKE speaks in a whisper, almost to himself. His whole tone changes. Very vulnerable, as though questioning a ghost.)

JAKE: Now. Why now? Why am I missing her now, Frankie? Why not then? When she was there? Why am I afraid I'm gonna lose her when she's already gone? And this fear—this fear swarms through me—floods my whole body till there's nothing left. Nothing left of me. And then it turns— It turns to a fear for my whole life. Like my whole life is lost from losing her. Gone. That I'll die like this. Lost. Just lost.

FRANKIE: It's okay, Jake.

JAKE: You liked her too, didn't you, Frankie?

FRANKIE: Yeah. I liked her.

(Pause)

JAKE: My back's like ice. How come my back's so cold?

FRANKIE: *(Moves right)* I'll get you a blanket.

JAKE: No! Don't leave.

FRANKIE: *(Stops)* All right.

(Pause)

You okay?

JAKE: Yeah. Just sit with me for a while. Stay here.

FRANKIE: *(Goes to chair, pulls it near couch)* Okay.

(FRANKIE sits in chair next to couch. JAKE stays on his belly, arm hanging limply over the side of couch, hand touching the floor.)

JAKE: Don't leave.

FRANKIE: I won't.

(Lights dim to black.)

SCENE 4

Lights up extreme left on MIKE *trying to help* BETH *walk. Her arm is around his neck. His arm around her waist and the other hand holding her hand. Her legs are very weak and keep going out from under her periodically. Sometimes he reaches down and moves one of her legs forward when she appears too weak to move. She stops now and then, breathing hard from the effort. She watches her bare feet the whole time, then once in a while her head jerks up and stares at the ceiling, then back down to her feet again—similar to the head movements of a blind person. The two of them keep struggling to walk in circles like this as they speak.* BETH's *voice now is very childlike and small.*

BETH: *(As she walks)* You won' hurd him, Mige. Yera kineness. Alla kineness. In for nah to me. Fine I kim it.

MIKE: *(Helping her walk)* Just try to keep moving. That's it. You're doing great.

BETH: Yera kineness, Mige. I'm onah too. Fo fo nahchoo. Inah laan tobit. In a laan.

MIKE: Try to pay attention to walking, honey. Just walking. You don't have to talk now. Doctor said that would come later. Slow. You don't have to worry about that now.

BETH: Jess walk. No makin' fan tat. Sant. Sant. *(She giggles.)*

MIKE: That's right.

BETH: Jess step. Ah kahn tah.

MIKE: Take it slow.

BETH: You won' hurd them. You won'. Nah can't a chile. A chile. Ah chile. *(Like "child")* You can hurd him, Mige. Hee a chile. Both.

MIKE: Don't think about him now. We'll worry about him later. Right now you just have to get strong. You have to learn how to walk first.

BETH: Heez nah weak. He bash me. *(She giggles.)* Bash me goot.

MIKE: *(Hard)* DON'T THINK ABOUT HIM!

(BETH stops, clasps her arms across her chest and folds completely forward. Her head drops. She starts to weep.)

(MIKE hugs her, trying to straighten her up.)

Beth, I'm sorry. I'm sorry. I—I just want you to concentrate so you can get better. That's all. Okay? I'm sorry. I want you to walk so we can take you home. You understand? Mom and Dad want to see you. Don't you want to get better?

(BETH shakes her head defiantly, stays folded up.)

Don't you want to get back home?

(Suddenly BETH pulls away from MIKE, takes a few steps on her own and falls. MIKE goes to her fast and picks her back up on her feet.)

BETH: *(Savage)* NO! DON' TUSH ME!

MIKE: *(Holding her up as she struggles)* I have to hold you up, Beth, or you'll fall over.

BETH: DON' TUSH ME! I won' fall! I won'.

MIKE: All right. If you want to stand on your own, that's great.

BETH: I won'.

MIKE: Okay.

(MIKE cautiously lets go of her and stands back a couple steps, ready to catch her if she topples. BETH just stands there for a while staring at her feet. She sways slightly from side to side.)

BETH: *(Quietly, staring at her feet)* I'm above my feet. Way above. Inah—I cah—

MIKE: Can you take a step?

BETH: How high me? How high—up?

MIKE: Try to take a step, Beth.

BETH: How high? Did they bury me in a tree?

MIKE: Try taking a step.

BETH: *(Abrupt, jerks her head toward MIKE)* You! You ztep.

(Pause)

MIKE: You want me to take a step?

BETH: *(Staying in the same place)* You ztep.

MIKE: If I take a step, will you take one?

BETH: You!

MIKE: All right.

(MIKE takes a step. BETH laughs. Stays in place.)

What's so funny?

BETH: You ztep. Fan tak. You.

MIKE: You want to try?

BETH: No! You.

MIKE: I just took one. Now it's your turn.

BETH: *(Clearly, rage)* I'M NOT A BABY! I'M NOT!

(Pause)

MIKE: I know you're not, Beth. I just want you to try to take a step. That's all.

BETH: NO!

(Pause as BETH stands there, rooted to the spot, but still swaying slightly.)

MIKE: Well, what're you gonna do, just stand there?

BETH: *(Fast, very clear, mimicking him exactly)* Well, what're you gonna do, just stand there?

MIKE: *(Moving closer to her)* Beth.

BETH: *(Screams)* DON' TUSH ME!

(MIKE stops. Stands off from her. BETH stays still, swaying, staring down at her feet. Pause.)

MIKE: I'm just trying to help you out.

(Pause. BETH's head jerks up. She stares at ceiling and stays.)

BETH: Hee killed us both.

MIKE: *(Moves toward her, then stops)* You're not dead, Beth. You're going to be all right.

BETH: *(Fierce, jerks her head toward MIKE)* I'M DEAD! DEAD! DAAAAH! HEEZ TOO.

MIKE: You gotta forget about him for now! You gotta just forget about him!

BETH: NAAH! You gan' stop my head. Nobody! Nobody stop my head. My head is me. Heez in me. You gan stop him in me. Nobody gan stop him in me.

MIKE: This guy tried to kill you! How can you still want a man who tried to kill you! What's the matter with you! He's the one who did this to you!

BETH: HEEZ MY HAAAAAAAAAAAAAAAART!!!

(Blackout. Moon stays green and full.)

SCENE 5

Lights up fast down right. Same props as Scene 3. Couch and lamp, suitcase, clothes, etc. But now more of the area is lit in front and to the sides of the couch with the couch remaining in very dim light. Just able to make out the shape of JAKE *lying belly down still, with his face turned away from audience, covered with blanket, arm still dangling out over the side.* FRANKIE, *his sister,* SALLY, *and their mother,* LORRAINE, *enter fast from upstage right of platform and cross down center into middle neutral territory. Scene is played out down center for a while.*

FRANKIE: *(On the move, entering from up right)* Just try to keep your voice down, Mom. This is the first time he's slept since I've seen him.

LORRAINE: Don't be so damn bossy.

FRANKIE: Well, he hasn't slept.

LORRAINE: I just wanna take a look at him is all.

SALLY: Mom—

FRANKIE: He's not lookin' too good right now, Mom.

LORRAINE: What'sa matter with him?

FRANKIE: He's lost a whole bunch of weight.

LORRAINE: Well, I'll make him up a batch a' that cream of broccoli soup. That'll put the weight back on him. That's his favorite.

FRANKIE: He won't eat.

LORRAINE: Whad'ya mean he won't eat. That boy'll eat the paint off a plate if you let him. Whad'ya been feedin' him?

FRANKIE: He's in big trouble, Mom.

LORRAINE: So what's new? Name a day he wasn't in trouble. He was trouble from day one. Fell on his damn head the second he was born. Slipped right through the doctor's fingers. That's where it all started. Back there. Had nothin' to do with his upbringing.

SALLY: Mom, just listen to Frankie a second. He's tryin' to tell you somethin'.

LORRAINE: I am listenin' but I'm not hearin' no revelations! What's the story here? My boy's sick. I'll make him some soup. We'll take him out to the Drive-In. Everything's gonna be fine. What's the big deal here?

SALLY: Mom! Jake might've killed Beth! That's what's goin' on. All right?

(Pause)

LORRAINE: Who's Beth?

(Pause)

SALLY: Oh, my God. Jake's wife. Beth. You remember her? Beth? Little, skinny Beth?

LORRAINE: Never heard a' her.

SALLY: Mom—Mom, you don't remember Beth?

LORRAINE: No. Why should I? I don't keep track of his bimbos.

SALLY: Great.

FRANKIE: We're not really sure about it yet, Mom. I mean—he's pretty emotional about the whole thing.

LORRAINE: He's an emotional boy. Always has been.

SALLY: He's not a boy. He's a big grown-up man and he might have killed his wife!

LORRAINE: He wasn't fit to live with anybody to begin with! I don't know why he ever tried it. Woman who lives with a man like that deserves to be killed. She deserves it.

FRANKIE: All right, knock it off! Both a' you! We gotta think about this thing now. Jake's the one who's in trouble here, okay? He's in bad shape. You understand that? He's in real bad shape. Every day he's gettin' worse.

SALLY: He's not gonna die or anything—

LORRAINE: My boy ain't gonna die. I'm goin' in there right now and nobody's gonna stop me.

(LORRAINE *moves directly onto stage-right platform toward the couch and* JAKE, *pushing past* FRANKIE, *who makes no attempt to stop her. Lights rise on couch now, equal to the rest of area. She stops beside couch and swats* JAKE *hard on the rump.* JAKE *doesn't move.* FRANKIE *and* SALLY *follow her onto platform.*)

Jake? Jake, it's your mother. Sit up, boy. Sit up and lemme take a look at your tongue. Come on, now. Sit up and face me.

(JAKE *rolls over slowly, facing out toward audience now. His face is pale white, eyes sunken and dark, radically changed from the last time he was seen.* LORRAINE *steps back.* FRANKIE *and* SALLY *move into couch area with* LORRAINE.)

(*To* FRANKIE)

What in the hell's he got? He looks like death warmed over.

SALLY: Jake?

(JAKE *just stares at them.*)

LORRAINE: *(To* JAKE*)* Your brother here's been tryin' to tell us that you're gonna pass on us. Now quit the shenanigans and sit up. Jake? Are you hearin' me?

SALLY: Just leave him be, Mom.

LORRAINE: He's just playacting. Used to do this all the time when he didn't get his own way. Mope around for days like a cocker spaniel. Got so bad sometimes I finally had to take a bucket a' ice cold rainwater and throw it right in his damn face. That worked every time. Maybe that's what we oughta do right now. *(To* FRANKIE*)* You got a bucket?

FRANKIE: I don't think rainwater's gonna do it, Mom. He's had the chills for three days now. He just shakes all through the night. Talks to himself and shakes.

LORRAINE: It's all pretend. He just wants some attention, that's all.

*(*SALLY *moves closer to* JAKE. *He smiles at her.)*

SALLY: Jake? You feelin' any better?

JAKE: *(Soft, loving)* How'd you ever get to be so beautiful?

SALLY: *(Short laugh)* You never used to think that when we were kids. Least you never admitted it. You always called me the Crayfish. You remember?

JAKE: *(Slow, slurred)* We were never gonna be apart.

SALLY: Jake, you know who I am, don't ya?

JAKE: We were gonna be tied together. *(Laughs.)* You remember when I tied you to me. That one night. You tried sneakin' off on me. In my sleep. Couldn't do it, could ya? Couldn't. Had you tied.

LORRAINE: *(Moving to* FRANKIE, *taking him aside so* JAKE *can't hear. To* FRANKIE*)* Has he been drinkin' or somethin'?

FRANKIE: No, I wouldn't buy him a bottle. Are you kidding?

LORRAINE: Well don't. Not unless you want someone else killed.

FRANKIE: I'm not gonna.

LORRAINE: Every time he gets near liquor he thinks it's his God-given duty to keep pace with his old man.

FRANKIE: I know that.

LORRAINE: Don't you dare buy him a bottle.

FRANKIE: I won't!

(JAKE reaches out suddenly and grabs SALLY by the wrist. She pulls back but his grip is powerful.)

SALLY: Jake, come on!

LORRAINE: *(Moving back to JAKE, to JAKE)* You let go a' yer sister!

JAKE: *(To SALLY, keeping hold of her wrist)* I was sure—I was so damn sure we both had the same idea. I was sure a' that.

SALLY: *(Pulling back slightly but caught)* I'm Sally, Jake. Your sister. Sally. Now let go a' me, all right?

LORRAINE: He knows who you are. Don't you believe for one minute that he don't know who you are. *(Approaching JAKE.)* You know who she is, now let go of her! Let go of her right now.

JAKE: You never did see me, did ya, Beth? Just had a big wild notion about some dream life up ahead. Somebody who was gonna save yer ass.

(JAKE starts to bear down on SALLY's wrist now and drags her closer to him.)

SALLY: *(Scared, struggling to get free)* I'm not Beth, Jake! Let go a' me. Let go a' me! You're hurtin' me!

LORRAINE: Let go a' your sister!

(LORRAINE takes off one of her shoes, charges JAKE and starts belting him over the head with it. JAKE keeps hold of SALLY's wrist. FRANKIE moves in and pulls LORRAINE away from JAKE from behind. She starts to beat FRANKIE with the shoe now.)

JAKE: *(To* SALLY*)* I'm gonna let go a' you! I'm gonna let go a' you
    once and for all!

(JAKE drops SALLY*'s wrist.* SALLY *backs away fast, rubbing her wrist.*
JAKE's arm falls limply to the floor again. His eyes close. He goes
unconscious. LORRAINE *stops beating* FRANKIE *with the shoe.* FRANKIE
lets go of her. They all stare at JAKE.*)*

LORRAINE: That boy's a maniac. Always has been. *(Pause)* What's he
    doin' now?

FRANKIE: He's out again. He goes in and out like that. All through the
    day. I don't know what's goin' on with him.

SALLY: He's crazy. He's just plain crazy.

LORRAINE: We gotta get him outa here. He's just goin' to seed in this
    dump. It's this place that's doin' it to him.

SALLY: We can't keep him at home, Mom.

LORRAINE: Why not? That's where he belongs. He belongs home.

SALLY: He's dangerous! That's why!

LORRAINE: He's dyin' here.

SALLY: He needs a doctor.

LORRAINE: He needs us is what he needs.

FRANKIE: If you could take him for a couple days, Mom, I could get
    back and find out what happened with Beth. You think you
    could do that? I just need a couple a' days. I gotta find out for
    sure what's goin' on.

LORRAINE: I'm gonna take him on a permanent basis. I'm not even
    gonna let him outa his room for a solid year. Maybe that'll teach
    him.

SALLY: What if he hurts somebody? He's liable to do anything in the
    state he's in.

LORRAINE: He's not gonna hurt us. We're related. Look at him. He's just a big baby. That's all he is. He's not gonna hurt us. Strangers he'll hurt. Strange women. Outsiders he'll hurt. That's guaranteed. But not us. He knows us.

SALLY: Mom, if you bring him in that house—I'm leavin'.

LORRAINE: Then leave, girl. This is my boy here.

(Blackout)

SCENE 6

Lights up left. BETH's *bed upstage in very dim light, just able to make out her form lying with her face turned away from audience, almost the identical position and attitude of sleep as* JAKE *in previous scene. A small fold-out hospital screen in front of bed that can be seen through. The perimeters of the area are more fully lit, revealing* MIKE, *his mother,* MEG, *and his father,* BAYLOR, *downstage.*

BAYLOR: What do ya mean, "brain damage"? How can they prove somethin' like that?

MIKE: She had an X-ray, Dad. They're not sure how bad it is yet. She's having a lot of trouble talking.

BAYLOR: She gone crazy, or what?

MIKE: No. She's had an injury to the brain. You understand? Doesn't mean it's permanent. Doesn't mean she's crazy either.

BAYLOR: Well, what the hell does it mean then? "Injury to the brain" sounds like a permanent situation to me.

MEG: Oh my goodness. How in the world could a thing like this ever happen?

MIKE: I told you, Mom. Jake beat her up. He beat the shit out of her.

BAYLOR: Watch your language.

MEG: Who's Jake?

MIKE: Her husband, Mom. Jake.

MEG: Oh.

MIKE: You remember Jake, don't ya?

MEG: Wasn't he the son of those people we don't talk to anymore?

MIKE: Yeah. That's right.

BAYLOR: Bunch a' Okies. Don't surprise me one bit.

MEG: I think I do remember him.

MIKE: You were there at the wedding.

MEG: I was?

BAYLOR: I wasn't.

MIKE: *(To BAYLOR)* No, you stayed away. You made a point a' that.

BAYLOR: I was fishin'.

MEG: I think I do remember that. There was cars all over the place. Lots of cars. I kept wondering how come they had to park on the lawn. Why'd they have to do that?

MIKE: I don't know, Mom.

MEG: Wasn't there a parking lot or anything?

BAYLOR: Well, when're we gonna be able to see her?

MIKE: She's sleeping right now.

BAYLOR: Well, wake her up. We drove all the way down here from Billings just to see her. Now wake her up.

MIKE: I wish you'd have called me or something before you came down.

BAYLOR: Why should I call you?

MIKE: She's having a kind of a rough time right now, Dad. She needs a lot of rest.

BAYLOR: Listen, I got two mules settin' out there in the parkin' lot I gotta deliver by midnight. I'm supposed to be at the sale by six tomorrow mornin' and those mules have to be in the stalls by midnight tonight.

MIKE: You brought mules down here?

BAYLOR: Yeah. Why not? Might as well do a little business long as I'm gonna be down in this country anyway. That all right by you?

MEG: They made so much noise. I was so embarrassed once we hit the city. Felt like such a hick. There we are pulling mules in an open trailer and everyone's staring at us like we made a wrong turn or something.

BAYLOR: Looks like we did make a wrong turn if we can't even see our own daughter. What's the story here, anyway? They got her locked up or something?

MIKE: This is a hospital, Dad. They don't lock you up in a hospital.

BAYLOR: Oh, they don't huh.

MEG: They locked me up once, didn't they, Dad?

BAYLOR: That wasn't you. That was your mother.

MEG: Oh.

BAYLOR: That was a long time ago, anyhow.

MEG: It wasn't me?

MIKE: Maybe we could go down to the cafeteria and have some coffee or something. She might be awake by the time we get back.

BAYLOR: I ain't gonna drink any a' that damn hospital coffee. And I'm not talkin' to no doctors either. I wanna see my daughter!

MIKE: You don't have to talk to any doctors.

BAYLOR: I didn't come all the way down here to be made a fool of in front of a bunch a' college boys.

MIKE: Nobody's interested in making a fool out of you, Dad. Beth's sick. She needs attention. And everybody here is doing the best they can for her.

BAYLOR: Well, that sounds like ya don't need us then. Sounds like you got all the bases covered here. Come on, Meg, let's head back home then.

(BAYLOR takes MEG by the elbow)

MEG: Well, we just got here, didn't we?

BAYLOR: I gotta get those mules out to the fairgrounds. Now let's go. We're wastin' our time here.

MIKE: Dad, wait a second. There's no reason to get offended.

BAYLOR: I'm not offended! What the hell, I'm just a dumb rancher. What do I know? I don't know the first damn thing about "brain damage." They got specialists for that. Ain't that right? They got boys back there with diplomas tall as a man. What am I supposed to know about it?

MIKE: If you can just wait—if you can just stay for an hour or so—

BAYLOR: I can't wait. I got stock to feed. Now let's go, Meg.

MIKE: Well, then, let Mom stay with me. Beth needs to see her. I'll bring her back home in a few days.

MEG: That would be nice.

(Pause)

BAYLOR: Where's she supposed to stay?

MIKE: She can stay with me.

BAYLOR: *(To MIKE)* How're you gonna watch out for her and your sister both. That's more'n one man can handle. More'n two men can handle.

MIKE: It's not that big a problem. They've got nurses here.

BAYLOR: You're gonna drive all the way back north with her? You're gonna wanna do that? Bring her all the way back up north?

MIKE: Just let me worry about it, okay?

BAYLOR: Well, what am I supposed to do, talk to myself all the way back home? That's a five-hundred-mile truck trip.

MEG: They got good radio between here and Billings, Dad.

BAYLOR: Good radio? All they got is that Eddie Jackrabbit. You call that music.

MEG: I liked it.

BAYLOR: All right. All right. *(To* MEG*)* You wanna stay?

MEG: I'd like to.

BAYLOR: All right. *(To* MIKE*)* How many days you think it'll be?

MIKE: Two or three.

MEG: I'll be fine, Baylor.

BAYLOR: You'll be fine. You'll be fine. Sure. All right. I'll go out and get your jacket out of the truck. Be right back.

MEG: I won't need it.

BAYLOR: *(As he exits)* You'll need it. You always need it.

(BAYLOR *exits.* MEG *turns and smiles at* MIKE.)

MEG: He's right.

(BETH *suddenly rolls over facing audience. Spotlight on her face. The rest of her body in dim light.)*

BETH: Mom?

(Blackout)

SCENE 7

Lights up upstage right. JAKE, *propped up with pillows, facing audience in a single bed that's now too short for him. He's in boxer underwear and a sleeveless T-shirt now and covered with an old Mexican blanket. Face even whiter than before, sunken eyes, hair slicked back as if he's just had a shower. Plastic model airplanes covered in dust and cobwebs of World War Two fighters and bombers hang from the ceiling directly above the bed.* LORRAINE *sits beside him on a chair stage left of bed, spoon-feeding him from a bowl of her cream of broccoli soup.* JAKE *refuses to eat.*

LORRAINE: *(Holding spoon of soup at his mouth)* Here now, come on. Just try a sip. That's all I'm askin'. Just a simple sip. I'm not askin' for the whole bowl. We'll work up to that slow. Just a little tiny old sip for now. Jake? *(Harder)* Sit up here and drink this soup! I'm sick of babyin' you. This is your favorite. Cream of broccoli. I made it special in the blender.

(Pause. JAKE *refuses soup.)*

I don't know why in the world you insist on gettin' so worked up over a woman. Look at you. I have never in my life seen you lookin' so let-down. You musta lost a good thirty, forty pounds. A woman ain't worth that kind of a loss. Believe you me. There's more pretty girls than one in this world. Not that she was such a looker. I can't even remember what she looked like to tell you the truth, but she couldn'ta been all that great. You'll find someone else sooner or later. You're a strong, strappin' man yet. Got a little age on you now but that don't matter when you got a strong frame. Your daddy was still lookin' good at the age of sixty, even though the bottle had walked across his face a few times over. His face was a mess, I'll admit that. I'll be the first to admit that. But he still had that big stout frame on him, just like you got. Still managed to twirl my ticket, I'll tell ya that much. Somebody's bound to come along, just dyin' to be encircled by them big bony arms. Don't you worry about that one bit. Now, come on, just try this soup. Just do me a little favor, all right? Do you want me to play helicopter with it like we used to?

(She raises the spoon of soup over his head and starts making helicopter sounds as JAKE *watches the spoon from below.)*

LORRAINE: *(In a pinched cartoon voice)* Man overboard! Man overboard! Looks like he could be drownin'! Better lower down the life-support. Take it slow, we don't wanna lose him now.

*(*JAKE *suddenly knocks the spoon out of her hand and sends it flying. He rips the blanket and sheet off himself, grabs the bowl out of her hand, stands on the bed, holds the bowl high above his head and sends it crashing down on the mattress. Then he begins to stomp on the soup, jumping all over the bed, exhaling loudly and grunting like a buffalo.* LORRAINE *backs off fast and stands there watching him.* JAKE *finally expends all his energy and just stands there limply on the bed, bent forward at the waist, arms dangling and gasping for air.)*

LORRAINE: *(Away from him, keeping her distance)* What in the name of Judas Priest is the matter with you, boy! I spent hours makin' that stuff. I slaved over the blender tryin' to get it creamy and smooth, just how you like it! Look what you've done to that soup!

*(*JAKE *looks down at his feet, covered in soup. He just stares at his feet.)*

Look what you've done to your bed. *(She moves toward bed.)*

JAKE: *(Staying on bed)* STAY AWAY FROM MY BED!

*(*LORRAINE *stops. Pause. They stare at each other.)*

LORRAINE: You got everybody buffaloed, don't ya? Everybody's worried sick that you've gone off yer cake, but you don't fool me one bit. You scared your sister so damn bad she quit the house.

JAKE: Sally? Where'd she go?

LORRAINE: She left. I don't know where. Just packed up and left. Probably just as well.

JAKE: *(Still standing on bed)* She shouldn't a' left me! She'll regret that.

LORRAINE: Who wants to be around you, the way you act. Your brother's run off to God-knows-where, tryin' to hunt up that dingbat woman a' yours.

(JAKE gets off the bed fast, moves away from it, charges across stage as though he's going somewhere, then stops short.)

JAKE: Frankie? Where'd he go? Where is Frankie? I knew that would happen! Soon as I'm outa the picture.

(LORRAINE goes to bed and starts ripping the sheets and blanket off it, cleaning up the mess. JAKE moves around the space, lost.)

LORRAINE: He went back to wherever in the hell she's from. Montana or somethin'. Weren't they originally from Montana? I don't know. I can't keep track of it anymore.

JAKE: I told him not to go back there!

LORRAINE: What difference does it make?

JAKE: She's dead! I told him that already. She's dead!

LORRAINE: Just cool your britches down.

JAKE: He's got no business foolin' around in this thing! This was strictly between me and her. Where's my pants?

(He starts to search for his pants)

LORRAINE: You're not goin' anywhere. You're sick.

JAKE: Where's my goddamn pants! He's sneakin' behind my back. I gotta go catch him before he gets there.

LORRAINE: You can't go outside in your condition. You wouldn't last a day.

JAKE: I need my pants now! I NEED MY PANTS!

(JAKE *stops suddenly again, gasping for breath. He looks around the space, not seeming to recognize where he is. He stares at the model airplanes. Pause.*)

LORRAINE: Look at ya. You haven't got any wind to speak of. How're you gonna go out in the world like that?

JAKE: I can't stay here.

LORRAINE: Why not? You never should a' left in the first place. This was the first room you ever had to yourself.

JAKE: Where were we before?

LORRAINE: You mean, before here?

JAKE: Yeah. Before. Where were we before?

LORRAINE: You-Name-It-U.S.A. Those were the days we chased your daddy from one air base to the next. Always tryin' to catch up with the next "Secret Mission." Some secret. He was always cookin' up some weird code on the phone. Tryin' to make a big drama outa things. Thought it was romantic I guess. Worst of it was I fell for it.

(JAKE *wanders around space, trying to recognize it.*)

JAKE: What code?

LORRAINE: Oh, I can't remember them now. There was lots of 'em. It was so many years ago. He'd make 'em all up.

JAKE: Why'd he use a code?

LORRAINE: He said it was because they didn't want him to reveal his location.

JAKE: Did you believe him?

LORRAINE: Yeah. Why shouldn't I of?

JAKE: Maybe he was lyin'.

LORRAINE: Why would he do that?

JAKE: So you wouldn't know what he was up to. That's why. Why do you think men lie to women?

LORRAINE: That was back when we were in love.

JAKE: Oh.

LORRAINE: That was back before things went to pieces.

JAKE: *(Still moving around space)* But we finally tracked him down, huh?

LORRAINE: Yeah. 'Course we tracked him down. Turned out not to be worth the trip, but we found him all right.

JAKE: Where?

LORRAINE: Different places. You were pretty little then.

JAKE: Little.

LORRAINE: Just a spit of a thing. I used to pack you to sleep in a dresser drawer. You were that tiny.

JAKE: You didn't close the drawer, did ya?

LORRAINE: No. 'Course not.

(JAKE *stops and stares at her. Pause.*)

JAKE: Where's that box?

LORRAINE: What?

JAKE: That box they put him in. You said you'd save that box for me. That little leather box.

LORRAINE: Oh—the ashes?

JAKE: Yeah.

LORRAINE: Now, how can you remember somethin' like that and not remember this room?

JAKE: Some things stick in your mind. Where's the box!

LORRAINE: It's here. It's right under the bed, there. You said save it, so I saved it.

JAKE: I wanna see the box.

LORRAINE: All right. Don't get so excited. It's right under here, unless the mice have gotten to it. I never looked at it again once I stuck it under here.

(She goes to bed, kneels down on floor and reaches under it. She digs around through various items under the bed.)

JAKE: How come you kept it under the bed?

LORRAINE: Couldn't figure out where else to put it. Couldn't stand lookin' at this stuff anymore and I was afraid to throw it away.

JAKE: How come?

LORRAINE: I don't know. Superstition, I guess.

(She pulls out a dusty American flag, folded in a triangle military-style. She hands it to him. JAKE takes it and stares at it.)

Here's the flag they gave you at the service. You remember that? Some government guy in dark glasses said a prayer over him and then he gave you that flag.

(She goes back to searching under the bed for the box as JAKE stares at the flag. He wipes the dust off it.)

JAKE: Dusty.

LORRAINE: *(As she searches under bed)* Yeah, well, like I said, I haven't touched a thing under here for years.

JAKE: You coulda dusted it off.

LORRAINE: Here it is.

(She pulls out a small leather box covered with dust. She blows the dust off the top and wipes it clean with the hem of her dress. She stands and hands the box to JAKE.)

I told ya I'd save it. 'Case you ever wanted it back someday.

JAKE: *(Holding box on top of flag)* This is him?

LORRAINE: What's left of him.

JAKE: *(Feeling weight of box)* He's kinda heavy.

LORRAINE: Well, he's a lot lighter than he was.

(LORRAINE picks the sheets and blanket back up off the floor.)

JAKE: Is this all that's left?

LORRAINE: Naw, there's a box a' medals and a leather flying jacket under there. More stuff in the garage. You can have it all. Take the whole kaboodle. I don't want it. Never did. I only saved it for you.

(JAKE moves to bed and sets the flag and box down on it, then he kneels down beside bed, reaches under and pulls out a cardboard carton full of Air Force medals and a leather flying jacket with small red bombs scratched into one of the sleeves. He sets the carton up on bed, then sits beside it and starts digging through the medals, holding them up to the light. LORRAINE watches him with her arms full of sheets.)

Jake, you can stay here as long as ya want to. I don't mind, really. I'm still your mother. You can just live in this room again. Just like you used to. I'll bring ya stuff. We can have conversations. Tell each other stories. You don't ever have to go outa this room again if you don't want to.

(JAKE stares up at the model airplanes, then down at the leather jacket. He puts the jacket on. He scratches at the red bombs on the sleeve. Pause.)

JAKE: How was it he died?

(Pause. They stare at each other.)

LORRAINE: Jake, you remember all that.

JAKE: No. I don't remember. I don't remember it at all.

LORRAINE: Jake—

JAKE: JUST TELL ME!

(Pause)

LORRAINE: He burned up.

JAKE: His plane crashed?

LORRAINE: No. He was no hero. Got hit by a truck. Drunk as a snake out in the middle of the highway. Truck blew up and he went with it. You already know that.

(JAKE leaps to his feet but stays by the bed.)

JAKE: DON'T TELL ME I ALREADY KNOW SOMETHIN' I DON'T KNOW! DON'T TELL ME THAT! HOW COULD I KNOW SOMETHIN' THAT I DON'T KNOW?

(Pause. They stare at each other.)

LORRAINE: *(Quietly)* Because you were there, Jake. You were right there with him when it happened.

(JAKE just stays there, staring at her. LORRAINE pulls the sheets up into a tight bundle, close to her.)

You just try and get some rest now, okay? I gotta go do this laundry. I'll be right out on the back porch if you need me. You just holler. Best thing you can do now is rest. Don't think about a thing, Jake. Just rest. Don't think about nothin'.

(LORRAINE exits upstage, out of the light, carrying the sheets. JAKE stays in place, staring out across to stage left. Very softly light begins to come up on BETH's hospital bed, now made up with blue satin sheets. BETH is alone, sitting on the upstage side of the bed with her back to JAKE. She is naked from the waist up with a blue silk dress pulled down around her waist and blue high heels with stockings. She is uninjured now—no bandage, her hair soft and beautiful. She is oiling her shoulders and chest from a small bottle beside her. JAKE just stares across at her as the light very slowly rises on her. She continues oiling herself slowly and seductively, unaware of JAKE. She is simply his vision. The light on her is continuously rising but remains very low.

Suddenly JAKE makes a move toward her and the light on her blacks out. She disappears. He stops short. Stares into the blackness, then turns and stares at his bed. All the rest of the lights black out except for a tight spotlight on his father's box of ashes. JAKE crosses back to the box, picks it up, opens it and stares into it for a second. He blows lightly into the box, sending a soft puff of ashes up into the beam of the spotlight. Spotlight fades slowly to black.)

Act II

SCENE 1

Lights up, stage-left set. Living room in BETH's PARENTS' *house. Same black platform as Act I but now two walls are flown in, stage left and upstage. The upstage wall has a swinging kitchen door mounted to stage right and an open hallway entrance to stage left, with no door, that leads off to an upstairs bedroom. The space visible through open hallway entrance is black and void. Same with space seen through kitchen door when it swings open. A small porch landing with three steps and a handrail is added onto the down-right corner of platform. A window with curtains, dead center of stage-left wall, with black void again seen through window. A well-worn sofa sits under the window, stage left, angled slightly toward audience. A stuffed armchair upstage of sofa, facing audience. An old-fashioned stand-up reading lamp between armchair and sofa. An oval rag rug on floor in front of sofa. A wooden gun rack center of upstage wall. Nothing else. The impression should be very simple and stark yet maintain a sense of realism. If wallpaper is used, it should be subdued and very faded.*

    BETH *is sitting on edge of sofa dressed in one of* BAYLOR's *faded red plaid shirts, way too big for her. It hangs outside her jeans, to the knees. Bare feet. No bandage now. Short hair. Her bruises almost healed up.* MEG *approaches her, entering through kitchen door, with a pair of fuzzy slippers in one hand and a pair of heavy work boots in the other. Before lights rise, the sound of a dog defending his territory is heard in the distance off right. Two distant voices of men arguing. The words unintelligible.*

MEG: Here we go, honey. I've got slippers or boots. Warm, fuzzy slippers. How 'bout these? They're very kind to the skin. Like having little lambs wrapped around your toes.

BETH: *(Distracted by outdoor sounds)* No, my feet are fine. I like them fine. Naked. They can move.

MEG: But the floor's so cold. This time a' year the floor's cold as ice. I used to even put socks on the dogs when they came in. Then your father put a stop to that, of course.

BETH: *(Standing, looks toward direction of voices)* Where—who's out there?

MEG: Outside? I don't know, honey. Mike wouldn't tell me.

BETH: Mike? Heez out there?

MEG: Yes. He's been out there all morning talking to that man.

BETH: *(Moving downstage to porch, looking out)* What man?

MEG: Some man. I don't know. He just showed up.

BETH: Whatz his voice?

MEG: What, honey?

BETH: Whatz his voice? Someone I know. Iz voice I know.

MEG: I couldn't see him from the front door. Mike wouldn't let him come up to the house.

BETH: *(Turns fast to MEG)* Who'ze—who'ze?

MEG: Don't you wanna try these slippers, honey? They'd keep you nice and cozy.

BETH: Tha's a voice of someone. Before. Someone with a voice before. Someone—I know.

MEG: I'm not sure who it is. Mike doesn't like him, that's for sure. I just wish he'd go away so the dog would quit.

BETH: *(Moving back toward sofa)* Someone with Jake. Jake's voice. Iz—a man with hiz voice. Same. Heez come to see me? Haz he come to see me?

(The sounds outside stop.)

MEG: Honey, I can't ask Mike. You know how he gets. He gets just like your father. There's no point in asking.

BETH: I—I—can I go? Can I go out to see? I want to see. Can I?

MEG: No, honey. It's freezing out there. The ground's solid ice.

BETH: He can't go. He can't. Don't let him go. I want to see.

MEG: Honey, it's nothing but a man. A stranger. Some stranger.

> (MIKE *enters fast from upstage center space, moves down to stairs and enters from porch. He's in a heavy jacket, gloves, wool cap, boots with snow on them; carries shotgun. He unloads shotgun and sets it on gun rack upstage wall, stomps his boots and takes his gloves and jacket off.*)

Oh, we were just now talking about you, Mike. I thought you were down by the road.

MIKE: Son of a bitch wanted to come right up to the goddamn house. Can you believe that? Walk right up to the house like a neighbor or somethin'. I can't believe it. Who do these guys think they are, anyway?

MEG: Don't swear in the house, Mike. I've told you that since you were a little boy. Keep the language outdoors.

BETH: *(To Mike)* Who'ze he? Who'ze he?

MIKE: Nobody. Just—just a guy. I don't know.

BETH: Jake?

MIKE: *(Turning on* BETH*)* No!! It's not Jake! All right? He's got nothin' to do with Jake. Just some guy. When're you gonna stop thinkin' about Jake for Christ's sake!

BETH: You lie to me! You lie like I'm dead. I'm not dead.

MIKE: Oh, so now you're *not* dead. Today you're not dead. Yesterday you were dead but today you're not. I gotta keep track a' this. Makes a big difference who you're talkin' to—a corpse or a live person.

MEG: Please don't yell in the house. The walls can't take it.

BETH: I'm not the one who's dead.

MIKE: *(To* BETH*)* You just settle down, all right! You just settle down now. I've about had it with you. I've been out there all night long in zero cold tryin' to protect you!

BETH: You're not the guard of me!

MIKE: Well, who is then? Who's gonna protect you? I'm the only one left around here.

MEG: There is no reason to scream. Screaming is not the thing we're born for.

(Pause)

BETH: Haz he gone now?

MIKE: Yeah. Yeah, he's gone.

(Pause)

BETH: *(To* MIKE*)* You—you. You don' let me come back. Why don' you let me come back?

MIKE: *(Moves toward her)* Beth—

BETH: *(Stiffens, stands back)* No! You make—you make a war. You make a war. You make an enemy. In me. In me! An enemy. You. You. You think me. You think you know. You think. You have a big idea.

MIKE: I'm just trying to keep you out of trouble. Can't you get that in your head? I'm tired of going through this with you.

BETH: You—you have a feeling. You have a feeling I'm you. I'm not you! This! *(Points to her head.)* This didn't happen to you. This! This. This thought. You don't know this thought. How? How can you know this thought? In me.

MEG: Beth, your brother's only trying to help you. He's only doing what he thinks best. Now don't get so excited. You'll only get yourself all worked up again.

BETH: *(To* MEG, *softens)* You—you a love. You—you are only that. Only. You don' know. Only love. Good. You. Mother. You. Always love. Always. *(To* MIKE*)* But he lies to me. Like I'm gone. Not here. Lies and tellz me iz for love. Iz not for love! Iz pride!

MIKE: Okay. Okay, I'll tell you exactly the truth. I'll tell you. You wanna know? It was Jake's brother. Okay? That's who it was. Jake's little lousy brother.

BETH: Jake?

MIKE: HIS BROTHER! NOT JAKE! HIS BROTHER!

MEG: Mike!

MIKE: *(To* MEG*)* Well, goddamnit! She wants to know the truth. She says—"tell me the truth, you're lying to me." I tell her the truth and she turns it into a lie. I'm sick and tired of this shit. *(To* BETH*)* What do you wanna know? You want me to tell you it was Jake? Okay, it was Jake. How's that? You're gonna believe whatever you want to anyway. What do you wanna believe?

BETH: It was not Jake.

MIKE: It was his brother! His pathetic little brother. Sniveling up here to our doorstep, asking for forgiveness.

BETH: Why'z he gone?

MIKE: What'd you expect me to do? Huh? Did you want me to invite him in for hot chocolate or something? Cookies? Pretend nothing ever happened? He's just on a friendly visit? Sometimes I think you must've enjoyed getting beat up. Maybe that's it. Maybe you get some kind of kick out of it.

(Pause)

MEG: You don't need to be cruel, Mike.

MIKE: This whole thing is cruel.

(Long pause as BETH stares at her shirt, touches the sleeves. Her whole tone shifts.)

BETH: What's this shirt?

MEG: That's Baylor's, honey. You wanted that one. That's the one you picked out of the closet.

BETH: Smells like him. Baylor.

MEG: He used to always wear that fishing. That was his favorite shirt. He said you could have it.

BETH: Smells like fish.

MIKE: So, now what? We're gonna talk about shirts now? *(To BETH)* What is goin' on with you? You shift streams faster than a trout in heat.

BETH: *(Soft, to MIKE)* If something breaks—broken. If something broken—parts still—stay. Parts still float. For a while. Then gone. Maybe never come—back. Together. Maybe never.

(Sound of single shot from a deer rifle in distance stage right.)

(BETH's head jerks toward sound.)

Zaat?

MIKE: Dad. Hunting.

MEG: He's been out there all night again. I just don't understand how he can take the cold like that. Sometimes I think he'd rather live out there in that hunting shack year-round. He's got everything he needs out there. His magazines. His flashlight. His radio. He even eats his meals out there, anymore. I don't know when all that started.

MIKE: All what?

MEG: Him moving out. When did that start?

MIKE: He hasn't moved out. He's hunting. Every year he hunts. You know that.

MEG: Sometimes I think he's hiding from us.

(Pause. MIKE goes to armchair, sits, takes his boots off and stretches his legs out—continuous as he speaks.)

MIKE: Well, there's only one day left in the season and he hasn't got his buck yet.

MEG: I don't know if I can take another winter of venison. Last year we had venison three times a day. Venison, venison, venison. It still wasn't gone by spring. God, how I hate that meat. Even bacon can't hide the taste.

MIKE: It's not that bad if you don't smell it.

MEG: Funny thing is, I don't think he likes the meat either. He never eats it. Poor excuse for killing a live thing if you ask me.

BETH: *(Staring around at space)* This—this—this is where I used to be?

MEG: Where, honey?

BETH: Here? Inside here. This room?

MEG: Yes. This is our home. You recognize it, don't you?

BETH: This room was—where we all were—together.

MEG: Yes. That's right. Christmas, Thanksgiving, Easter. We were always here.

MIKE: You're safe here. Long as you stay with us.

BETH: What's "safe"?

MIKE: Safe. Safe from injury. You won't get hurt here.

BETH: I hurt all over.

MEG: But it's getting better, honey. Every day it's getting a little bit better.

BETH: What is?

MEG: The brain. They say the brain heals itself just like the skin. Isn't that amazing? It just keeps healing itself. That's what they told us at the hospital.

BETH: What brain?

MEG: Your brain, honey.

BETH: Where? In me.

MIKE: In your head. The brain in your head. Inside your skull.

BETH: Iz hiding in there?

MEG: No, I woudn't say that exactly. The brain can't hide.

BETH: Iz in there like a turtle? Like a shell?

MEG: Not really. It's—what does a brain look like, Mike?

MIKE: It don't know what it looks like. It's gray. That's about all I know about it.

MEG: Yes. It's a gray thing. Kind of like a snail, isn't it, Mike? It's kind of curled around itself like a big snail.

MIKE: You got me.

BETH: Snail.

MEG: Yes. I think so. I't all lumpy. I saw pictures of it once. They took pictures of my mother's brain. They showed them to me once.

BETH: We can't see it?

MIKE: Not when you're alive. You can't see it when you're alive.

BETH: Why?

MIKE: Because—you'd be dead if you could see it. It'd be sticking out.

BETH: You can see the head? The face.

MIKE: Yeah. That's right. But not the brain. The brain's inside the head. Covered up.

BETH: Where?

MIKE: *(Slaps his forehead)* Inside! Here! Inside! Behind the skull!

(BAYLOR'S VOICE heard offstage.)

BAYLOR: *(Offstage)* Just try to keep your weight off it. That's it. Don't put yer weight down on it. Hang on. Just keep ahold of my neck now.

(BAYLOR enters from upstage, then up porch stairs, wearing hunter's orange from head to toe and a camouflage hunting vest, rifle in one hand. He helps FRANKIE on stage, who is hopping on his right leg, arm around BAYLOR's neck, a hole about the size of a quarter in his left thigh with a little patch of blood—nothing more. As they enter, MIKE immediately gets up and grabs his shotgun, sticks the shells back in it and snaps the barrels shut. BAYLOR assists FRANKIE over to the sofa. FRANKIE collapses onto sofa holding his left thigh in pain.)

MEG: Oh, my goodness, Baylor. What in the world happened here? We heard you shooting.

BAYLOR: Aw, this yayhoo was out there in the damn woods without a lick a' orange on him. Came crashing through that stand of aspen like a freight train and I shot him.

MEG: You shot him? Oh, my God, Baylor.

BAYLOR: Nailed him clean through the thigh. Look at that. Bullet passed right on through and out the other side. Never touched the bone or nothin'.

MEG: *(To Frankie)* But it still must hurt. Doesn't it hurt?

FRANKIE: Yeah. It hurts.

MEG: It must.

BAYLOR: Hurts me too. Wrecked my entire day a' shootin'. I got one day left to bag my limit and this bonehead comes along and scares every damn deer in four counties.

FRANKIE: I'm sorry. I was looking for my car.

BAYLOR: Your car? Where'd you park it, in the lake?

MEG: Oh, my goodness.

BAYLOR: Stop staying "Oh, my goodness, Oh my God," all the time. Think up somethin' different for a change.

MIKE: *(Approaching* FRANKIE*)* You were tryin' to circle back around, weren't you? Isn't that what you were doin'? Thought you'd come up around the back side? I thought I told you to take a hike, buddy.

FRANKIE: *(Staring at* BETH*)* I just wanted to see her. That's all. All I wanna do is see her. *(To* BETH*)* My brother thinks you're dead, see. I gotta go back and tell him now.

BETH: Before—you. I know you. We—

MIKE: Beth, you go on up to the bedroom now. Go on!

BAYLOR: Aw, let her talk to him. Christ. What difference does it make now. He's not gonna do much harm with that hole in his leg. Mother, help me off with these boots.

*(*BAYLOR *sits heavily in armchair.* MEG *kneels in front of him and helps pull his boots off.)*

MIKE: I'll give him a ride down to the emergency.

BETH: No—he—he can stay. I know him.

MIKE: He's not stayin' in this house! I'll tell you that right now!

BAYLOR: *(To* MIKE*)* You keep yer voice down, boy! You forget whose house this is. *(Pause)* No point in movin' him around right now. Long as the blood's stopped. Best to prop that leg up and let him set for a while.

MEG: *(Stands, to* FRANKIE*)* I'll get something to put your foot on.

BAYLOR: *(To* MEG*)* Let Beth get it! You help me off with this gear now. I've never seen anybody get so easily distracted as you. Just keep yer mind on yer business now.

(MEG *kneels again in front of* BAYLOR, *finishes with his boots and starts pulling off his orange outer pants, as* BAYLOR *pulls them down from his waist. Underneath he's wearing heavy dungarees.*)

MEG: *(As she helps* BAYLOR*)* Beth, go get that little footstool out of the kitchen for the man.

BETH: Kitchen.

MEG: Yes. In the kitchen, honey. The little footstool. Bring it in here for him.

(BETH *exits through kitchen door upstage.*)

MIKE: *(As he puts his jacket, cap and gloves back on)* I got an idea. Why don't we just move him on up to the bedroom. Huh? We got an extra bedroom empty don't we? Let's just move him up there. Then we can serve him breakfast in bed. We can move the TV up there for him. How 'bout that? We can get the electric blanket. He could even share the room with Beth, maybe. That'd be nice and cozy.

BAYLOR: *(To* MIKE*)* Hey! You just cool yourself down, buster.

MIKE: I'm not stayin' in the same house with the brother of the man who tried to kill my sister! I'm not doin' that.

BAYLOR: I'm the one who shot him! All right? Since I'm the one who shot him, I'm gonna see to it that he stays alive. I'm too old to go to jail just yet. Thank you very much.

MEG: *(Still helping* BAYLOR *undress)* Can't we just talk in a normal tone?

BAYLOR: Soon's it gets normal we'll talk normal!

MIKE: *(Moving toward porch)* You just lemme know. You lemme know when he's outa here.

BAYLOR: Where you goin'?

MIKE: Out to the shack.

BAYLOR: *(To* MIKE*)* Wait a second. Take the 30-30. You see any deer out there, let 'em have it. There's only one day left.

MEG: *(To* MIKE*)* Just try not to shoot any more people please.

*(*BAYLOR *reaches for deer rifle, across* MEG, *and hands it to* MIKE. MIKE *takes it. He stares at* FRANKIE.*)*

MIKE: *(To* FRANKIE*)* You wormed your way in, didn't you? Pretty cute. But I'm not forgettin' anything. Everybody else might forget but I'm not. Far as I'm concerned you and your brother are the same person.

*(*MIKE *leans the shotgun against the sofa, then snaps the lever on the 30-30 and engages a bullet. He stares at* FRANKIE, *then exits out porch and upstage into blackness.)*

BAYLOR: *(To* MIKE *as he exits)* Don't mess that shack up. I spent all afternoon sweepin' the mouse shit out of it.

MEG: You shouldn't oughta make him go out in that cold, Baylor.

BAYLOR: Wasn't my idea. It's his.

*(*BETH *enters from kitchen door upstage with small footstool. She crosses fast downstage and just stands there, holding it. She stares at audience. Pause.)*

Well, take it on over to the man, Beth. Take it over and set it down for him. Don't just stand there with it. Not gonna do him any good while it's in the air.

MEG: *(Stands to help* BETH*)* Here, honey, I'll take it.

BAYLOR: No! *(Stops* MEG*)* Let her do it. She can do it. 'Bout time she starts doin' things by herself. You keep babyin' her she's never gonna get any better.

*(*BETH *stays in same place, holding stool. She turns and stares at* FRANKIE. MEG *kneels and goes back to helping* BAYLOR.*)*

BAYLOR: *(Deliberate)* Beth—take the stool over to the man and set it down for him. What're you starin' at?

(Pause. BETH moves slowly over to FRANKIE and stops in front of him but keeps holding stool. She stares at FRANKIE.)

BAYLOR: *(To BETH)* That's right. Now set it down on the floor. Right in front of him.

(BETH sets the stool down on floor in front of FRANKIE.)

That's the ticket. Now help him get his leg up on it.

FRANKIE: That's all right. I can do it.

(FRANKIE struggles to get his leg up on stool but can't do it.)

BAYLOR: *(To FRANKIE)* She can help you. Good for her to help somebody else out for a change. Make her realize she's not the only cripple in this world.

MEG: Baylor—

BAYLOR: *(To MEG)* What? She knows all about it. She knows somethin's gone wrong.

MEG: I know but you don't have to—

BAYLOR: What? Speak the plain truth? Everybody's been tiptoeing around here like she can't handle the plain truth. And she knows all about it. Don't ya, Beth?

(BETH helps FRANKIE get his injured leg propped up on the stool.)

FRANKIE: Thanks.

BAYLOR: *(To MEG)* There now. See that? Now she's got the experience of helping somebody else out. And you woulda robbed her a' that, see. You wanna just keep on lettin' her believe that she's never gonna pull outa this thing.

MEG: That's not true.

BAYLOR: That's good, Beth. Now why don't you go on in the kitchen and make us up a nice big pot a' black coffee.

MEG: She can't make coffee, Baylor. She'll burn herself.

BAYLOR: See, there ya go again.

MEG: Well, why take the risk of her getting hurt? She can't make coffee.

BAYLOR: That's right. "Why take the risk?" Why take the risk of her getting better? Why not just let her stay the same?

MEG: She is getting better.

BAYLOR: Nah. We'll be right back in the same boat we were in with your mother. Another invalid. House full a' invalids. I'll be the only one left in this joint that can function.

MEG: Well, you're never around anyway.

BAYLOR: I'm around. I'm around plenty. But I'll tell ya one thing—I'm not gonna be the caretaker of a nursing home here. I got better things to do.

MEG: Like shooting men.

BAYLOR: That was an accident.

MEG: Well, I don't understand how a man can be mistaken for a deer. They don't look anything alike.

BAYLOR: He was crashin' through the woods, hell bent for leather. How was I supposed to know?

MEG: Didn't you look? He doesn't have antlers or anything. He doesn't look anything like a deer.

BAYLOR: You don't make an examination before you shoot somethin'. You just shoot it.

FRANKIE: It was my fault.

BAYLOR: Yer darn tootin' it was your fault. Yer just lucky I'm as old as I am. In my prime you'da been dead meat, son.

BETH: *(To* FRANKIE*)* You have voice I know.

(Pause)

FRANKIE: 'Scuse me?

BETH: You have voice.

BAYLOR: *(To* FRANKIE*)* You understand what's happened to her, don't
ya?

MEG: Baylor, please—

BAYLOR: *(To* MEG*)* Aw, knock it off. What in the hell are we tryin' to
pull here? Beth, you go ahead and tell him. Go ahead. Tell the
man what happened to you. Go on.

(Pause)

BETH: I—

FRANKIE: That's all right. I just mainly wanted to know if you were
alive. My brother's worried sick about you. He said to tell you he
just misses you a lot.

(Pause. Silence MEG *stands.)*

MEG: Maybe I'll make that pot of coffee, Baylor.

BAYLOR: All right. Why not. And bring me in that tin of Mink Oil for
my feet. They're startin' to crack again.

MEG: Do you want to come in and help me, Beth?

*(*BETH *shakes her head, "no.")*

BAYLOR: *(To* MEG*)* Leave her be!

*(*MEG *exits through door upstage.* BETH *stands there staring at* FRANKIE.
BAYLOR *stays in armchair.)*

BAYLOR: *(To* FRANKIE*)* Christ, there's gotta be a borderline between
polite and stupid. I swear to God. Her mother was the same way.
Drive you crazy with politeness. *(Pause. To* FRANKIE*)* How's that
leg doin'?

FRANKIE: It just burns a little.

BAYLOR: I'll bet it does. You took a helluva lick.

BETH: *(Very simple to* FRANKIE*)* This—this is my father. He's given up love. Love is dead for him. My mother is dead for him. Things live for him to be killed. Only death counts for him. Nothing else. This—This—*(She moves slowly toward* FRANKIE.*)* This is me. This is me now. The way I am. Now. This. All. Different. I—I live inside this. Remember. Remembering. You. You—were one. I know you. I know—love. I know what love is. I can never forget. That. Never.

(Lights fade. All three stay in place. Lights to black.)

SCENE 2

Sound of electric shaver in darkness, stage right. Lights up slowly (cross fade with Scene 1 ending), on stage-right bedroom set—JAKE's bed with model airplanes above. Walls in. JAKE is standing extreme downstage on the very edge of the stage, facing audience, stage right of center. He is in his boxer shorts underwear, sleeveless T-shirt under his father's leather pilot's jacket. The jacket is covered with all the medals from the cardboard box now. He wears the American flag from his dad's funeral draped around his neck. He is shaving his face with a cordless electric shaver, staring straight in front of him as though there were a mirror. His face is pale white, eyes sunken. Lights up full. He finishes shaving. Shuts off shaver. Takes the cap off it and blows the whiskers out then replaces cap and stares in "mirror". He speaks to himself in a loud whisper as he looks at his face in the imaginary mirror.

JAKE: *(Whisper)* Don't think about her feet or her calves or her knees or her thighs or her hips or her waist or her ribs or her tits or her armpits or her shoulders or her neck or her face or her eyes or her hair or her lips. Especially not her lips. Don't think about any of these things. You'll be much better off.

(He turns upstage just as SALLY enters through up left door, wearing a jacket, jeans and western boots and carrying a suitcase. They both stop and stare at each other. Pause. SALLY closes the door, then turns back to JAKE. She keeps hold of the suitcase.)

SALLY: How're you feelin', Jake?

JAKE: Me?

(Pause. He moves fast to the bed, pulls the flag off his neck as he crosses, kneels down beside bed, stuffs the flag under bed, pulls out a small black toilet case, unzips it, puts the shaver inside, zips it back up and shoves it back under the bed. He rises to his feet, then sits on the edge of the bed, facing SALLY, and rubs his knee as he stares at her. Pause.)

SALLY: *(Sets suitcase on floor)* Where's Mom?

JAKE: *(Rapid speech)* I don't worry anymore where anybody is. I don't think about that. Anybody can move wherever they want. I just try to keep track of my own movements these days. That's enough. Have you ever tried that? To follow yourself around? Like a spy. You can wind up anywhere. It's amazing. Like, just now I caught myself shaving. I was right over there. Shaving my face. I didn't know I was doing that until just now. It's kinda scary, ya know.

SALLY: Scary?

JAKE: Yeah. I mean there's a possibility that you could do something that you didn't even know about. You could be somewhere that you couldn't even remember being. Has that ever happened to you?

SALLY: No. No, it's the opposite with me. Everything just keeps repeating itself.

JAKE: Oh. Well, then you don't know what I'm talkin' about.

(Pause. She stares at him. He grabs his knees and stares at the floor.)

SALLY: Um—I decided to come back and see if I could maybe help you out, Jake. You don't mind, do ya?

JAKE: Me? Help me out?

(He gets off the bed fast, as though he's just remembered something important. He kneels down on floor again, pulls toilet case out, unzips it, digs around in case and pulls out a toenail clipper. He zips case back up

and shoves it under bed. Then he sits on edge of bed, facing SALLY, *and starts clipping his toenails.* SALLY *just stands there watching him, stuffs her hands in her pockets.)*

SALLY: I was out there—I was driving around in the car out there and—

JAKE: Where were you headed?

SALLY: I was just—I was driving around the house. In circles. Real slow. I couldn't make up my mind.

JAKE: No, I mean where were you headed originally? Before you decided to come back?

SALLY: I wasn't sure. I mean—I was thinkin'—at first I was thinkin' I'd go up and try to see Beth, and then—

*(*JAKE *stands suddenly. Starts moving around the room.* SALLY *just stands there.)*

JAKE: Beth? You were gonna' go and try to see Beth? Nobody believes me!

SALLY: Now wait a second—

JAKE: NOBODY BELIEVES ME! Bunch a' traitors for family. Did you talk to Frankie about her before you left?

SALLY: No! Why would I talk to Frankie?

JAKE: You're a liar. You wouldn't have thought to go see her unless you'd talked to Frankie first. Why would you think to go see her? She's dead! Didn't I tell ya that already?

SALLY: Yeah. But I thought I'd go see her anyway.

JAKE: A dead person? You wanted to go see a dead person?

SALLY: There was other times when you said you'd killed her—when you thought you'd killed her—remember?

*(*JAKE *stops, stares at her. Pause.)*

JAKE: So what'd you come back here for?

SALLY: I don't know exactly. I started thinkin' about this whole thing. This family. How everything's kinda—shattered now.

JAKE: Now? What d'ya mean "now"? When wasn't it shattered?

SALLY: I don't wanna start fightin' with you just when I walk in the door. I didn't come back for that.

JAKE: (Crossing back to bed) Why not? What else are we gonna' do? Huh? You got some brave ideas? You got some brave ideas about mending things up. Is that it? I'll tell ya the only idea that's gonna work. I been sittin' here in this room for days thinkin' about it and I finally came up with it.

SALLY: What's that.

JAKE: (Sits on bed, quieter) I'm not goin' outdoors anymore. I'm not leavin' this room. Mom brings me food. I don't need the outside. All I do is get in trouble out there.

SALLY: Well, you can't just stay locked up in here, Jake. That's crazy.

JAKE: No. Out there is crazy. Out there. Soon's you step out that door.

(JAKE goes back to clipping his toenails again. He ignores her. Pause. SALLY watches him. Pause.)

SALLY: (Turning toward her suitcase) All right. I guess I was wrong. I thought there might be a chance I could talk to you and see if we could be friends or somethin', but I guess I was dead wrong.

JAKE: Wait a second, Sally. Come on.

SALLY: Naw, you make it impossible. You're gonna sit around here pretending to be crazy. Tryin' to make everyone believe you're crazy. Is that what you're gonna do? Well, it's not gonna change what you did. You already got away with that once, didn't you?

JAKE: Sally—

SALLY: Don't worry. I'm not gonna give you away.

JAKE: We made a promise.

SALLY: Yeah.

JAKE: Don't forget.

(Pause)

SALLY: I won't.

JAKE: Look, I need an ally. Just one. Just one good, solid ally that I can rely on. Everyone else is against me.

SALLY: No! I'm not doin' that again for you. Never again.

JAKE: *(Suddenly in a whisper)* Frankie called here. He called here. I heard Mom talkin' to him on the phone.

(Pause. SALLY stares at him. She sets suitcase down.)

SALLY: So what if Frankie called? Why shouldn't he call? He's your brother.

JAKE: *(Whisper)* He didn't ask to talk to me!

SALLY: Why are you whispering now? What's gotten into you?

JAKE: *(Whisper)* Mom.

SALLY: What about her?

JAKE: *(Whisper)* She's with him. Her and Frankie are together. They've got a pact.

SALLY: What're you talkin' about?

JAKE: *(Whisper)* They're tryin' to make me believe that Beth's alive.

SALLY: She probably is.

JAKE: Are you with them too?

SALLY: I'm not with anybody, all right! I'm all by myself.

JAKE: Then you can help me. There's no reason why you couldn't help me.

SALLY: Look, I went through this once with you, Jake. With Dad. I already went through this.

JAKE: *(Moving to her, pleading, in a whisper)* No, no, no. It's not the same. They wanna make me suffer. Don't you know that? Frankie thinks I deserve to suffer. So does Mom.

SALLY: Nobody wants to make you suffer. It's just you.

JAKE: *(Whisper)* It's that whole family too. Beth's family. You remember how they hated me.

SALLY: Will you please stop whispering! It's makin' me nuts!

(Pause. JAKE stops and stares at her.)

JAKE: *(Normal voice now)* You're afraid a' me, aren't ya? *(Pause)* Aren't ya!

SALLY: I'm not afraid of you.

JAKE: Yeah, you are.

SALLY: Only because you remind me of Dad sometimes.

JAKE: Dad? *(Pause)* Dad?

SALLY: Yeah. You do. Sometimes you sound just like him.

JAKE: I don't sound anything like him. I never sounded like him. I've made a point not to.

SALLY: You do. The way you get that creepy thing in your voice.

JAKE: What creepy thing?

SALLY: That high-pitched creepy thing like you're gonna turn into an animal or something.

JAKE: What animal?

SALLY: I don't know what animal!

JAKE: What kind of animal?

SALLY: Not any special kind. Just an animal sound in general.

(Pause. They stare at each other.)

JAKE: A bear?

SALLY: Don't get cute.

JAKE: You remember how he used to try to dance with you when he was drunk? How he'd pull you right up tight against his chest and breathe into your neck. You remember all that?

SALLY: What're you tryin' to do?

JAKE: He'd put on Lefty Frizell and twirl you around the kitchen until you got so dizzy you had to run into the bathroom and puke. I remember lyin' awake listening to you with the dry heaves and listening to him bellowing down the hallway at Mom. Warning her not to go in and help you out. I remember all that!

SALLY: Yeah! Then you remember the night he died too, don't ya?

(JAKE stops. They stare at each other. Pause.)

JAKE: No! *(Pause)* That's the part I forgot.

(LORRAINE enters quickly with a metal serving tray and wearing an apron. She stops when she sees SALLY. Pause.)

LORRAINE: *(To SALLY)* Oh. I thought you might've come back. I saw that car out there and I said to myself: "I bet she's back."

SALLY: That's pretty sharp, Mom.

LORRAINE: Just puttin' two and two together. *(Crosses to bed and starts putting the dirty breakfast dishes on tray.)* What'sa matter, you get homesick or somethin'? Don't tell me you got homesick for yer little ole family. Out there all alone on the big bad American road.

SALLY: Not exactly. No.

LORRAINE: Well, what was it then? You forget somethin'?

JAKE: *(To LORRAINE)* Were you listening to us out there?

LORRAINE: Out where?

JAKE: Outside the door! Were you out there, breathing on the door-knob, listening to us?

LORRAINE: Why? Have you all got some big terrible secret or somethin'? Talkin' behind my back again probably. Don't take long for the conspiracy to start, does it?

JAKE: You were, weren't you? *(To* SALLY*)* See, that's what I mean.

LORRAINE: What's what you mean?

JAKE: *(To* LORRAINE*)* I'm talkin' to her!

SALLY: *(To* LORRAINE*)* He thinks you and Frankie are in cahoots against him.

JAKE: *(To* SALLY*)* Don't tell her that!

SALLY: Why not? That's what you told me, isn't it?

JAKE: I didn't tell you that so you could tell her! That was private.

LORRAINE: So there *is* a secret.

SALLY: *(To* LORRAINE*)* He thinks you've got some kind of a plot going to make him suffer.

JAKE: Sally, you shut up!

LORRAINE: Suffer?

JAKE: I didn't say anything like that.

(JAKE *stops. Pause.* JAKE *and* SALLY *look up and stare at each other like two dogs with their hackles up.* LORRAINE *watches them but continues to slowly collect the breakfast plates off the bed.)*

LORRAINE: Well—looks like you're just gonna have to stay away for a spell, Sally. We can't have him gettin' upset like this. Not in his condition. He wasn't like this until you showed up.

SALLY: *(Still with her eyes on* JAKE*)* I'm not leavin'. I'm sick to death of leavin'. Every time I pack, I tremble now. I start to tremble. It's in my body. My whole body shakes from the memory of all this leavin'. It feels like a leaving that will last forever. This is my home as much as his.

LORRAINE: But we're in a state of emergency here now, with your brother like this. This is a crisis. You have to be a little flexible in a crisis.

SALLY: I'm not leavin'!

LORRAINE: How can you be so mule-headed stubborn and selfish!

JAKE: *(To* LORRAINE, *moving away from* SALLY*)* She can stay if she wants to.

(Pause)

LORRAINE: There's not enough room, Jake.

JAKE: There's room. This is my room and she can stay if she wants to.

(Pause)

LORRAINE: Well this isn't gonna' be much fun, is it?

JAKE: *(To* LORRAINE*)* I want Sally here, where I can see her. Where I can keep an eye on her. She's not gonna be sending any messages for you anymore.

LORRAINE: Messages?

JAKE: Yeah, that's right. You can tell Frankie that she's not coming back there. She's staying with me. There's not gonna be any more codes sent.

LORRAINE: *(To* SALLY*)* What kinda trash have you been puttin' in his head?

JAKE: I'm just bein' careful, that's all. I want you to stay here. Right here in this room, Sally.

SALLY: Just like old times, huh? Okay. Okay. I will. Maybe that's just what I need to do. Take the tiger by the tail. I'll stay right in here with you. We'll just camp out.

LORRAINE: Well, I'm not doin' the cookin' anymore. I'll tell ya that much. I'm not runnin' a boardinghouse here.

SALLY: I'll cook.

LORRAINE: *(Moves to SALLY)* Why can't you just leave! Why can't you just get your fanny out in the wide world and find yourself somethin' to do. Stop mopin' around here gettin' everybody's dander up.

SALLY: Where do you want me to wind up, Mom? Somewhere down the road?

LORRAINE: You'll find somethin'. Everybody finds somethin' sooner or later.

SALLY: Like what?

LORRAINE: A town or somethin'.

SALLY: What town?

LORRAINE: I don't know what town! There's lots of towns around. This is a country full a' towns. There's a town for everybody. Always has been. If there's no town, then start one of your own. My granddaddy started a town on a mesquite stump. He just hung his hat on it and a whole town sprang up.

SALLY: That was a whole other time.

LORRAINE: Time's got nothin' to do with it.

SALLY: I'm stayin'.

(Pause)

LORRAINE: *(Moves to JAKE)* Jake, look—we were doin' just fine, weren't we? We had everything workin' smooth as butter here. We had our system. We were self-sufficient, weren't we, Jake? What do we need her for?

JAKE: I can trust her.

(Pause)

LORRAINE: (Laughs) I have been doin' my best to pull you out of this thing. I went outa my way to bring you back here. I fixed up your room, just like it used to be. I've been cookin' all your meals.

JAKE: It's just a trap.

LORRAINE: For what? Why would I wanna trap you? Have you got your mind so twisted up that you can't even recognize your own mother's good intentions?

JAKE: (About SALLY) I recognize her. I remember her real good. We went through somethin' together.

(JAKE fixes on SALLY as he speaks about her. SALLY's back is toward stage left. Very slowly, as this scene continues, light begins to rise on the stage-left set. A soft pool of light on the sofa where FRANKIE lies on his back with his head Upstage. BETH is kneeling on the floor next to FRANKIE, wrapping the shirt she wore in the first scene around FRANKIE's wounded leg. Her gestures are very soft and loving. She wears jeans and a bra. FRANKIE is sweating hard and his face is extremely pale, like JAKE's now. JAKE slowly approaches SALLY as he speaks to her. SALLY, LORRAINE and JAKE pay no attention to the stage-left light.)

LORRAINE: Well, so did we, Jake. I've known you a lot longer than she has.

JAKE: (Approaching SALLY slowly) Where was that, Sally? Where was that? Where were we when that happened?

SALLY: You don't wanna know.

JAKE: We drove all night long.

SALLY: Just forget about it now.

(SALLY moves away from JAKE, crosses to bed and sits on it. JAKE stays where he is, facing stage left. Now he begins to see BETH and FRANKIE in the dim light but he regards them as a distant vision in his mind. LORRAINE and SALLY ignore the stage-left action. JAKE remains fixed on BETH and FRANKIE.)

JAKE: *(Staring at BETH and FRANKIE)* We listened to the radio.

(LORRAINE crosses to SALLY carrying the tray of dirty plates.)

LORRAINE: *(To SALLY)* See the state you've got him in now. See what you've done.

SALLY: *(Sitting on bed)* I haven't done a thing but come back home.

(SALLY reaches under the bed and pulls out the flag. She spreads it across her lap.)

LORRAINE: *(To SALLY)* You did it on purpose. You knew this was gonna happen. He was doin' so well with me lookin' after him. He was gonna stay. He was just gonna live here like he used to. Now you've got his mind all driftin' away again.

JAKE: *(Still fixed on BETH and FRANKIE)* We drove a thousand miles and never said a word.

LORRAINE: *(After pause, to SALLY)* Well, you stay then. You suit yourself. I'll just wait you out. I can wait a whole lot longer than you can. Believe you me. I've been a lifetime at it. He'll come back around to me. You wait and see. He'll come back.

(LORRAINE exits upstage with tray and plates. JAKE stays fixed on BETH and FRANKIE. SALLY stares at JAKE's back. Pause.)

JAKE: *(With his back to SALLY)* You gotta help me escape, Sally. I gotta get back there. She's still alive.

(SALLY watches JAKE awhile, then reaches down under bed and pulls out the leather box of ashes. She holds it in her lap and opens it as JAKE remains staring stage left.)

SALLY: What's this?

(JAKE *slowly turns around facing* SALLY. *They stare at each other as lights fade on them to black. Lights are rising on* BETH *and* FRANKIE *simultaneously.*)

Play task :

Scene task: In order to ~~overcome~~ fulfil my
dream of normality I wish to convince
a gentle and attractive brother-in-law. to take a chance on me.

Obstacles: I Like Frankie,

Frankie resists, Jake

⚹ pace   Mike, Brain damage

SCENE 3

Lights remain up on stage-left set with FRANKIE *on his back stretched out on sofa, head upstage, and* BETH *on her knees beside him, wrapping* BAYLOR'S *shirt around his injured leg.*

FRANKIE: Uh—look—Beth—don't you think you oughta put your shirt back on?

BETH: You need it. *I mollycoddle you.*

FRANKIE: I don't. Really. I don't. It's stopped bleeding. It hasn't bled for a long time now.

BETH: It could start again. *I caution you.*

FRANKIE: It just aches a little. It's not bleeding anymore.

BETH: It's going up your leg now. *I ~~inform~~ alert you*

FRANKIE: *(Sits up fast)* What is?

BETH: Black line. That's bad. *I warn you,*

FRANKIE: What's that mean? A black line.

*(*FRANKIE *pulls his pant leg up. Looks at his leg.)*

BETH: It's bad. Poison. *I scare you*

FRANKIE: *(Pushing his pant leg down again)* Look—please, just leave it alone and put your shirt back on. Your dad might come back in here.

BETH: He's asleep. *I ~~entice~~ invite you*

FRANKIE: Well, then your mother or your brother could come. Somebody could come in here. *I oblige you*

BETH: Doesn't matter. *I ~~invite~~ you*

FRANKIE: It does matter! I'm on thin ground as it is without them seeing you on your knees with your shirt off. What're they gonna think if they walk in here and find you rubbing my leg with no shirt on? Please stop rubbing my leg now!

BETH: Don't you like it? *I like your*

FRANKIE: Just stand up. Stand up on your feet and put your shirt back on. Please, Beth. Just act like we're having a conversation or something.

BETH: You don't have to be afraid of them. They're afraid of you.

FRANKIE: How do you figure that? *I comfort you   I ~~edit~~ you*

BETH: They tell it in their voice. *I enlighten ~~inform~~ you.*

FRANKIE: They want to kill me.

BETH: Only Mike. But he won't. *I ~~educate~~ unease you.*

FRANKIE: What makes you so sure about that? *I placate you.*

BETH: (Quick) Because only half of him believes you're what he hates. The other half knows it's not true. *I persuade you*

(Pause. FRANKIE stares at her.)

FRANKIE: I thought you couldn't uh—

BETH: What? *— I encourage you*

FRANKIE: (Lies back down) I don't know. I thought you couldn't talk right or something. You sound okay to me.

BETH: I do? *— I beckon you.*

FRANKIE: Yeah. Your dad said there was—I mean you were having some kind of trouble.

BETH: Oh. There was that time. I don't know. I get them mixed. I get

— I verify you.   `I confuse myself   `I inform you

- I brief you

the thought. Mixed. It dangles. Sometimes the thought just hangs with no words there.

FRANKIE: But you can speak all right?

- I enlighten you

BETH: It speaks. Speeches. Speaking. In me. Comes and goes. Again. I don't know why. You hear me? Now?

FRANKIE: Yes. You sound all right. I mean it sounds like you're doing pretty good.

BETH: Sounds like it. *- I back you.*

FRANKIE: Yeah.

BETH: You can speak? Speech. *- I quiz you.*

FRANKIE: Me, Yeah, sure.

BETH: But you can't walk. *I mock you.*

FRANKIE: No. Not right now.

tease/

BETH: I would rather walk than talk. *I enlighten you.*

FRANKIE: Yeah—do you—would you mind getting up off the floor, please, and putting your shirt back on?

BETH: Maybe they'll have to cut your leg off. *- I diagnose you.*

FRANKIE: (*Sits up fast again*) What? Who do you mean?

BETH: Maybe cut. Like me. Cut me. Cut you out. Like me. See?

I tutor you

(*She bends her head forward and pulls the hair up on the back of her neck to show* FRANKIE *a nonexistent scar.* FRANKIE *looks at the place on her head that she's showing him.*)

- I beckon

BETH: (*Showing* FRANKIE *back of her head*) See? Tracks. Knife tracks.

FRANKIE: (*Looking at her head*) What? There's nothing there. There's no scar there.

BETH: (*Straightens her head again*) No brain. Cut me out. Cut. Brain. Cut.

FRANKIE: No, Beth, look—they didn't—they didn't operate did they? Nobody said anything about that.

BETH: They don't say. Secret. Like my old Mom. Old. My Grand Mom. Old. They cut her. Out. Disappeared. They don't say her name now. She's gone. Vanish. *(She makes a "whooshing" sound like wind.)* My Father sent her someplace. Had her gone.

FRANKIE: They wouldn't just go in there and operate without your consent. They can't do that. It's a law. They need written consent or something. Somebody has to sign something.

BETH: Mike.

FRANKIE: What?

BETH: Mike did.

FRANKIE: No, Beth. I don't think you've got this right. Mike wouldn't do something like that.

BETH: He wants me out.

FRANKIE: He's your brother. He loves you.

BETH: *(Stands, moves away from FRANKIE)* You don't know him!

FRANKIE: Well, there's no scar there, Beth. *(Unwraps the shirt from his leg and offers it out to her.)* Here, take this shirt back. Please. Come and take it.

(Pause. Slowly BETH bends down and takes shirt. She stands with it and holds it out away from herself. She giggles to herself.)

BETH: *(Holding shirt out)* Look how big a man is. So big. He scares himself. His shirt scares him. He puts his scary shirt on so it won't scare himself. He can't see it when it's on him. Now he thinks it's him.

(She giggles and puts the shirt back on. Buttons it up. FRANKIE watches her, still sitting on sofa.)

Jake was scared of shirts. You too?

FRANKIE: No. I'm only scared of people.

(BETH starts moving in circles, pulling the front of the shirt out away from herself and looking at the buttons and fabric.)

BETH: *(Referring to shirt)* This is like a custom. Big. Too big. Like a custom.

FRANKIE: A what?

BETH: Custom. Like a custom.

FRANKIE: A custom?

BETH: For play. Acting.

FRANKIE: Oh. You mean a "costume"?

BETH: Costume.

FRANKIE: Yeah. A "costume." I get what you mean.

BETH: Pretend.

FRANKIE: You were in a play, right? I mean you were acting.

BETH: *(Moving, playing with shirt)* Pretend is more better.

FRANKIE: What do you mean?

BETH: Pretend. Because it fills me. Pretending fills. Not empty. Other. Ordinary. Is no good. Empty. Ordinary is empty. Now, I'm like the man. *(Pumps her chest up, closes her fists, sticks her chin out and struts in the shirt.)* Just feel like the man. Shirt brings me a man. I am a shirt man. Can you see? Like father. You see me? Like brother. *(She laughs.)*

FRANKIE: Yeah. You liked acting, huh?

(BETH *keeps moving, finding variations of the shirt to play with.* FRANKIE *sits on sofa watching her.*)

BETH: Pretend to be. Like you. Between us we can make a life. You could be the woman. You be.

FRANKIE: What was the play you were in? Do you remember?

BETH: *(Moving toward* FRANKIE*)* You could pretend to be in love with me. With my shirt. You love my shirt. This shirt is a man to you. You are my beautiful woman. You lie down.

(BETH moves in to FRANKIE and tries to push him down on the sofa by the shoulders. FRANKIE resists.)

FRANKIE: Now, wait a second, Beth. Wait, wait. Come on.

(BETH keeps trying to push FRANKIE back down on sofa but FRANKIE stays sitting.)

BETH: *(Giggling, pushing FRANKIE)* You fight but all the time you want my smell. You want my shirt in your mouth. You dream of it. Always. You want me on your face.

(FRANKIE pushes her away hard, then sits on edge of sofa. BETH stands away from him.)

FRANKIE: *(Pushing her away)* Now cut it out!

(Pause as BETH stares at him from a distance.)

Now, look—I can't hang around here. I didn't come here to fool around. I've gotta get back home and talk to Jake about this. That's the whole reason I came here. He's gonna think something went wrong.

BETH: Jake.

FRANKIE: Yeah, He's gonna think somethin' happened to me.

BETH: Your other one. You have his same voice. Maybe you could be him. Pretend. Maybe. Just him. Just like him. But soft. With me. Gentle. Like a woman-man.

(BETH starts moving slowly toward FRANKIE. FRANKIE stands awkwardly, supporting himself by the sofa, on his bad leg.)

FRANKIE: I need to find some transportation outa here! I need to find my car! I can't hang around here, Beth.

BETH: *(Moving toward FRANKIE)* You could be better. Better man. Maybe. Without hate. You could be my sweet man. You could. Pretend to be. Try. My sweetest man.

(As BETH *gets closer,* FRANKIE *starts to move around the sofa, hopping on his bad leg and trying to keep the sofa between him and* BETH.*)*

FRANKIE: *(Hopping away from her)* No, Beth. This is not something I want to do right now. It's not good for my leg. I should be resting it. I have to be getting out of here now.

BETH: *(Moving after him slowly)* You could pretend so much that you start thinking this is me. You could really fall in love with me. How would that be? In a love we never knew.

FRANKIE: You're Jake's wife. We've got no business messing around like this! Now it's time for me to go. I have to go now. I have to find my car.

BETH: It's buried.

FRANKIE: What?

BETH: There's a blizzard. It's buried. We have to stay together now. Us. That's funny how we wind up. *(Laughs.)*

FRANKIE: A blizzard? What're you talking about, a blizzard. How long was I asleep?

BETH: *(Moving toward porch, pointing out)* See? Look. Out there. Everything's white.

FRANKIE: *(Trying to move away from sofa, toward porch)* When did that happen?

BETH: We have to stay alone. Together. Here. Us.

*(*FRANKIE *takes a couple of hopping steps and falls to the floor.* BETH *moves to him.)*

FRANKIE: *(On floor)* Goddamnit!

*(*FRANKIE *clutches his leg in pain.* BETH *kneels beside him and starts to take her shirt off again.* FRANKIE *stops her, reaches out and grabs her wrists.)*

No! Look—don't take your shirt off again! Don't do it. The shirt
is not gonna do my leg any good. It's useless. Understand? The
shirt is no help. So just leave it on. Okay? Just leave the shirt on,
Beth.

(He lets go of her wrists. She stops trying to take the shirt off.)

BETH: Maybe they'll cut. Cut.

FRANKIE: Stop saying that! I don't like the sound of it. It's not as bad
as all that. Amputation is not the answer here. Is there any way
you could make a phone call for me?

(BETH stands, moves to sofa and sits. She watches FRANKIE on the floor.)

BETH: *(Sitting on sofa)* You can only think of far away? Only thoughts
of where you came from? Nothing here? Nothing right here?
Now.

FRANKIE: I'm in a situation here that I didn't expect to be in. You
understand me? I didn't expect to be stuck here.

BETH: Stuck. Like me. Stuck.

FRANKIE: This is your home. You live here. I don't.

BETH: But you have brain.

FRANKIE: What?

BETH: Brain. In you. Thinking.

FRANKIE: So do you!

BETH: No. Mike took it. My father told him to.

*(She gets up from sofa and crosses past FRANKIE to porch. She looks out.
FRANKIE on floor behind her.)*

FRANKIE: Beth, that's just not true. That's not true. I don't know
where you got that idea from. You'd be dead if you didn't have a
brain. You can't live without one.

BETH: *(Looking out over porch)* Then why is this so empty? So empty now. Everything. Gone. A hole.

(Sounds of MIKE *breathing heavily offstage.)*

FRANKIE: What's that? Beth? What's that sound? Is someone out there? Beth.

*(*BETH *continues looking out over porch.)*

Help me get back on the couch now. There's somebody coming.

*(*MIKE *enters from the porch, covered in snow and carrying the severed hindquarters of a large buck with the hide still on it. He carries the butchered deer over his right shoulder with his rifle in his left hand.* MIKE *sees* FRANKIE *on the floor. He stops. Pause. He stares at* BETH, *then back to* FRANKIE. MIKE *flops the hindquarters down on the floor in the middle of the room, then props his rifle on top of the meat. He pulls his gloves off and starts warming his hands by blowing into them.* FRANKIE *stares at* MIKE *from the floor.* BETH *stares at the deer parts. Pause.)*

MIKE: *(To* BETH, *but staring at* FRANKIE*)* Tell Dad I kept the rack for myself. It's a trophy buck. He can have the meat but I'm keepin' the rack.

BETH: *(Still staring at deer)* He doesn't eat the meat. Momma says he doesn't eat the meat.

MIKE: Then he can feed it to the dog. I don't care what he does with it. *(Pause. To* FRANKIE*)* What're you doin' on the floor?

FRANKIE: I can't get up.

MIKE: *(To* BETH*)* He didn't try nothin', did he?

(Pause. BETH *keeps staring at the deer.)*

Beth!

BETH: Huh?

MIKE: He didn't try to pull anything on ya, did he?

FRANKIE: I fell.

MIKE: *(To FRANKIE)* I'm askin' her!

BETH: *(Staring at deer)* You cut him in half?

MIKE: Beth, I'm askin' you a question!

(MEG *enters from up left in nightgown and bathrobe, slippers. She just appears, drowsy from sleep.*)

MEG: Why is there so much noise now? Your father's trying to get some sleep.

MIKE: He should try sleepin' at night like everybody else.

FRANKIE: *(To MEG)* Mam—

MEG: *(To FRANKIE)* Why aren't you up on the sofa? You're gonna catch your death of cold on the floor like that.

BETH: Mama? Daddy doesn't eat the meat, does he?

(MEG *looks at* BETH, *then she sees the deer carcass on the floor. She approaches it slowly, stepping over* FRANKIE.)

Mike said to give it to Daddy but he doesn't eat the meat.

MEG: *(Staring at deer quarters)* Mike—what in the world? Can't you take it down to the freezer?

MIKE: Tell Dad to do it when he gets up. I shot it for him, he can dress it out. I'm goin' back out there. There's deer all over the place.

MEG: Well, you can't just leave it here in the middle of the living room floor.

MIKE: Why not? It's frozen solid. Won't thaw out for hours yet. I thought I'd surprise him.

MEG: He'll be surprised all right.

FRANKIE: *(Still on floor, trying to crawl to sofa)* Mam, is there any chance you could make a phone call for me?

MEG: I suppose so. Is it long distance?

MIKE: Nobody's makin' any phone calls for you, buddy. The lines are frozen solid. You're stuck. You're stuck right here. It's snowin' like there's no tomorrow out there.

MEG: *(Moving toward porch, looking out)* Is it that bad? I must've dozed off. It wasn't snowing that hard when I went upstairs.

FRANKIE: *(Reaching sofa, trying to pull himself up)* I have to get back home! I can't stay here anymore! I have to get back home!

MEG: *(Staring out over porch at snow)* Please, don't scream in the house. This house is very old.

FRANKIE: *(Clawing his way up onto sofa, to MIKE)* Look—look—you want me outa here, right? Everybody wants me outa here? I don't belong here, right? I'm not part of your family. I'm an enemy to you? Isn't that right? I am willing to go. Now. I'm ready. I'm ready to go now! Just get me outa here whatever way you can. I'll do whatever's necessary. I'll pay you. Just get me outa here!

(MIKE smiles and stares at FRANKIE, puts his gloves back on, picks up his rifle. BETH crosses slowly over to FRANKIE. FRANKIE collapses, exhausted, on sofa.)

BETH: *(Beside FRANKIE now, she pats him softly on his head)* Your whole life can turn around. Upside down. In a flash. Sudden. Don't worry. Don't worry now. This whole world can disappear. Everything you know can go. You won't even recognize your own hands.

(BETH, as she exits, moves slowly upstage and exits through hallway entrance.)

Night, Mama.

MEG: Good night, dear.

MIKE: (*To* MEG) It's not night! It's daytime! Jesus Christ, can't you see it's daytime out there.

(MEG *turns slowly and stares out over porch.* MIKE *exits out porch, down stairs and disappears upstage with his rifle.* MEG *stays looking out over porch.*)

FRANKIE: (*Yelling to* MIKE *as he exits*) Wait a second!

(*Pause.* FRANKIE *and* MEG *are left alone,* MEG, *with her back to* FRANKIE, *staring out at snow.* FRANKIE *stares at her back.*)

MEG: (*Keeping her back to* FRANKIE, *staring out*) I never get tired of seeing snow. Isn't that funny?

(*Lights fade to black.*)

SCENE 4

Lights up on stage-right set. Night. Moon is full. SALLY *is in* JAKE*'s bed with the blanket pulled up around her neck, lying on her back.* JAKE *is standing in the middle of the room in his underwear still, leather jacket with medals. He's draping the flag around his neck and over his shoulders, holding the leather box of ashes in one hand.*

SALLY: This isn't gonna fool her, Jake.

JAKE: *(Moving to bed)* Just tuck yourself in. Tuck the blanket tight around you so she sees there's a body in there.

(He goes to SALLY *and starts tucking the blanket tightly around her with her arms inside and only her head sticking out.)*

SALLY: But my body doesn't look anything like your body.

JAKE: Doesn't matter. She's not gonna look that close. Turn over on your stomach so she doesn't see your face.

SALLY: She'll see my hair then.

JAKE: Put your head under the pillow. Turn over and put your head under the pillow. Come on, Sally. You gotta do it.

*(*SALLY *turns herself over on her stomach as* JAKE *keeps tucking the blanket around her tightly.)*

SALLY: This is really stupid, Jake. Where'd you see this, in some old prison movie?

JAKE: *(Tucking blanket around her, then putting pillow over her head)* Now when she comes in, in the morning—she'll come in with the breakfast. She'll come in and she'll say somethin' like: "Rise and shine—it's coffee time!" You just stay under the pillow. You can kinda moan or somethin'—make a few little movements, but don't say anything to her.

(SALLY takes the pillow off her head and throws it on floor.)

SALLY: *(Throwing pillow)* I can't breathe under here! I feel like a mummy.

(JAKE picks up pillow.)

JAKE: Sally, you gotta cover your head or she'll know right away.

SALLY: All right, just hand me the pillow. When I hear her comin', I'll put it over my head.

JAKE: What if you fall asleep? You could fall asleep and forget.

SALLY: I won't forget. Just hand me the pillow.

(Pause. JAKE tosses the pillow on her head. SALLY takes it and moves it to one side. Pause.)

You better go through the bathroom window. She'll see you if you try to cross the porch.

JAKE: I know how to escape. Don't worry.

SALLY: Aren't you gonna wear any pants?

JAKE: She hid 'em. She thinks that's gonna stop me.

SALLY: You're gonna try to get to Montana in your underpants with an American flag wrapped around your neck?

JAKE: I'll travel by night.

SALLY: *(Laughs)* Oh boy, Jake. I hope ya make it.

JAKE: I'll make it all right. There's nothin' gonna stop me. Not Frankie or Mom or that family of hers or—

(He stops himself. Stares into space.)

SALLY: What'sa matter, Jake?

JAKE: *(Staring)* There's this thing—this thing in my head.

(SALLY rises up slowly on one elbow in the bed and stares at him. He whispers now.)

(Whisper) This thing that the next moment—the moment right after this one will—blow up. Explode with a voice. A scream from a voice I don't know. Or a voice I knew once but now it's changed. It doesn't know me either. Now. It used to but not now. I've scared it into something else. Another form. A whole other person who doesn't see me anymore. Who doesn't even remember that we knew each other once. I've gotta see her again, Sally.

(Suddenly BETH screams from out of the darkness, stage left.)

BETH: *(In dark)* JAAAAAAAAAAAAAAAKE!

(Lights black out stage right.)

Act III

SCENE 1

Stage-right set. LORRAINE *is in* JAKE*'s bed bundled up in blankets to her neck. She shakes all over with the cold chills and her face is pale and sweating. The model airplanes still hang overhead.* SALLY *sits in the chair, stage left of the bed, with a bowl of soup on her lap and a spoon in her hand. A cup of coffee sits steaming on the side table.* SALLY*'s voice is heard first in darkness.*

SALLY: *(In dark)* Rise and shine! It's coffee time!

> *(Lights sweep up fast to bright morning.* SALLY *offers* LORRAINE *a spoonful of soup.)*

LORRAINE: Did he tell you to say that? He probably did, didn't he? Where is the humiliation supposed to end?

SALLY: Just try a little sip of soup, Mom. Just a little sip.

LORRAINE: Not from you.

SALLY: Look, you can't keep blaming me forever. He's gone. There was nothin' I could do about it.

LORRAINE: Is there any good reason in this Christless world why men leave women? Is there? Is there any good reason for that? You tell me. You tell me. Isn't there enough to suffer already? We got all kinda good reasons to suffer without men cookin' up more.

SALLY: There's always a chance he might come back.

LORRAINE: He won't come back now. Thanks to you. Not now. I know him. He's like a stray dog. He's home for a while and you pet him and feed him and he licks your hand and then he's gone again. I know where he's gone too. Straight to that girl. You can bet yer bivey on that. She's got a hold on his mind.

SALLY: Well, Frankie'll bring him back then. He'll find him.

LORRAINE: Frankie can't even find his own zipper. How's he gonna find his brother?

SALLY: Just try a little soup, Mom.

LORRAINE: I don't want any a' that slop! Stop tryin' to pawn it off on me.

SALLY: It's the same batch you made for Jake.

LORRAINE: I know. Smells like it.

SALLY: *(Smelling soup)* Smells all right to me.

LORRAINE: It's ripe.

SALLY: Well, you gotta eat somethin'.

LORRAINE: My son's abandoned me! Can't you understand that? He's abandoned me. And you put him up to it.

SALLY: I didn't put him up to nothin'. What was he gonna do? Stay here and rot in this room. He woulda left sooner or later.

LORRAINE: He's run off to the wild world when he could've stayed here under my protection. He could've stayed here forever and no one could've touched him. Now he's gonna wind up right back in prison. In prison, where they'll eat him alive.

SALLY: *(Offering spoon to LORRAINE)* Just take a little bit on your tongue. See if you like it.

(LORRAINE sits up fast and knocks the spoon out of SALLY's hand. SALLY stands and moves left, away from LORRAINE.)

LORRAINE: *(As she knocks spoon away)* Get that stuff away from me! What'sa matter with you! I'm not interested in food. I'm not interested in keeping something alive that's already dead.

SALLY: You're not dead yet! You won't get out of it that easy!

(Pause)

LORRAINE: I know what's gonna happen. I can see it plain as day. They'll find him by the highway. That's what'll happen. Crumpled up. Busted open like a road dog. Then maybe you'll be satisfied.

SALLY: I don't want anything to happen to him any more than you do. He couldn't stay here.

LORRAINE: I'll get a call. Cop will come to my door. Just like before. Just like with his daddy. I'll wait for that cop. I'll wait right here. Long as I have to.

SALLY: Now don't start imagining things.

LORRAINE: There's nothin' imaginary about it. I can see it.

SALLY: What can you see?

LORRAINE: Maybe the same cop will come. The very same cop. I never could figure that out. Why they'd send a cop? Why should a cop be a messenger of death? It's like sending a fireman.

(LORRAINE lies back down in bed again. She pulls the blankets up around her neck. Pause.)

SALLY: You can't let yourself get so worked up over this. You're gonna make yourself sick.

LORRAINE: You sent that cop, didn't you? Back then. Jake never woulda done somethin' like that. He'da come and told me face to face.

SALLY: We were miles away. Mexico. It happened in Mexico. Remember?

LORRAINE: I remember! Don't talk to me like I'm an idiot.

SALLY: We tried to call you that night it happened. We both tried to call you but they said the police had to do it. It was international. I never wanted to send a cop. They said it had to be official.

LORRAINE: Doesn't matter. Official, unofficial, it's the same news. Dead is dead. Nobody can make it un-dead.

(Pause)

SALLY: You didn't really care one way or the other, did you? You'd let him go a long time ago.

LORRAINE: He left me! All right? Get that straight in your noggin. *He* left *me*! Not the other way around.

SALLY: You never tried to find him.

LORRAINE: *(Sitting up again)* Are you kidding? Man runs off. Into the night. No word. No note. No phone call. Disappears like an apparition and I'm supposed to go track his ass down. Not me, sister. No sir. Not this one. Let him stagger around, lost and wild-eyed if he wants to. Let him bang his head up and down the alleyways moanin' like a baby about some mystery he doesn't even have a clue to. You can't save the doomed! You make a stab at it. You make the slightest little try and you're doomed yourself. Take a look at your brother if you don't believe me.

SALLY: But you never even tried, did you?

LORRAINE: Tried what? Who are you to be judgin' me now? Who are you? You don't even have a man. Never did.

SALLY: You're not recommending it, are you?

LORRAINE: Just don't go accusing me of neglecting your father. You don't know nothin' about it.

SALLY: You never even asked me about it.

LORRAINE: About what?

SALLY: Our trip down there. Me and Jake made a special trip. Remember? We found him in his trailer down there.

LORRAINE: *(Lies back down)* So what? Ya want a medal or somethin'? You're his kids, not his wife. Why shouldn't you try to find him. I don't wanna hear about that stuff now.

SALLY: We really surprised him. I don't think he'd had a visitor for months.

LORRAINE: Who'd visit him?

SALLY: He didn't even know who we were at first. Just stood there at the screen door, kinda staring at us like we might be burglars or something.

LORRAINE: Probably drunk. As usual.

SALLY: Nope. Stone cold sober. Didn't have any money to drink. He looked real weak and vulnerable. The opposite of how he was when he was drinking.

LORRAINE: He was always weak. That never changed.

SALLY: He took us inside and the smell almost knocked me over. No windows. Smelled like dirty laundry and cigarettes and something else. Something almost sweet.

LORRAINE: Booze.

SALLY: Maybe.

LORRAINE: Tiger Rose. That was his baby. Tiger Rose. I musta tripped over a million a' them skinny green bottles.

SALLY: He had all these pictures of us taped to the walls. Baby pictures and 4-H Club pictures and pictures of Jake running with a football. But they were all squeezed in between these other pictures. Pictures of Bing Crosby and Ginger Rogers and Ida Lupino and Gene Autry and Louis Armstrong. And there we were kinda peeking out between the cracks of these faces. I got the feeling he must've spent a lot of time talking to these faces. Maybe even introducing the pictures of us to the pictures of all these stars. Trying to make a family out of us all. So we'd know each other.

LORRAINE: Yeah, well he shoulda tried that at home first.

SALLY: You can't condemn him now. He's dead.

LORRAINE: I'll condemn him right up to my last breath! He shaped my whole life. Vengeance is the only thing that keeps me goin'.

SALLY: How can you get revenge out of a dead man?

LORRAINE: Because—he's still alive in me. You understand that? He's still walkin' around inside me. He put stuff into me that'll never go away. Ever. He made sure a' that.

SALLY: That's not him. That's you. If you hadn't had him, you'da found somebody else to throw the blame on.

LORRAINE: Yeah, well you didn't know him like I knew him.

SALLY: Guess not. Because what I saw down there with Jake was a man who was totally innocent.

LORRAINE: Innocent! That's a hot one.

SALLY: Didn't you ever wonder about him? About what became of him?

LORRAINE: Who?

SALLY: Dad.

LORRAINE: *(Sitting up)* Wonder? Did I ever wonder? You know a man your whole life. You grow up with him. You're almost raised together. You go to school on the same bus together. You go through tornadoes together in the same basement. You go through a world war together. You have babies together. And then one day he just up and disappears into thin air. Did I ever wonder? Yeah. You bet your sweet life I wondered. But you know where all that wondering got me? Nowhere. Absolutely nowhere. Because here I am. Here I am. Alone. Just the same as though he'd never even existed.

SALLY: I thought you said he was still in you.

LORRAINE: Not him. Some disease he left behind.

SALLY: But there must've been a time when you loved him. Before.

LORRAINE: Love. Whata crock a' shit. Love! There's another disease. Only difference is it's a disease that makes ya feel good. While it lasts. Then, when it's gone, yer worse off than before you caught it.

SALLY: Well, I don't think there's a whole lot we can do about it, is there?

LORRAINE: Yes there is. Oh, yes there is. You can resist. You can look it right square in the kisser and resist.

(LORRAINE *lies back down. Pause.*)

SALLY: Maybe. Maybe *you* can. That's what Jake tried to do. He's a lot like you I guess. He started squirming in that trailer. Making up reasons why we had to get outa there. Get back across the border before it got dark. Dad kept wanting us to stay but he didn't have anything to offer us. And that's when Jake made a desperate move. He didn't even know he was doing it. He was so desperate to get out of that situation, that he stands up and he offers to take Dad and me out to a bar. For a drink! I couldn't believe it. Dad's whole face lit up. I've never seen his face like that. He smiled like a little kid and grabbed his hat.

LORRAINE: You can't stop a drinkin' man from drinkin'. All he needs is an idea and he's gone. Just the idea of straddling a bar stool in some honky-tonk somewhere in his mind. He's gone.

(LORRAINE *slowly pulls herself up to a sitting position and listens more intently to* SALLY.)

SALLY: They started right off with double shots of tequila and lime. At first it was like this brotherhood they'd just remembered. But then it started to shift. After about the fourth double shot it started to go in a whole different direction.

LORRAINE: That figures.

SALLY: There was a meanness that started to come outa both of them like these hidden snakes. A terrible meanness that was like— murder almost. It *was* murder.

LORRAINE: Whad'ya mean, murder?

SALLY: Their eyes changed. Something in their eyes. Like animals. Like the way an animal looks for the weakness in another animal. They started poking at each other's weakness. Stabbing. Just a little bit at a time. Like the way that rooster used to do. That rooster we had that went around looking for the tiniest speck of blood on a hen or a chick and then he'd start pecking away at it. And the more he pecked at it the more excited he got until finally he just killed it.

LORRAINE: Yeah, we had to boil that one. Tough son of a gun.

SALLY: They locked into each other like there was nobody else in the bar. At first it was all about sports. About which one of them could throw a hardball faster. Which one could take the toughest hit in football. Which one could run the fastest and the longest. That was the one they decided would be the big test. They decided to prove it to each other once and for all. So they downed a couple more tequilas and crashed out through the doors of the place into the street.

LORRAINE: I thought you said he could barely stand up.

SALLY: Who?

LORRAINE: Your father.

SALLY: That was before. Before he'd had a drink. Now it was like he'd had a transfusion or somethin'. That tequila went right into his blood and lit him on fire. He crouched down in a racing position right beside Jake. And they were both deadly serious. And then they took off. Dad took about four strides and fell flat on his face in the street but Jake never stopped. He ran like a wild colt and never once looked back. Straight into the next bar up the block. I went over and tried to help Dad up but he turned on me and snarled. Just like a dog. Just exactly like a crazy dog. I saw it in his eyes. This deep, deep hate that came from somewhere far away. It was pure, black hate with no purpose.

LORRAINE: That was him all right.

SALLY: He wouldn't let me help him. He just crawled up the street toward the bar that Jake went into. And there I was following along behind. I felt so stupid. He kept turning and snarling at me to keep back. But I didn't wanna fall too far back 'cause I was afraid somethin'—

(She starts to break down but stops herself.)

LORRAINE: What?

SALLY: *(Trying to control it)* I was afraid somethin' bad might happen to him and—it happened anyway.

LORRAINE: What happened?

SALLY: Jake came up with a brilliant idea. He said, since we were only about a mile from the American border we should hit every bar and continue the race until we got to the other side. First one to the other side, won. First one to America! But we couldn't miss a bar. Right then I knew what Jake had in mind.

LORRAINE: What?

SALLY: Jake had decided to kill him.

(Pause)

LORRAINE: *(Throws the blankets off and struggles to sit up)* What in the world are you talkin' about!

SALLY: It was just the same—it was just the same as if he'd had a gun. He knew what was gonna happen. Dad couldn't even walk anymore. He couldn't stand. His knees were all bloody. Jake knew that all he had to do was push him over the edge. Just a few more drinks and he'd be gone.

LORRAINE: *(Struggling to stand by bed, supporting herself)* That is the most lamebrained, idiotic piece of claptrap I ever heard in my life! Jake might be a lot a' things. He might be crazy. He might be wound a little loose in some areas but he would never, ever, in this world, try to kill his own father! How can you say somethin' like that?

SALLY: I was there! I was right there and I saw every inch of it. I saw him killed! I saw it happen. I saw him splattered all over the road like some lost piece of livestock. He was trying to run down the middle of a highway. He was trying to beat his own son to the border. He didn't even know what country he was in anymore! Jake murdered him! And he never even looked back. He was already sitting in some bar down the road ordering the next round of drinks. He never even got up when he heard the sirens.

LORRAINE: It was an accident! That's all. Just an ordinary accident. Couldn't be helped.

SALLY: No, Mom. It was no accident.

LORRAINE: He didn't know what he was doin', any more than his father did!

SALLY: He knew. He still knows. He made me promise. That's how come he didn't tell you face to face. That's why the cop came to your door.

LORRAINE: He is not a murderer! My son is not a murderer! Why is everyone trying to make him into this criminal? First, that woman of his. He never shoulda got tied up with that woman in the first place. She's the cause of all this. And now you've turned against him.

SALLY: I'm just tellin' you what I saw with my own eyes.

LORRAINE: What you saw? What you saw! You stood there and watched your own father get run over by a truck in the middle of a Mexican highway and you're tryin' to tell me that Jake murdered him?

SALLY: That's the way it happened.

LORRAINE: What about you! Jake was nowhere near him you said. What were you doin'? Standin' there helpless? You were the only one sober and there was nothin' you could do? Is that the story?

SALLY: Dad wouldn't let me near him. I couldn't get near him.

LORRAINE: You couldn't have gone for help? Were your legs broke or somethin'?

SALLY: There was nowhere to go! Jake had the keys.

LORRAINE: Jake! Jake! Jake! *You're* the one who killed him, not Jake!! You're the one. If he was that drunk, you could've taken care of him. You coulda got him off the road. You coulda dragged him. You coulda done somethin' other than just stand there and watch. It was you. Wasn't it? It was you that wanted him dead. It's you that wants Jake dead too!

SALLY: No!

LORRAINE: It's you that wants to undermine this entire family! Drag us down one by one until there's no one left but you.

SALLY: I'm just sick of coverin' up for him. I'm sick to death of covering everything up. I'm sick of being locked up in this room. In our own house. Look at this room. What're we doin' in here? This was Jake's room when he was a kid. What're we doin' in this room now? What're we supposed to be hiding from?

(Long pause. LORRAINE stands there staring at SALLY, then slowly turns her head up and stares at the model planes.)

LORRAINE: *(Staring at planes)* I know one thing for sure. All these airplanes have gotta go. All these airplanes are comin' down. Every last one of 'em. All the junk in this house that they left behind for me to save. It's all goin'. We'll make us a big bonfire. They never wanted it anyway. They had no intention of ever comin' back here to pick it up. That was just a dream of theirs. It never meant a thing to them. They dreamed it up just to keep me on the hook. Can't believe I fell for it all those years.

SALLY: I didn't want him to die, Mom.

LORRAINE: Doesn't matter now. He was one a' them hopeless men. Nothin' you can do about the hopeless. *(Pause)* You know what I miss more than anything now?

SALLY: What?

LORRAINE: The wind. One a' them fierce, hot, dry winds that come from deep out in the desert and rip the trees apart. You know, those winds that wipe everything clean and leave the sky without a cloud. Pure blue. Pure, pure blue. Wouldn't that be nice?

(Lights fade slowly to black.)

SCENE 2

Lights up, stage-left set. Night. FRANKIE *asleep on couch, curled up, his back to audience with a dark blanket wrapped around him. Just as lights rise, we see* BAYLOR *drop himself heavily into the armchair, exhausted. He's wearing a gray long-john top, heavy dark woolen pants with suspenders (dark bloodstains on pants and shirt), heavy wool socks with the same boots from Act II but with the laces untied. He breathes heavily and makes a feeble attempt to lean forward and take his boots off but gives up and collapses back into the comfort of the chair, giving out a defeated exhale.* MEG *enters quickly from up left still in nightgown, bathrobe and slippers from Act II.*

MEG: Baylor, could you please come upstairs and talk to Beth? She's got me worried sick.

BAYLOR: Help me off with these boots, would ya? My back's killin' me. Some hunter. Leave all the work up to someone else. Easy enough to shoot the damn thing. Dressin' it out's another matter.

(MEG moves to BAYLOR, kneels and pulls his boots off. She stands again and keeps hold of the boots.)

MEG: *(Standing in front of him with boots)* Baylor.

BAYLOR: What! Stop houndin' me, will ya! "Baylor, Baylor, Baylor!" I never get a moment's peace around here.

MEG: I want you to come upstairs and talk to Beth.

BAYLOR: Tell her to come down here if she wants to talk. I'm not gettin' outa this chair for the duration of the night.

MEG: She won't come down.

BAYLOR: Then have her send me a letter. There's nothin' wrong with her body is there? Last time I saw her, she was walkin' around.

MEG: She's talking in a whole different way now. About stuff I never even heard of. I don't understand a thing. It's like she's talking to someone else.

BAYLOR: Well, she wasn't exactly an open book before.

MEG: I know, but now she's just scaring me really bad.

BAYLOR: Scarin' you? She's your own daughter for Christ's sake.

MEG: Well, she doesn't act like it anymore. She's like a whole different person.

BAYLOR: She's the same person. Just leave her be for a while. She needs some time to herself. Yer always fussin' with her so much she never has a chance to just be by herself. That's the only way she's gonna be able to face this thing.

MEG: I'm afraid to leave her alone, though.

BAYLOR: Stop bein' afraid! Yer afraid a' this—yer afraid a' that. You spend all yer time bein' afraid. Why don't ya just save all that fear up for when the real thing comes along.

MEG: What's that?

(Pause)

BAYLOR: Well, we're not gonna last forever, are we, Meg? Have ya ever given that any thought? One a' these days our parts are gonna give out on us and that'll be it. Now that's somethin' to be afraid of.

MEG: I'm not afraid a' that. I don't care one way or the other about that. I'm afraid for my daughter. She's disappearing on us. All I recognize anymore is her body. And even that's beginning to change.

BAYLOR: How do ya mean?

MEG: The way she stands now. With her shoulders all slumped forward and her head slung down. Her eyes staring at the ground all the time. She never used to be like that.

BAYLOR: She's had a big shock to her system. Whad'ya expect?

MEG: I expect her to get better. I expect her to come back to herself. She's a million miles away now.

BAYLOR: Well, we handled yer mother for all those years. We can handle Beth, too, I suppose.

MEG: My mother was an old, old woman. Beth's still a baby.

BAYLOR: She's not a baby.

MEG: She's a young woman! She's young yet, Baylor.

BAYLOR: I know she's young. What's that got to do with it? You think the powers that be hang around waiting for the right time, the right moment to bear down upon us? You think they're all sittin' up there consulting with each other about her age? "Oh, she's young yet. She's a baby. Let's hold off for a while." They couldn't give a shit about her predicament or any of us. We're all gonna get clobbered when we least expect it.

MEG: *(Moving to exit up left)* Well, I can't talk to you about it. That's clear.

BAYLOR: Where you goin'?

MEG: Upstairs.

BAYLOR: Bring me in that Mink Oil before you go up there. You think you can remember that? Last time you forgot. My feet are startin' to bleed.

(MEG exits up left through hallway with BAYLOR's boots. BAYLOR gives another deep exhale, then turns his head and stares at FRANKIE, who's still asleep. Pause. BAYLOR kicks the couch with his left foot, then flinches with pain, but FRANKIE remains asleep.)

BAYLOR: *(To FRANKIE)* Soon's the plow comes through, you're outa here, pal. This ain't a motel.

(BAYLOR kicks the couch again and flinches but FRANKIE remains asleep.)

You hear me?

(MEG re-enters from the hallway with a tin of Mink Oil, crosses to BAYLOR and hands the tin to him.)

(To MEG) We gotta get this character outa the house. He's dead weight. All he does is sleep now. *(To MEG, taking tin)* Thanks. Help me off with these socks, would ya? I can't bend an inch.

(MEG kneels and pulls BAYLOR's socks off while BAYLOR struggles to open the tin.)

MEG: Beth's been talking about him. Saying his name. Did we know this man before, Dad?

BAYLOR: *(Slamming tin into the arm of the chair)* Goddamn these tins! They make everything nowadays so they won't come open! Nothin' comes open anymore.

MEG: Here, let me do it.

BAYLOR: *(Hands tin to MEG)* You do it.

MEG: *(Taking tin)* I am doing it.

(MEG pops open the tin easily and hands it back to BAYLOR.)

BAYLOR: How'd you do that?

MEG: I've done it before.

BAYLOR: Well, I can never get the damn thing to pop open. They used to have a little trigger on the side. Little metal pry gizmo.

MEG: They still do.

(BAYLOR turns the tin around until he discovers a little metal hinged bar.)

BAYLOR: I'll be darned. Thought they'd eliminated that.

MEG: No. They still have it.

BAYLOR: Well, I'll be darned. Would you mind puttin' this on my feet, Meg? My back is so sore from carving that meat, I can't bend over.

(BAYLOR hands the Mink Oil tin back to MEG. MEG takes it. She hesitates.)

MEG: I should get back upstairs and check on Beth.

BAYLOR: Just do my feet, would ya please!

(MEG kneels and starts to rub Mink Oil into BAYLOR's feet. BAYLOR lays his head back on the chair and closes his eyes.)

MEG: She's just been talking so funny. Mixing things up. I can't follow her thoughts anymore.

BAYLOR: Aah. Boy, I'm tellin' ya, that is as close to heaven as I been in a long time.

MEG: *(As she rubs his feet)* Doesn't it sting?

BAYLOR: Little bit.

MEG: I should think it would. Your toes are cracked wide open. How can you do that to yourself?

BAYLOR: I didn't do it. The cold did.

MEG: But you sit out there in that shack for hours on end letting your feet freeze. That doesn't make any sense, Baylor.

BAYLOR: I can't stalk deer anymore, at my age. I gotta wait for 'em to come to me.

MEG: Isn't there some other hobby you could take up?

BAYLOR: It's no hobby. Where'd you get that idea? Hunting is no hobby. It's an art. It's a way a' life. Everything gets turned into a hobby these days.

MEG: Well, it's not necessary to injure yourself like this.

BAYLOR: What's "necessary" got to do with it?

MEG: Well, I mean, we're living in the modern world. We've got the grocery store just four miles down the road. We don't need to kill animals anymore to stay alive. We're not pioneers.

BAYLOR: There's more to it than that.

MEG: Well, what is it? I'd like to know. I mean what is the big fascination about standing out there in the cold for hours on end waiting for an innocent deer to come along so you can blast a hole through it and freeze your feet off in the process?

BAYLOR: It's deer season. You hunt deer in deer season. That's what you do.

MEG: Look at this. You've got blood all over your pants and shirt. You look like you've been in a war or something.

BAYLOR: Just rub that stuff into my feet and stop tryin' to pick a bone with me. I'm too tired to argue.

(Pause. MEG keeps rubbing BAYLOR's feet. BAYLOR keeps his eyes closed.)

MEG: *(After pause)* Maybe you just wanna be alone. Maybe that's it. Maybe it's got nothing to do with hunting. You just don't want to be a part of us anymore.

BAYLOR: *(Eyes closed)* You've still got the greatest hands in the world.

MEG: Maybe it really is true that we're so different that we'll never be able to get certain things across to each other. Like mother used to say.

BAYLOR: Your mother.

MEG: "Two opposite animals."

BAYLOR: Your mother was a basket case.

MEG: She was a female.

(Pause. BAYLOR opens his eyes, looks at MEG, shakes his head, then closes his eyes again.)

BAYLOR: *(Eyes closed)* Meg, do you ever think about the things you say or do you just say 'em?

MEG: She was pure female. There wasn't any trace of male in her. Like Beth—Beth's got male in her. I can see that.

BAYLOR: I'm her father.

MEG: No. She's got male in her.

BAYLOR: *(Opens eyes, leans forward, points to himself)* I'm male! I'm her father and I'm a male! Now if you can't make sense, just don't speak. Okay? Just rub my feet and don't speak.

(BAYLOR leans back, closes his eyes again. MEG keeps on rubbing his feet. Pause.)

MEG: She was like a deer. Her eyes.

BAYLOR: Oh, brother. How do you manage to get things so screwed up? No wonder yer daughter's in the shape she's in. A deer is a deer and a person is a person. They got nothin' to do with each other.

(Pause)

MEG: Some people are like deer. They have that look—that distant thing in their eyes. Like mother did.

BAYLOR Your mother had that distant thing in her eyes because she'd lost her mind, Meg. She went crazy.

MEG: She was just old.

BAYLOR: Yeah, she almost took us to the grave with her. You and me'd be a lot younger today if we'd stuck her in a rest home when the whole thing started.

MEG: *(Still rubbing his feet)* I know what it is.

(*Pause.* BAYLOR *opens his eyes.*)

BAYLOR: What! What's what *what* is?

MEG: The female—the female one needs—the other.

BAYLOR: What other?

MEG: The male. The male one.

BAYLOR: Oh.

MEG: But the male one—doesn't really need the other. Not the same way.

BAYLOR: I don't get ya.

MEG: The male one goes off by himself. Leaves. He needs something else. But he doesn't know what it is. He doesn't really know what he needs. So he ends up dead. By himself.

(BAYLOR *sits up fast. Pulls his feet away from* MEG, *grabs the tin away from her and starts trying to put the lid back on it.*)

BAYLOR: All right. All right! Stop rubbing my feet now. Go on up-stairs! Go on. I've heard enough a' this.

(MEG *stands.*)

MEG: Did I put enough on?

BAYLOR: Yeah, that's fine. Go on upstairs now.

MEG: You know, that stuff's not really for feet.

BAYLOR: What?

MEG: That Mink Oil. That's for boots. It's not made for feet.

BAYLOR: I know that! Don't ya think I don't know that!

MEG: I just thought maybe you didn't know that.

(BAYLOR starts reaching for his socks but can't quite get to them.)

BAYLOR: WILL YOU PLEASE GO ON UPSTAIRS NOW!!! GET OUTA HERE!

(Pause. MEG just stands there staring at him as BAYLOR trembles with rage, trying to reach his socks.)

MEG: You think it's me, don't you? You didn't used to think it was, but now you think it's me. You think your whole life went sour because of me. Because of Mother. Because of Beth. If only your life was free of females, then you'd be free yourself.

BAYLOR: Well, you sure know how to speak the truth when you put yer mind to it, don't ya?

MEG: All these women put a curse on you and now you're stuck. You're chained to us forever. Isn't that the way it is?

BAYLOR: Yeah! Yeah! That's exactly the way it is. You got that right. I could be up in the wild country huntin' antelope. I could be raising a string a' pack mules back up in there. Doin' somethin' useful. But no, I gotta play nursemaid to a bunch a' feeble-minded women down here in civilization who can't take care a' themselves. I gotta waste my days away makin' sure they eat and have a roof over their heads and a nice warm place to go crazy in.

MEG: Nobody's crazy, Baylor. Except you. Why don't you just go. Why don't you just go off and live the way you want to live. We'll take care of ourselves. We always have.

(MEG turns to go.)

BAYLOR: Wait a second!

(MEG stops, turns to him. Pause.)

Come and reach me my socks for me. I can't bend over.

(Pause. MEG *looks at socks, then to* BAYLOR.*)*

Just pick 'em up for me. You don't have to put 'em on me. I can do that by myself.

*(*MEG *crosses slowly over to his socks, picks them up off the floor, holds them up in the air. Pause.)*

Gimme my socks! My feet are freezing!

*(*MEG *moves slowly to* BAYLOR *with the socks and drops them in his lap, then turns and exits up left through hallway.* BAYLOR *struggles to put his socks on as he rages to himself but he can't get them on.)*

BAYLOR: *(To himself, struggling with socks)* Everything should be reversed! Everything should be reversed! The worst part of your life should come first, not last! Why do they save it for last when yer too old to do anything about it. When yer body's so tied up in knots you can't even stand up to yer own wife.

*(*BAYLOR *throws his socks down in defeat. He kicks the sofa and yells at* FRANKIE.*)*

BAYLOR: *(To* FRANKIE*)* Hey! Hey! *(Kicks couch again.)* Hey, you goddamn freeloader! Nap time is over!

*(*FRANKIE *stays asleep.* BAYLOR *reaches out and pulls the blanket off him.)*

Get up! Get up outa that sofa before I drag you out of it with my own two hands!

*(*FRANKIE *stays asleep. Finally* BAYLOR *reaches out with his foot and pokes* FRANKIE *hard in the rear. Suddenly* FRANKIE *sits up, not knowing where he is. He grabs a corner of the blanket and tries to pull it back around himself but* BAYLOR *grabs the other end and they have a tug of war.)*

BAYLOR: *(Pulling on blanket)* No more blankets! No more free rides! It's time for you to leave! Let go a' this blanket!

(BAYLOR finally yanks the blanket away from FRANKIE. FRANKIE just sits there, rubbing this hands on his shoulders from the cold. He shivers. His eyes dart around the room, trying to figure out where he is.)

Now get up. Get outa that sofa and reach me my socks.

(FRANKIE just stares at BAYLOR. Keeps rubbing his shoulders, shivering.)

BAYLOR: *(Pointing to his socks)* See the socks?

(FRANKIE stares at the socks but makes no move toward them.)

Do you see 'em or not?

(FRANKIE nods.)

Then pick 'em up for me, would ya and put 'em on my feet. My back's seized up and my wife's abandoned me.

FRANKIE: I—I don't think I can get up. I can't feel my leg anymore.

BAYLOR: My feet are turnin' to ice, here! I need my socks!

FRANKIE: Wrap the blanket around them.

(Pause. BAYLOR considers for a moment, then wraps the blanket around his feet. Pause.)

How's that?

BAYLOR: It's not the same as my socks.

FRANKIE: Well, I'm sorry. I just can't get up.

BAYLOR: Yer not injured that bad.

FRANKIE: *(Sudden recognition)* You're the one who shot me, aren't you?

BAYLOR: Don't go gettin' any fancy notions about suing me. I had every right to shoot you. You were on my land.

FRANKIE: I remember you now.

BAYLOR: You won't get anywhere with that Big City stuff back here, boy. That don't hold water in the back country. There's not a lawyer within six hundred miles a' this place.

FRANKIE: I'm not gonna sue you.

BAYLOR: Last lawyer who tried to come back in here, we cut his nuts off.

FRANKIE: Hey look! Hey! I've got a bullet hole in my leg! All right? I've got a bullet hole clean through my leg! And you did it! And it's not gettin' any better. It's gettin' worse, in fact. So don't try to scare me with this stuff about lawyers, because I'm not buyin' it. I've got a serious injury here!

BAYLOR: Aw, stop complainin', will ya. I've had my belly full a' complaints in this house.

FRANKIE: Look—I don't know why it is but nobody around here will make any effort to try and get me outa here. How come that is? My brother—I've got a brother with a real short fuse. He gets weird ideas in his head. It doesn't take much to tip him over the edge. Now I've been here way too long. Way, way past the time I was supposed to get back. And he's gonna start gettin' the wrong idea about me and your daughter. I mean, your daughter is his wife. You know that, don't ya? I mean I suppose you know that but it's hard to tell anymore if anybody knows anything about anybody else around here. Like her, for instance. Your daughter. She is getting very strange with me. Very strange. I mean she started talkin' to me like I was him. Like I was my brother. To her, I mean. Like she thought I was him and not me. Your daughter. Beth. I mean I don't even know if she knows who I am anymore but—she thinks—she thinks her brother—your son and you, in fact—even you—she includes you in this too—she thinks you and him, your son and you, are somehow responsible for taking her brain out. For removing her brain. Did you know about all this?

BAYLOR: Nope.

FRANKIE: No. See? See, that's what I mean. Nobody knows. Nobody seems to know. Nobody seems to have the slightest idea about what's goin on. And meanwhile—MEANWHILE—I AM STUCK HERE TRYING TO GET BACK HOME! AND NOBODY IS MAKING ANY EFFORT TO HELP ME!

BAYLOR: Aw, pipe down, will ya for Christ's sake! Jesus God Almighty! You're worse than all the women in this house put together.

FRANKIE: If I die on you here—If I die, you're gonna be in big trouble, mister. You and everybody else in this family.

BAYLOR: Don't threaten me in my own house! Don't you try and threaten me in my own goddamn house! This isn't Southern California. This is Montana, buster!

(MEG appears again up left in same costume.)

MEG: *(Soft)* Baylor?

BAYLOR: *(Pause, turns to her, leans back in chair)* What is it now?

MEG: Beth's coming down. She wants to talk to you.

(FRANKIE suddenly reaches out for the blanket and jerks it off BAYLOR's feet, wraps it around himself. BAYLOR tries to grab it back but he's too late.)

BAYLOR: Gimme that blanket back! Give it back! That doesn't belong to you.

(FRANKIE keeps blanket, wraps it tightly around himself so he's covered completely with just his head sticking out. Like a mummy.)

MEG: She's coming down here now, Baylor.

BAYLOR: Let her come, for Christ's sake! What in the world is the big fuss all about? She lives in this house. *(Turns back to FRANKIE.)* Gimme back that blanket!

(In the course of this last rant by BAYLOR, BETH *appears beside* MEG *but* BAYLOR *doesn't notice her.* FRANKIE *sees her and tightens his blanket around his shoulders.* BETH *is dressed in a bizarre combination of clothing. She wears black high heels with short woolen bobby socks, a tight pink skirt—below the knee, straight out of the fifties—a fuzzy turquoise-blue short-sleeved, low-cut sweater, green tights. She wears lots of charm bracelets and a silver chain around her neck with a St. Christopher medal, a gold cross and a rabbit's foot.*

She has various kinds of snap earrings encircling her left ear. Her hair is piled high with a small white ribbon tied in a bow at the top. Her face is heavily made up with thick glossy pink lipstick, blue mascara and dark, outlined eyebrows. MEG *takes her hand as she enters and* BETH *just stands there holding hands with her mother. After pause,* BAYLOR *still hasn't seen her.)*

BETH: *(Soft)* Daddy?

*(*BAYLOR *turns to* BETH. *No reaction. Just stares at her for a while.)*

(To MEG*)* Who's this?

BETH: Daddy, I wanna ask you somethin' special.

BAYLOR: *(Another pause, staring at* BETH*)* What in the sam-hell have you got on? What is that getup!

BETH: I wanna get married, Dad.

BAYLOR: You go upstairs right now and take that crap off a' you! Take it all off and go jump in the shower. You look like a roadhouse chippie.

(Pause. BETH *lets go of* MEG*'s hand and crosses slowly over to* FRANKIE. FRANKIE *recoils on the sofa, wrapped tightly in the blanket.* BETH *stops in front of him and stares at him.* MEG *stays where she is.* BAYLOR *stays in chair.)*

MEG: Baylor, she's been tryin' for hours to get up the courage enough to come down here and ask you. You don't have to be so hard.

BAYLOR: Beth, are you hearin' what I said?

BETH: *(Staring at* FRANKIE*)* This is my man. This is the one. We're gonna get married, Daddy. I've decided.

BAYLOR: You're already married to one idiot!

(Sudden sound of shot from deer rifle in distance. Immediately on sound of shot, both FRANKIE *and* BAYLOR *stand with a jolt.* FRANKIE *stands straight up on sofa, still keeping the blanket wrapped around him, supporting himself on his bad leg by holding on to back of sofa.* BAYLOR *supports himself by holding arm of chair. They both stare in direction of sound out toward porch.* BETH *keeps staring at* FRANKIE. MEG *and* BETH *pay no attention to the gunshot.)*

BAYLOR: *(Referring to* MIKE*)* He's got another one. How d'ya' like that. I sit out there for weeks on end, freezin' my tail off and come up empty. He gets two in one day. Life is not fair.

*(*MEG *moves slowly toward* BAYLOR.*)*

MEG: Maybe we could have the wedding here, Baylor. That would be nice, wouldn't it? Soon as the weather thaws.

FRANKIE: *(To* MEG*)* She's married to my brother! She's already married! You were there at the wedding. Don't you remember?

MEG: *(To* BAYLOR*)* We could have it up on the high meadow. That would be beautiful. Just like the old times.

FRANKIE: I AM NOT GETTIN' MARRIED TO MY BROTHER'S WIFE!

*(*MIKE *comes running up porch steps into house carrying deer rifle.)*

MIKE: *(As he enters)* I got him! I got him! He's right out there in the shed. I got him good. He's right out there now. He's not goin' anywhere. He walked right into it. Right smack dab into it.

*(*MIKE *crosses slowly over to* FRANKIE, *who remains standing on sofa.* BAYLOR *sits slowly back down in armchair.)*

BAYLOR: *(Sitting)* Well, I'm not dressin' this one out for you. Not me. You can have the pleasure your own self. You think it's so damn smart to go around shootin' game without doin' the labor. It's time you put two and two together, boy.

MIKE: *(To FRANKIE)* Guess who I got tied to the stove? He's out there, snivelin' like a baby.

FRANKIE: Jake?

MIKE: *(Goes to BETH)* He's gonna apologize to you, Beth. He's gonna make a full apology. Anytime you're ready. He promised me.

BETH: Can you come to the wedding too, Mike? I want everybody to be there. I want the whole family there.

MIKE: *(Moving to MEG)* He's gonna apologize to all of us. You too, Mom.

MEG: Who is it? Nobody has to apologize to me. Nobody has ever offended me in any way.

MIKE: *(Moving to BAYLOR)* He's already begging. I got him beggin'. He's on his knees out there, Dad.

FRANKIE: You didn't shoot him too, did you? What're you tryin' to do? Kill my whole family off?

MIKE: *(Moving to FRANKIE)* I didn't have to shoot him. I just scared him. Soon as he saw me, he broke down.

BAYLOR: What'd you do with that rack? I want that rack! It belongs to me. I'm gonna put that rack on the wall.

MIKE: It's out there too. It's all out there. We can all go out and visit him. One at a time. He'll confess to us. I broke him down good. You shoulda seen him. He was crawlin'. I just kept him on his knees. I kept him there. You shoulda seen it, Dad. Every time he'd try to stand up, I'd knock him back down. Just hammer him down until he gave up completely. He gave himself up to me. He's my prisoner now. You wanna see? Just come out on the porch and I'll go back down there and turn him loose. You watch. He'll do anything I say now. I've got him trained.

BAYLOR: I just want the rack. That's all I wanna see.

MIKE: *(Moving toward porch)* I'll go get him. I'll go get him and bring him up here to the house. You won't believe it when you see him. He's not gonna bother any of us again. I guarantee ya that.

(MIKE exits. Pause. They all remain. Silence.)

FRANKIE: Why did it have to snow!

(Suddenly BAYLOR makes a lunge for FRANKIE, grabs hold of the blanket and rips it off FRANKIE. FRANKIE just stands there on the sofa. BAYLOR slowly wraps himself in blanket all the way up to his neck and sits back down in the chair slowly. Pause. Then BETH very softly moves in on FRANKIE, who just stands there, staring off in the direction of MIKE's exit.)

BETH: *(To FRANKIE)* It's all right. Once we're together, the whole world will change. You'll see. We'll be in a whole new world.

(BETH embraces FRANKIE around his waist and puts her head gently on his stomach as FRANKIE remains standing, looking out. Pause. MEG looks at them.)

MEG: I think it would be wonderful up on the high meadow. We could invite the whole family. We could even have a picnic up there. Cake and lemonade. We could have music. We haven't had a real wedding in so long.

(Lights fade . . .)

SCENE 3

Lights up, stage-right set, on LORRAINE *and* SALLY. LORRAINE *is dressed up
in a dark suit, white blouse, with a bow around her neck, a dressy hat, high heels
and stockings. She lies on top of the bedclothes with her back propped up with
pillows, poring through one of several travel brochures. The kind with lots of
foldout color photographs of European landscapes. Her purse is slung over one of
the bedposts. Two large, open suitcases lie on the floor at the foot of the bed, half
packed with clothes.* SALLY's *suitcase is beside the bed, ready to go. The chair is
pulled out into the middle of the room surrounded by cardboard boxes full of odd
papers and paraphernalia from the men.* SALLY *sits on the chair in a dress and
high heels facing audience, picking through the boxes and throwing different items
into a large pile of junk—in a metal bucket on the floor in front of her. Included
in the pile are all the model airplanes which used to hang over the bed. As lights
rise on them, the two women continue their separate activities for a little while,*
LORRAINE *avidly looking through the brochures and, every once in a while,
making notes with a pen in a small dimestore notebook beside her. She also sips
from a cup of coffee.* SALLY *keeps throwing papers into the pile, once in a while
reading parts of an old letter to herself, chuckling, then crumpling the paper up
and tossing it, then reaching into a box for another one. Now and then she comes
across an old photograph, stares at it and throws that away, too. Once this quiet,
introverted mood is established,* SALLY *picks out another photo from a box, stares
at it, then holds it up for* LORRAINE *to look at.*

SALLY: *(Holding up photo, still sitting)* You wanna save this?

> *(*LORRAINE *lowers the brochure she's involved with and squints toward the
> photo.)*

LORRAINE: What is it?

SALLY: Picture of you in some parade. I don't know.

LORRAINE: *(Going back to her brochure)* Naw, toss it.

(SALLY throws photo into pile, digs into another box.)

LORRAINE: *(Lowers brochure again)* Wait a second. What parade?

SALLY: I don't know. How many were you in?

LORRAINE: Quite a bunch. Lemme see it.

(SALLY gets up from chair, picks through pile of junk and locates photo again. She picks it up and takes it over to LORRAINE.)

SALLY: *(Looking at photo, as she crosses)* Looks like the forties or something.

LORRAINE: *(Taking photo and holding it away from herself, squints at it)* Lemme see. *(Stares at photo.)* Oh—I know. This was down in Victorville. Had a big "Frontier Days" blowout there. Big to-do. That was my sorrel mare.

SALLY: What year was that?

LORRAINE: Musta been 'forty-five, 'forty-six. Right around the end of the war. Yeah, big barbecue, square dance. The whole fandango. Pretty little mare, isn't she?

SALLY: Yeah. Were you in a lot of parades?

LORRAINE: Every chance I'd get. Used to just love gettin' out there with the sequins and jing-a-bobs and all that Spanish music. We had us a great old time.

SALLY: Dad went too?

LORRAINE: Yeah, he'd ride right alongside me. He had that big dumb gray gelding you had to throw down on his side every time you went to reshoe him. Dumb as a post.

SALLY: I didn't know you did all that.

LORRAINE: Oh, yeah. We lived pretty high there for a while.

SALLY: I never knew that. You wanna save this one, then?

LORRAINE: *(Hands photo back to* SALLY*)* Naw, burn it.

SALLY: *(Taking photo)* You sure?

LORRAINE: What do I wanna save it for? It's all in the past. Dead and gone. Just a picture.

*(*LORRAINE *goes back to her brochures as* SALLY *crosses back to pile of junk, holding photo.)*

SALLY: *(Reaching chair, looking at photo)* Okay if I keep it?

LORRAINE: *(Reading brochure)* Fine by me. Don't know what good it's gonna do ya.

SALLY: I just like the picture.

LORRAINE: Sure, go ahead and keep it. That was one heck of a little mare, I'll tell ya. She'd go anywhere, anytime.

SALLY: *(Putting photo in her purse, hanging on the chair)* What ever happened to her?

LORRAINE: She went with the rest of 'em. One day he just decided he was sick a' feedin' livestock and he loaded everything into the trailer and hauled 'em all off someplace. That was the last I saw of her. Probably wound up in a dog dish.

(Pause. SALLY *goes back to rummaging through the boxes, throwing things on the pile.* LORRAINE *studies her brochures.* SALLY *pulls an old letter out of one of the boxes, opens it and starts to read it to herself.)*

SALLY: *(After reading to herself for a while)* Here's a letter from Frankie, right after he won that baseball scholarship.

LORRAINE: I found it. Here it is. Right here. Sligo County. Connaught.

*(*LORRAINE *starts pointing excitedly at a big colorful map of Ireland. She holds it up to show* SALLY*.)*

I'll be darned. There it is, right there.

SALLY: Is that where we're goin'?

LORRAINE: That's it. I've still got some people back there if I can ever track 'em down. Been so long since anybody's ever heard from 'em.

SALLY: What's their names?

LORRAINE: Skellig. Mary Skellig and there was a Shem or Sham or somethin' like that. Shem Skellig, I think it was. Probably her husband.

SALLY: How're we gonna find 'em?

LORRAINE: Oh, those little tiny villages back there. Everybody knows everybody. All we gotta do is ask. They're real friendly folks back there.

SALLY: You've never been there before, have you?

LORRAINE: Nope. But I used to remember my grandma talk about it. She said they were all real friendly. We shouldn't have much trouble.

(SALLY *continues going through the boxes and tossing things out as they talk.*)

SALLY: Did you talk to a travel agent about this?

LORRAINE: They gave me all this stuff down at the Irish Embassy, or whatever you call it. That building with the green flag in the window. It's not gonna be a problem. All we gotta do is get there and ask around.

(LORRAINE *is now poring through a book and some other pamphlets as she keeps referring back to the map of Ireland. Pause.*)

SALLY: What happens when we do find them?

LORRAINE: Whad'ya mean?

SALLY: I mean, if you haven't had any contact with them for so long, maybe they won't even know who we are.

LORRAINE: They'll know. All I gotta do is tell 'em my maiden name and they'll remember.

SALLY: Are we gonna live with them?

LORRAINE: No, no. We'll just stay for a little visit. Save on motel bills.

(Pause as they continue their respective activities.)

SALLY: Who are these people?

LORRAINE: What people?

SALLY: The uh—Skelligs.

LORRAINE: Relatives. Ancestors. I don't know.

SALLY: Maybe they're all dead.

LORRAINE: People don't just all die. They don't just all up and die at once unless it's a catastrophe or somethin'. Someone's always left behind to carry on. There's always at least one straggler left behind. Now we'll just ask around until we find out who that is. We'll track him down. And then we'll introduce ourselves. It's not gonna be that difficult a task.

(Pause. They continue activities. SALLY pulls out a blue rosette ribbon, slightly faded, won at some livestock show. She holds it up for LORRAINE to see, then tosses it into bucket.)

SALLY: *(Standing behind pile of junk and boxes)* How're we gonna haul all this junk outa here, Mom?

LORRAINE: We're not gonna haul it. We're gonna burn it.

SALLY: I know, but we've gotta get it outa the house somehow.

LORRAINE: What for?

SALLY: Well, what're we gonna do, burn the house down?

LORRAINE: Why not?

(Pause. SALLY stares at LORRAINE.)

SALLY: We're gonna burn the whole house down?

LORRAINE: That's right. The whole slam bang. Oughta make a pretty nice light, don't ya think? Little show for the neighbors.

(SALLY starts to laugh.)

What's so damn funny?

(SALLY stops laughing.)

SALLY: How're we gonna do it?

LORRAINE: Well, ya light one a' them Blue Diamond stick matches and toss it in there and run. That's the way I always did it.

SALLY: You mean we're just gonna run away and let it burn?

(LORRAINE picks up a box of wooden matches and approaches the pail of junk.)

LORRAINE: Nah—maybe we won't run. Maybe we'll just stand out there on the front lawn, the two of us, and watch it burn for a while. Sing a song maybe. Do a little jig. Then we'll just turn and walk away. Just walk.

SALLY: Well, we're not gonna have any place to come back to, Mom.

LORRAINE: Who's comin' back?

(Lights dim slowly as LORRAINE strikes a match and lights the pile of papers in the bucket. The fire in the bucket keeps glowing. Simultaneously, lights are rising center stage. From deep upstage center, JAKE emerges into the light, walking on his knees straight toward the audience with the American flag between his teeth and stretched taut on either side of his head, like a set of driving reins for a draft horse. Behind JAKE, holding an end of the flag in each hand, MIKE walks along, clucking to JAKE like a horse and shaking the "reins" now and then. The deer rifle is tucked under MIKE's arm. They continue this way with MIKE driving JAKE downstage center. Lights reach their peak. MIKE reins JAKE in to a stop. JAKE remains on his knees. Fire keeps burning in bucket stage right.)

MIKE: *(Pulling back on flag)* Ho! Ho, now!

(JAKE *stops.*)

That's it.

(JAKE *stays in one place on his knees as* MIKE *comes up beside him and takes the flag out of his mouth and rolls it up in a ball around his rifle. Now and then, he pats* JAKE *on the head, as he would an old horse.*

JAKE *is silent. He has deep bruises around his eyes and jaw. His knees are bleeding and the knuckles on both hands. He's in same costume as at end of Act II.)*

MIKE: *(Removing flag, patting* JAKE*)* Atta boy. You're gonna do just fine. Pretty soon we can take you right out into the woods. Drag some timber. You'll like that. *(Rolling flag up around the rifle.)* Now, I want you to stay right here. You understand?

(JAKE *nods his head.*)

I don't want you wanderin' off. I want you to wait right here for me. I'm gonna go inside and get Beth. You remember her, don't ya?

(JAKE *nods.*)

You remember what you're gonna say to her?

(JAKE *nods.*)

You're not gonna forget?

(JAKE *shakes his head.*)

You're gonna tell her everything that we talked about, aren't ya?

(JAKE *nods.*)

Good. And you're not gonna touch her. You're not gonna even think about gettin' close to her.

(JAKE shakes his head.)

Good. Now, just stay right here and wait for me. Don't move an inch.

(JAKE remains on his knees, staring out toward audience. MIKE crosses with rifle wrapped in flag, toward stage-left set. Lights rise on set as MIKE moves toward it. BAYLOR is asleep in chair with blanket wrapped tight around him. Only his head and feet stick out. MEG is absent. BETH, in same costume as at end of Scene 2, Act III, is tucking the throw rug from the floor around FRANKIE, who lies on his back, shivering violently on the sofa, head upstage, staring at ceiling. Light remains up on JAKE. MIKE walks up the porch steps and onto landing. He stops there and speaks to BETH, who remains involved with FRANKIE.)

MIKE: He's ready now, Beth. You can come outside and he'll apologize to you. You just stay on the porch with me. He won't come near you.

BETH: *(Referring to FRANKIE)* He's shaking all over. I don't think he's getting any better, Mike. We can't keep him here. Maybe we could get married in the hospital.

MIKE: Beth! Forget about him now. Okay? I want you to come out here and listen to what your husband's got to say. I went to a lot a' trouble gettin' him to come around to my way a' thinkin'.

(Pause. BETH turns to MIKE.)

BETH: Who's out there?

MIKE: Jake! The one you've been askin' about all this time. The one you couldn't live without. Your old pal, Jake! He's right outside there and he wants to tell you something.

BETH: He's dead.

(Pause. MIKE *stares at her.)*

MIKE: All right.

*(*MIKE *makes a sudden, violent move toward her and grabs her by the arm. He starts to drag her toward the porch.* BETH *resists.)*

BETH: DADDY! HE'S TRYING TO TAKE ME AWAY! DADDY!

*(*BAYLOR *suddenly wakes up and stands abruptly. The blanket falls to his feet.)*

BAYLOR: *(To* MIKE*)* What's goin' on here?

BETH: He's trying to take me outside. I don't wanna go outside now.

*(*BETH *pulls away from* MIKE *and runs back to* FRANKIE. *She kneels beside him by the sofa and strokes his head.* BAYLOR *seems totally disoriented for a moment, then focuses on* MIKE*'s rifle with the flag wrapped around it.)*

MIKE: Beth, you get back here!

BAYLOR: *(Referring to rifle)* What're you doin' with that?

MIKE: Dad, I've got the bastard right outside on his knees. He's agreed to make an apology to the whole family. Where's Mom?

BAYLOR: Never mind that. What're you doin' with that rifle? What's that wrapped around it?

MIKE: It's just a flag. He had it on him. He had it all wrapped around him. I wanted Beth to come out so he could—

BAYLOR: *(Pause. Taking a step toward* MIKE, *kicking blanket away)* It's not just a flag. That's the flag of our nation. Isn't that the flag of our nation wrapped around that rifle?

MIKE: Yeah, I guess so. I don't know. I'm tryin' to tell you somethin' here. The flag's not the issue!

BAYLOR: You don't know? You don't recognize the flag anymore? It's the same color it always was. They haven't changed it, have they? Maybe added a star or two but otherwise it's exactly the same. How could you not recognize it?

(BAYLOR *is slowly moving in on* MIKE, *who backs up slightly as he approaches, keeping the rifle pointed low.*)

MIKE: Dad, I'm tryin' to tell you that I've got him turned around. I've got him totally convinced that he was wrong. He wants to confess to all of us. He owes it to us.

BAYLOR: Don't let that flag touch the ground!

(MIKE *quickly raises the rifle so it's pointed directly at* BAYLOR *but only accidentally.* MIKE *is still backing up as* BAYLOR *moves slowly toward him.*)

Don't point it at me! What's the matter with you! Have you lost your mind?

(MIKE *quickly raises the rifle over his head.*)

MIKE: I've got Jake out there on his knees. The guy who beat up your daughter!

BAYLOR: Gimme that flag! Hand it over to me! Hand it over.

(MIKE *lowers the rifle, takes the flag off it and hands it to* BAYLOR. BAYLOR *snatches it out of his hands.* BETH *goes to the blanket unnoticed by* BAYLOR *and takes it back to* FRANKIE, *covering him with it tightly like a mummy.*)

BAYLOR: (*Folding the flag up and tucking it under his arm*) What do ya think yer doin', using the American flag like a grease rag. Gimme that rifle.

MIKE: Dad—

BAYLOR: Gimme that rifle!

(MIKE *hands the rifle over to* BAYLOR.)

Haven't you got anything better to do than to monkey around with weapons and flags? Go outside and make yerself useful.

(BAYLOR turns away from MIKE and heads back for his chair with the rifle and flag. Pause.)

MIKE: So it doesn't make any difference, is that it? None of it makes any difference? My sister can get her brains knocked out and it doesn't make a goddamn bit a' difference to anyone in this family! All you care about is a flag? *(He points out toward JAKE.)*

It was him who was wearin' it! He's the traitor, not me! I'm the one who's loyal to this family! I'm the only one.

BAYLOR: *(Approaching chair, disoriented)* What's happened to my blanket now?

MIKE: Doesn't anybody recognize that we've been betrayed? From the inside out. He married into this family and he deceived us all. He deceived her! He lied to her! He told her he loved her!

(Short pause as BAYLOR stands by the chair searching for his blanket, still with flag, oblivious to everything else.)

BAYLOR: *(Looking behind chair for blanket)* How do things disappear around here?

(MIKE suddenly bursts across the set and picks up BETH in his arms. She clings to the blanket and as MIKE tears her away from FRANKIE, she drags the blanket with her. BAYLOR pays no attention.)

BETH: *(Being dragged away by MIKE)* NOOOOOOOOOO!!!!

(MIKE carries BETH across the set to the porch and down the steps to JAKE, who remains on his knees facing audience. He sets BETH down on her feet, facing JAKE, and forces her to look at JAKE.)

MIKE: *(Holding BETH in place)* Now look at him! Look at him! Isn't that the man you love? Isn't that him? Isn't that the one you say is dead?

(BETH shakes her head.)

MIKE: *(Shaking her by the shoulders)* Look at him! *(To JAKE)* Get up on your feet. Stand up!

(MIKE grabs JAKE by the collar still holding on to BETH. JAKE struggles to stand.)

Get up on your feet and tell her what you're gonna say. Tell her everything we talked about in the shed. Go ahead and tell her now. Go ahead!

(Pause as JAKE stands there, trying to maintain a vertical position. He stares at BETH. He tries to form the words but falters on them.)

JAKE: *(Softly)* I—I—I—I love you more than this earth.

(Pause. Then MIKE lets go of BETH and grabs JAKE by the shoulders. Shakes him. JAKE offers no resistance.)

MIKE: *(Shaking JAKE)* That's not what you were gonna say! Tell her what you were gonna say! We had it all memorized!

(BETH suddenly runs back up the steps, still holding on to the blanket, and enters the set again. She stops and stares at BAYLOR. FRANKIE rolls toward her on the sofa.)

MIKE: *(Staying with JAKE)* BETH!!

BAYLOR: *(To BETH)* What're you doin' with that blanket?

BETH: *(Looking at FRANKIE)* I was gonna—I wanted to keep him warm.

BAYLOR: *(Moving to BETH)* Gimme that blanket.

(BAYLOR snatches the blanket out of BETH's hand and heads for the chair. He tosses the blanket on the chair but keeps hold of the flag. BETH stays where she is.)

BETH: *(As BAYLOR moves away from her)* Daddy—

(BETH *stays marooned in one spot with her back to* JAKE *and* MIKE, *facing* FRANKIE *and* BAYLOR. BAYLOR *starts to try to fold the flag up but makes a mess of it.*)

Daddy, there's a man—

(MIKE *turns* JAKE *facing into the stage-left set.*)

MIKE: *(Behind* JAKE, *hands on his shoulders, whispers in his ear)* Look! Look in there. You see them? You can go right on in there now. They won't mind. They won't even notice. They won't even know you're an enemy. Your brother's in there, too. See him in there? He's with her now. He's with Beth. They've been sleeping together ever since he got here. I'll bet you didn't know that, did ya? They've been sleeping together right there on that sofa. Nobody cares, see. Dad doesn't care. Mom doesn't. Nobody cares. They've just all lost track of things. Go on in there and introduce yourself. I'll bet they take you right into the family. You could use a family, couldn't ya? You look like you could use a family. Well, that's good, see. That's good. Because, they could use a son. A son like you. Go ahead.

(MIKE *pats* JAKE *on the back, and exits upstage into darkness, leaving* JAKE *at the bottom of the porch steps facing into the stage-left set.* MEG *enters from up-left door.*)

MEG: Isn't anyone coming to bed? It's nighttime, isn't it?

BAYLOR: Meg, come here and help me fold this flag. You remember how to fold a flag, don't ya?

(BETH *takes a few steps toward* MEG, *but it's as though she's isolated in her own world now. Neither* MEG *nor* BAYLOR *recognizes her presence.*)

BETH: *(Moving toward* MEG, *then stopping again)* Mom—

MEG: *(Moving to* BAYLOR) I'm not sure. Did I ever fold one before?

(JAKE starts to move slowly up the steps and onto the landing. FRANKIE sees him now from the sofa. BETH still has her back toward JAKE. BAYLOR has handed one end of the flag to MEG as they back away from each other upstage, stretching the flag out between them.)

BAYLOR: *(To MEG)* Don't let it touch the ground now. Just back away from me and we'll stretch it out first. Don't let it touch the ground whatever you do.

MEG: I won't.

(JAKE keeps moving slowly, from the porch right into the set. FRANKIE props himself up on the sofa, staring at him.)

FRANKIE: Jake?

(BETH whirls around fast and sees JAKE. Their eyes lock. BETH stays where she is. JAKE keeps moving.)

I been tryin' to get ahold of you, Jake. I've been stuck here. For days. I couldn't get out.

BETH: *(Eyes still on JAKE)* Daddy, there's a man here. There's a man here now.

BAYLOR: *(With flag)* Now there's a right way to do this and a wrong way, Meg. I want you to pay attention.

MEG: I am.

BAYLOR: It's important.

BETH: THERE'S A MAN IN HERE! HE'S IN OUR HOUSE!

(BAYLOR and MEG pay no attention to the others but continue with the flag. JAKE now inside the stage-left set, stops and stares at BETH. They keep their eyes on each other. Pause. He takes a step toward her, then stops.)

JAKE: *(To BETH, very simple)* These things—in my head—lie to me. Everything lies. Tells me a story. Everything in me lies. But you.

You stay. You are true. I know you now. You are true. I love you
more than this life. You stay. You stay with him. He's my
brother.

*(JAKE moves to chair and picks the blanket up. He wraps himself up in it
around his shoulders. FRANKIE struggles to sit up on sofa. BETH stays close
to him.)*

FRANKIE: Jake! Wait a second. Jake! What're you doin'?

*(JAKE moves to BETH, wrapped in blanket. BETH pulls back away from
JAKE.)*

BETH: I remember now. The first time I saw you. The very first time I
ever saw you. Do you remember that too?

JAKE: *(To BETH)* Just one kiss. Just one.

*(Slowly JAKE leans toward BETH and kisses her softly on the forehead. She
lets him, then pulls back to FRANKIE. JAKE smiles at her, then turns and
exits across stage right, toward porch, with blanket. FRANKIE struggles to
stand with BETH holding on to him.)*

FRANKIE: *(To JAKE as he exits)* JAKE!! Jake, you gotta take her with
you!! It's not true, Jake! She belongs to you! You gotta take her
with you! I never betrayed you! I was true to you!

*(JAKE moves down the porch steps and exits upstage into darkness. He never
looks back. BETH very softly embraces FRANKIE and lays her head on his
chest. They remain there in the embrace as MEG and BAYLOR continue with
their flag folding.)*

BAYLOR: *(Folding flag with MEG)* Now, the stars have to end up on the
outside. I remember that much. Who's got the stars?

MEG: I do.

BAYLOR: Okay. Then I've gotta fold toward you. In little triangles.
You just stay put.

(BAYLOR folds the flag in triangles, military-style, toward MEG, who stays where she is, holding the other end.)

Now if everything works out right we should have all the stars on the outside and all the stripes tucked in.

MEG: Why do they do it like that?

BAYLOR: I don't know. Just tradition I guess. That's the way I was taught. Funny how things come back to ya' after all those years.

(BAYLOR finishes the last fold and holds the flag up.)

There! Look at that! We did it! We did it, Meg!

(BAYLOR picks MEG up and twirls her around, then sets her down and kisses her on the cheek, holding flag up.)

I'll be gall-darned if we didn't do it. It's letter perfect. Looks like right outa the manual.

(MEG holds her hand to her cheek where BAYLOR kissed her. She steps back away from him and stares around the room, bewildered. She doesn't notice FRANKIE and BETH.)

What'sa matter?

MEG: I believe that's the first time you've kissed me in twenty years.

BAYLOR: Aw, come on, it ain't been that long. Let's go on up to bed now.

(Pause as BAYLOR looks at MEG. She turns and stares out toward porch, keeping her hand to her cheek.)

Meg?

MEG: I'll be up in a while.

BAYLOR: Well, I'm goin' up. You shut the lights when you come. And don't dawdle. I don't wanna get woke up in the middle of a good dream.

(BAYLOR exits up-left door with flag. Pause. MEG moves slowly down right toward porch, still unaware of BETH and FRANKIE. She stares out across the stage to the fire still burning in the bucket. She moves out onto porch landing and stares into space. She stops. Pause.)

MEG: *(Still with hand to her cheek)* Looks like a fire in the snow. How could that be?

(Lights fade slowly to black except for fire.)

States of Shock

A VAUDEVILLE NIGHTMARE

"You might come here Sunday on a whim.
Say your life broke down. The last good kiss
you had was years ago. You walk these streets
laid out by the insane, past hotels
that didn't last, bars that did, the tortured try
of local drivers to accelerate their lives.
Only churches are kept up. The jail
turned 70 this year. The only prisoner
is always in, not knowing what he's done.

The principal supporting business now
is rage."

Richard Hugo

States of Shock was first presented by The American Place Theatre (Wynn Handman, Artistic Director) in New York City on April 30, 1991. It was directed by Bill Hart; the set design was by Bill Stabile; the costume design was by Gabriel Berry; the lighting design was by Pat Dignan and Anne Militello; the sound design was by J. A. Deane; and the production stage manager was Lloyd Davis, Jr. The cast was as follows:

COLONEL	John Malkovich
STUBBS	Michael Wincott
GLORY BEE	Erica Gimpel
WHITE MAN	Steve Nelson
WHITE WOMAN	Isa Thomas

States of Shock received its British première in the Salberg Studio at the Salisbury Playhouse on 16 June 1993. It was presented by the Royal National Theatre Studio in association with Salisbury Playhouse as part of 'Springboards', a season of new work. The cast was as follows:

COLONEL	David Burke
STUBBS	Corey Johnson
GLORY BEE	Naomi Wirthner
WHITE MAN	Carl Forgione
WHITE WOMAN	Serena Harragin

Directed by Deborah Paige
Designed by Lucy Hall
Music composed by Peter Salem
Lighting by Peter Hunter
Sound by Gina Hills

Bare stage. Cyclorama upstage covering entire wall and into ceiling. Simple café table and two chairs upstage right. Red Naugahyde café booth with table downstage left. Seated in the two chairs, upstage right, facing each other, are the WHITE WOMAN *and the* WHITE MAN. *The* WHITE MAN *sits slumped in his chair with his chin on his chest and his hands folded in his lap, facing stage right. He is not asleep but appears to be in a deep state of catharsis. Very still. The* WHITE WOMAN, *sitting opposite him at the table, is more upright but equally still, staring off into upstage space. Her hands are folded on the purse in her lap. They are both dressed completely in white, very expensive outfits, reminiscent of West Palm Beach. She has a wide-brimmed straw hat and elaborate jeweled dark glasses. Their faces and hands are also white and pallid, like cadavers.*

In the darkness, the sounds of two live percussionists situated behind the cyclorama, extreme right and left, opposite each other. Their driving rhythms slowly build in intensity as the cyclorama takes on an ominous tone. The cyclorama is lit up with tracer fire, rockets, explosions in the night. A cross-fade takes place in which the war panorama and drumming are exchanged for the stage light and the silence of the white couple who just sit there very still but not with the sense that they're frozen in time. A pause.

A referee's whistle is sharply blown off stage left. From stage left enters the COLONEL, *dressed in a strange ensemble of military uniforms and paraphernalia that have no apparent rhyme or reason: an air force captain's khaki hat from WW II, a marine sergeant's coat with various medals and pins dangling from the chest and shoulders, knickers with leather leggings below the knees, and a Civil War saber hanging from his waist. The* COLONEL *is pushing*

STUBBS *in a wheelchair with small American flags, raccoon tails,* *and various talismans and good-luck charms flapping and dangling* *from the back of the seat and armrests.* STUBBS *is dressed in a* *long-sleeved black shirt and black jeans. He's covered from the waist* *to the ankles with an old army blanket. A silver whistle hangs* *around his neck by a red string.*

They come to a stop downstage center. STUBBS *stares straight* *ahead and blows his whistle again. The white couple turn their* *heads toward* STUBBS *and the* COLONEL, *acknowledging their pres-* *ence, then return to their previous attitudes and postures—very still.* *Another pause.*

COLONEL: I believe this might be the deal right here, Stubbs. Might be just the ticket. (GLORY BEE, *a waitress in uniform,* *pencil stuck in her hair, carrying menus and a serving tray, enters* *from right.)*

GLORY BEE: Yessir. Two for lunch? Do you have a smoking preference?

COLONEL: I prefer smoking, don't you? Country was founded on tobacco. Don't see any reason not to support it.

GLORY BEE: That's fine, sir. Would you follow me, please. (*She* *moves toward booth, left.)*

COLONEL: What we'd like is something with a view. My friend here just got out of the hospital and he's been yearning to gaze into an open vista for some time now.

GLORY BEE: Would a booth be all right, sir? You can see the window from here. Best view in the house. (*She stops by the* *red booth and motions toward upstage.)*

COLONEL: How's that suit you, Stubbs? The booth? (STUBBS *just* *stares upstage at the cyclorama. Pause. To* GLORY BEE.) He's suffered a uh—kind of disruption. Temporary kind of thing, they say. Takes some time to unscramble.

GLORY BEE: I see.

COLONEL: Shot smack through the chest is what it was. Show the lady, Stubbs. *(STUBBS blows his whistle again and abruptly lifts his shirt to the armpits, revealing a massive red scar in the center of his chest. GLORY BEE looks away from it. STUBBS keeps his shirt held up.)* Took a direct hit from a ninety millimeter. Went straight through him. Killed my son who, unfortunately, was standing right behind him. Killed him dead. Stubbs is the lucky one. It's a wonder he's still with us. Isn't that right, Stubbs? *(STUBBS just stares with his shirt still up. To GLORY BEE.)* 'Course my son never knew what hit him. Thank the good Lord. But today, you see—today—what is your name, miss?

GLORY BEE: Uh—Glory.

COLONEL: Glory. Isn't that fine. "Glory."

GLORY BEE: "Glory Bee."

COLONEL: How 'bout that. "Glory Bee." Has a kind of a French ring to it. Well—anyhow, today happens to be the anniversary of my son's death. So, what I thought was I'd just pick up Stubbs here from the hospital and take him out for a dessert of some kind. Maybe a hot fudge sundae or something on that order.

GLORY BEE: That's fine. Um—is the booth—okay?

COLONEL: Booth's fine. Booth's gonna be just perfect. You can pull your shirt down now, Stubbs. We're gonna park it right here. *(STUBBS pulls his shirt down as COLONEL wheels him around to the upstage right side of the table. GLORY BEE lays the menus out on the table.)*

GLORY BEE: Would you like some coffee or a beverage of some kind, sir?

COLONEL: Coffee? Coffee, Stubbs? *(STUBBS nods. To GLORY BEE.)* You wouldn't happen to have any "Maker's Mark," would you? Kentucky bourbon? "Fighting Cock"? Something with a little sting to it?

GLORY BEE: No, sir. This is a family restaurant.

COLONEL: Families don't drink bourbon?

GLORY BEE: Well, we don't have a liquor license, sir. This is a coffee shop.

COLONEL: I see. Well, make it two coffees, then. That'd be just dandy. A "cuppa' joe."

GLORY BEE: Thank you, sir. I'll be back in just a minute. (GLORY BEE *exits right.* COLONEL *spits in his hand and smooths* STUBBS*'s hair carefully.*)

COLONEL (*as he tends to* STUBBS): This is a family restaurant, Stubbs. How 'bout that. Guess we got lucky. Could've wound up any old place. Wandered into a titty bar or roadhouse dive, but here we are in a family restaurant. God knows we've had worse luck on a Sunday. (COLONEL *settles into booth, handing one of the menus to* STUBBS *who just stares at it.* COLONEL *looks through the menu. The white couple turn their heads and stare at* STUBBS *and the* COLONEL. *Looking through menu.*) Let's just see what they've got here in the way of desserts. That's what you want now? You've made your mind up on that? No main course for you? (STUBBS *nods.*) Okee-dokee. (COLONEL *removes his hat and rubs his bald head.*) Grass don't grow on a busy street. Well, then, let's see— They've got a peach cobbler. That might be nice. Some kinda sauce on it. They got a key lime pie. Isn't that somethin'. Didn't think we were that far south for key lime pie. How's that sound to you, Stubbs? Key lime? (STUBBS *just stares at him. Pause.*) It's a pale green kind of a thing. (*No response from* STUBBS.)

WHITE WOMAN (*to* COLONEL, *out of the blue*): We've been waiting three quarters of an hour. Can you imagine that? (COLONEL *turns to her.*)

COLONEL: Excuse me?

WHITE WOMAN: My husband and I have been waiting three quarters of an hour for a simple order.

WHITE MAN: Clam chowder.

WHITE WOMAN: That's right. Two bowls of clam chowder. You'd think that would be simple enough.

COLONEL: You'd think so, wouldn't you.

WHITE WOMAN: I mean it's not as though we ordered a club sandwich or a turkey dinner with a lot of trimmings. *(Pause. COLONEL turns back to STUBBS and the menu. STUBBS suddenly blows his whistle and talks directly to the white couple, who just stare at him.)*

STUBBS *(to white couple)*: When I was hit— It went straight through me. Out the other side. Someone was killed. But it wasn't me. I'm not the one. I'm the lucky one. *(Pause. The white couple just stare at STUBBS for a moment, then turn back to their previous attitudes. STUBBS keeps staring at them as though waiting for a response. COLONEL refers to the menu.)*

COLONEL *(still studying menu)*: They've got your standard banana split. How 'bout that, Stubbs? No frills.

STUBBS *(to white couple)*: When I was hit—I never saw it coming. I never heard a sound. The sky went white. *(GLORY BEE enters from right, very slowly, balancing two cups of coffee on her tray which she is having great difficulty with. Coffee keeps sloshing over the edge of the cups as she stares intensely at them and moves inch by inch toward the COLONEL and STUBBS in the booth. The white couple stare at GLORY BEE as she makes her way. COLONEL keeps focused on the menu.)*

WHITE WOMAN: There she is.

WHITE MAN: She ought to be fired.

WHITE WOMAN: Oh, miss! Miss! *(GLORY BEE ignores them and keeps heading toward the booth with the coffee. All her attention on the cups.)*

GLORY BEE *(to herself, about spilling coffee)*: Dang it! Dang, dang, dang, dang, dang!

WHITE MAN: She's ignoring us.

WHITE WOMAN: MISS! *(GLORY BEE keeps heading painstakingly toward the booth, trying to balance the coffee.)*

COLONEL *(to STUBBS)*: What about a pair of banana splits? Or would you rather have the hot fudge? It's up to you, Stubbs.

STUBBS *(to white couple)*: When I was hit— The lights went out. It's been dark ever since.

WHITE WOMAN *(to GLORY BEE)*: We have better things to do this morning than wait three quarters of an hour for two bowls of clam chowder.

GLORY BEE *(to COLONEL, as she reaches booth)*: Excuse me, sir, but would you mind taking these for me. I have the darnedest time balancing liquids. I don't know what it is. Ever since I was very little.

COLONEL *(as he takes coffee off tray)*: That's because you stare at the cups.

GLORY BEE: Excuse me?

COLONEL: You can't stare at the cups. You've got to fix your attention on a point in space. You've got to ignore the cups altogether.

GLORY BEE: I see.

COLONEL *(placing cups on table)*: You've got to pretend the cups don't exist. There's a trick to it.

WHITE MAN: She's completely ignoring us.

COLONEL: Otherwise you're bound to spill.

GLORY BEE: I'll have to try that. *(STUBBS suddenly lifts his shirt again and shows his scar to GLORY BEE.)*

STUBBS *(to* GLORY BEE*)*: Right here is where it went through. It went clear through here and out the other side.

COLONEL: Stubbs, put your shirt down now. The lady's already seen that. *(*STUBBS *pulls his shirt back down and stares at the* COLONEL, *who continues perusing the menu.)*

GLORY BEE *(to* COLONEL*)*: Have you decided on something, sir?

COLONEL: Well, let's see—

WHITE WOMAN: We could have had most of our shopping done by now. We could be buying things as we speak.

COLONEL: I think what we're gonna do is have us a pair of banana splits. That okay by you, Stubbs? *(*STUBBS *just stares at him.)*

GLORY BEE *(writing down order)*: Two banana splits.

COLONEL: Yeah. I think that's right. And would you mind putting a little candle right in the center of each one of those. You've got those little birthday candles, don't ya?

GLORY BEE: Birthday candle.

COLONEL: Yeah. You know, those little pink and blue jobs like you have for the kids? Just to honor my son. Just as a kind of reminder.

GLORY BEE: You want two birthday candles?

COLONEL: One each. Right smack in the center. Just as a token.

GLORY BEE: You don't want me to sing or anything, do you? I'm capable of singing, but I don't like doing it at the drop of a hat.

COLONEL: Sing? No. No singing. This isn't his birthday.

GLORY BEE: Who?

COLONEL: My son. It's the anniversary of his death. Not his birthday.

GLORY BEE: Oh. I thought *this* was your son.

COLONEL: No, no. This is the man who attempted to save my son's life by placing his body in the way of incoming artillery fire. I already told you that.

GLORY BEE: I'm sorry. We've been very busy. I *can* sing though, if you want me to.

COLONEL: No singing. That won't be necessary.

STUBBS *(to GLORY BEE)*: When I was hit I could no longer get my "thing" up. It just hangs there now. Like dead meat. Like road kill. *(Short pause. GLORY BEE stares at STUBBS, then pulls away.)*

GLORY BEE: Two banana splits. With candles.

COLONEL: Don't forget those candles, now.

GLORY BEE: No, sir. *(She crosses back, right. The white couple stop her.)*

WHITE WOMAN: Miss!

GLORY BEE: Yes, ma'am?

WHITE WOMAN: What in the name of Christ has happened to our clam chowder? We've been waiting three quarters of an hour.

GLORY BEE: I offered you the "Express" and you turned it down.

WHITE MAN: We could be shopping as we speak. *(STUBBS blows his whistle, then suddenly screams at GLORY BEE.)*

STUBBS: MY THING HANGS LIKE DEAD MEAT!!! *(Pause. White couple turns and stares at STUBBS. The COLONEL ignores them. He's busy taking several toy soldiers, tanks, airplanes, and ships out of his bag and arranging them on the table in front of him. STUBBS just stares into space.)*

WHITE WOMAN *(to GLORY BEE)*: I thought this was supposed to be a family restaurant.

GLORY BEE: It is. *(GLORY BEE exits right. Pause.)*

COLONEL *(moving toys around on table)*: She thought *you* were my son. Now. When you were hit, Stubbs—you were backed up against the mountain. Is that right? Pretend the sugar is the mountain. Right here. Just pretend. *(COLONEL moves the sugar dispenser into position.)*

STUBBS: Backed up against the mountain.

COLONEL: You had heavy enemy artillery plus warships firing into you from offshore. Let's say the knives will represent the shoreline. *(COLONEL moves knives into position. STUBBS picks up a fork.)*

STUBBS: Fork.

COLONEL: Forks? All right—fine—forks. That's fine. We'll say the forks are the shoreline. Forks will do well enough. *(COLONEL exchanges the knives for the forks and marks the hypothetical shoreline.)* Now—from the top of the mountain— Let me get this straight, now. Only you can verify this because you were there, Stubbs. I'm just going on hearsay. From the top of the mountain you were backed up by your own defensive artillery plus militia. Is that right? *(STUBBS just stares at the forks and toys.)* Does that seem right to you? The way I've got it set up? You're the expert on this. *(STUBBS reaches over from his wheelchair and moves one of the toy pieces into a different position.)* Good. Is that pretty close to the way it was? *(STUBBS just stares at the table.)* So, in effect, you were caught in a cross fire? Isn't that fair to say? You were backed up against the mountain, being fired upon by enemy artillery while your own defense continued to pound them from behind you. Firing across your heads. There was nowhere to run.

STUBBS: When I was hit—

COLONEL: Now hold your horses. Just wait a second. We'll get to that. I want to reconstruct everything up to that moment.

I know we've done this before, but there's certain particulars that still escape me.

STUBBS: When I was hit there was no sound.

COLONEL: I realize that! You're jumping the gun. That's not important now. What I'm trying to figure out is the exact configuration. The positions of each element. A catastrophe has to be examined from every possible angle. It has to be studied coldly, from the outside, without investing a lot of stupid emotion.

STUBBS: I was hit in silence.

COLONEL *(slamming table with his fist)*: THAT MAKES NO DIF-FERENCE!! *(An explosion offstage in the distance. Pause. Silence. They stare at each other. The white couple is staring at them. Suddenly STUBBS backs his wheelchair up and then wheels himself over to the white couple. He parks the wheelchair upstage of their table. Still in booth.)* Stubbs! Don't be childish. We have to face this thing together. You know that as well as I do. There's no point in running off in a huff. Sooner or later we have to face it.

STUBBS *(to white couple)*: The middle of me is all dead. The core. I'm eighty percent mutilated. The part of me that goes on living has no memory of the parts that are all dead. They've been separated for all time. They'll never have a partner. You're lucky to have a partner.

COLONEL: Stubbs! Front and center! Scat like a scalded dog! *(STUBBS wheels himself away from the white couple and returns to the booth where the COLONEL is pouring some whiskey from a silver flask into the two cups of GLORY BEE's coffee. STUBBS parks by the booth and the COLONEL.)* Now, look, Stubbs—let's have an understanding here—all right? We're in a public situation. We have to use a little diplomacy. Some discretion. Restraint. You have to remember that the enemy is always sneaking. Always slimy. Lurking. Ready to snatch the slightest secret. The smallest slipup. Here— Have a drink. I've doctored it up some. Go ahead. It'll open your pipes. (COLO-NEL *offers a cup of coffee laced with whiskey out to* STUBBS. STUBBS *takes it but hesitates to drink. Pause.*) Well, go ahead. It's perfectly good whiskey. I've never steered you wrong on that score, have I? After all, you're not exactly a candidate for assassination, are you? Let's not get carried away with ourselves. (STUBBS *drinks.*) That's the ticket! No point in getting worked up over nothing. We're in this together. Let's have a toast. (*They click cups and drink together.*) TO THE ENEMY!

STUBBS (*holding his cup high*): TO THE ENEMY!

COLONEL: Exactly. WITHOUT THE ENEMY WE'RE NOTHING!

STUBBS (*toasting*): WITHOUT THE ENEMY WE'RE NOTH-ING!

COLONEL: Exactly. Where would we be today without the enemy?

STUBBS: I don't know . . . where would we be?

COLONEL: THE ENEMY HAS BROUGHT US TO-GETHER!

STUBBS: THE ENEMY HAS BROUGHT US TOGETHER!

COLONEL: Exactly right. Now, there's no point in pouring your heart out to strangers, Stubbs. You oughta know that by now. No future in it. Where has it ever gotten you? No-where. Plain and simple. Absolutely nowhere. We have to stick together in this. We've got a history. Nobody knows that better than you and me. Best a stranger can do is pretend and we're both past that, aren't we, Stubbs?

STUBBS (*toasting*): WE'RE BOTH PAST THAT!

COLONEL: That's the truth of it. Pretending is not for us. What we're after is the hard facts. The bare bones.

STUBBS *(toasting)*: THE BARE BONES!

COLONEL: Exactly.

WHITE WOMAN: Would you both pipe down over there. This is a family restaurant.

WHITE MAN: That's absolutely right. *(COLONEL turns and stares at WHITE WOMAN and takes another drink, then turns back to the toys and speaks to STUBBS in a hushed, conspiratorial tone. WHITE WOMAN leans out of her chair toward the COLONEL, trying to eavesdrop.)*

COLONEL *(hushed)*: Now look, Stubbs— The placement of these two figures right here is the key to the whole thing. You see these two? *(COLONEL holds up two toy infantrymen and shows them to STUBBS.)* The red one is you and the white one is my son. Have you got that? Here— Take a look at them. Check them over carefully and memorize the colors. Try to study every detail. Every nuance. Let nothing escape your scrutiny. *(STUBBS takes the two toys and turns them over in his hands, examining them closely. Pause.)* Red and white. Red is you. White's my son. Okay? Have you got that? Are we on the same wavelength? *(STUBBS just stares.)* Now, what I'm gonna ask you to do is place those figures down in exactly the right positions for me. Only you can know this, Stubbs. Place them exactly where you and my son were standing when the artillery struck you.

STUBBS *(holding toy soldiers)*: Red and white.

COLONEL: That's correct.

STUBBS: And blue.

COLONEL: No! No blue. Just red and white.

STUBBS: And blue.

COLONEL: NO BLUE, STUBBS! NO BLUE!

WHITE WOMAN: We're trying to have a peaceful time here, if you don't mind. (COLONEL *crosses to* WHITE WOMAN, *whispers in her ear, then returns to the booth.*)

COLONEL *(to* STUBBS*)*: Place them down in the battlefield exactly as you were positioned on that fateful day. Now, just remember that the sugar is the mountain and the forks are the . . .

STUBBS: Shoreline.

COLONEL: Go ahead. (GLORY BEE *enters from right with the banana splits on her tray. She is carrying them much the same way as she was trying to balance the coffee—moving very slowly with all her attention on the tray. Candles are burning in the center of each banana split. The candles are much bigger than birthday candles.*)

WHITE MAN: There she is.

WHITE WOMAN: She ought to be shot.

WHITE MAN: Oh, miss! (GLORY BEE *keeps heading for the booth with the banana splits, ignoring the white couple.*)

WHITE WOMAN: She's ignoring us again.

WHITE MAN: Is that our order? That's not our order, is it?

WHITE WOMAN: No, it's not. It's *their* order.

WHITE MAN: We've been here longer than them, haven't we?

WHITE WOMAN: We've been here forever. (GLORY BEE *keeps steadfastly heading toward the booth, balancing the banana splits.*)

COLONEL: Set them down, Stubbs.

STUBBS *(holding toys)*: Blue is me?

COLONEL: *White* is you! There is no blue. There's only red and white. Go ahead and set them down. (STUBBS *keeps staring at the table, holding the toys in his hand.*)

WHITE WOMAN: We'd like a word with the manager, miss. Oh, miss!

WHITE MAN: She's completely ignoring us. *(One of the candles blows out.)*

GLORY BEE: Oh, shoot! *(GLORY BEE turns and heads back.)*

WHITE WOMAN: We'd like to speak to your manager.

GLORY BEE: Eat my socks. *(GLORY BEE exits right with the banana splits.)*

WHITE MAN: What'd she say?

COLONEL: Stubbs, get ahold of yourself. It's a simple equation. All we're trying to do is re-create a moment in time. A catastrophic moment in our personal history. That's all there is to it.

STUBBS *(holding figures)*: When I was hit—

COLONEL: No! Not that! *Not* when you were hit! We know all about that. We're fed up with that. We're up to here with that. It's the moment before. The exact moment *before* you were hit. That's the important moment here. Can't you get that through your thick head? Where were you standing in the battlefield? Where was my son?

STUBBS: Behind.

COLONEL *(pointing to a spot on table)*: Here?

STUBBS: Far away. Long ago. When they said—it would all be over.

COLONEL: Who said?

STUBBS: When they said it would all be done in a day.

COLONEL: Who?

STUBBS: Long, long ago. When they said he would be removed.

COLONEL: When who said who would be removed?

STUBBS: The enemy.

COLONEL: Where were you standing, Stubbs!

STUBBS: Far, far away.

COLONEL: I'm not talking about the location of the conflict! I'm talking about the battlefield itself! Where exactly were you on the field of battle!

STUBBS *(toasting his cup)*: LONG LIVE THE ENEMY!

COLONEL: Give me those soldiers! Give them back! *(STUBBS refuses and clutches the toys with both hands, close to his chest. Pause.)* You don't want me to take them back by force, do you, Stubbs? You don't want that. *(Pause. STUBBS slowly, reluctantly relinquishes the toy soldiers to the COLONEL. COLONEL places them on the table, then pulls STUBBS away from the table and propels the wheelchair into the wall upstage left.)* Now— Since you seem to find it so impossible to follow the simplest directions—to answer the simplest questions—I'm going to have to experiment here with various positions. Various, hypothetical arrangements—seemingly random but nevertheless with a comprehensive knowledge and background in hand-to-hand combat and military strategy. *(STUBBS abruptly wheels himself across the stage and exits.)* Stubbs! Get back over here! The situation has to be faced! *(STUBBS reenters from right.)*

STUBBS: I was here. Facing the green sea. I was smelling it. Through the smoke. It didn't smell American to me. It smelled like a foreign sea. The birds were not American birds. I wanted to have a feeling for home but nothing called me back. I wanted to have a memory. I prayed for a memory. But nothing came but smoke and the smell of dead fish.

COLONEL: Stubbs, we don't have a hope in hell of understanding the catastrophe if you're going to allow your mind to wander through smoke and dead fish! You've got to pull yourself together now! Grab ahold of your bootstraps! *(STUBBS blows his whistle and crosses to centerstage.)*

STUBBS: I was here!

COLONEL *(pointing at table)*: You were *here*! Caught in a cross fire!

STUBBS *(facing audience)*: I couldn't remember the faces—the voices—of the ones. I wanted to see them but their faces never came to me. Never came back.

COLONEL *(jabbing the table)*: We have to pinpoint the location!

STUBBS *(remaining centerstage)*: America had disappeared. *(COLONEL stands suddenly, in a fury, and draws his saber.)*

COLONEL *(saber drawn)*: DON'T TALK FOOLISHLY! That's a blasphemous thing to say! It's a disgrace to the memory of my son! I'm not buying dessert for anyone who makes a comment like that! The principles are enduring. You know that. This country wasn't founded on spineless, spur-of-the-moment whimsy. The effects are international! UNIVERSAL! *(COLONEL smashes his sword down on the table, upsetting all the toys. An explosion close by, offstage. Immediately the percussionists and war sounds join in full swing. The cyclorama explodes with bombs, missiles, and blown-up planes. This time, silhouetted against the panorama of light, stylized shapes of tanks, infantry, and heavy artillery move from right to left, in the heat of battle. GLORY BEE enters again, from right, balancing the two banana splits with an even larger candle burning in the center of each one. She makes her way slowly across the stage toward the red booth, all her attention riveted to the tray and the desserts. The "war" keeps raging behind her. When she finally reaches the booth she sets the banana splits down on the table. All the sounds, images, and effects suddenly stop. Silence. The COLONEL's gaze is fixed on the candles. STUBBS remains staring out over audience. Pause.)*

GLORY BEE: I hope the candles are all right, sir. That's all I could find in the kitchen.

COLONEL: Candles are fine.

GLORY BEE: We keep a supply on hand for the blackouts.

COLONEL: They're just fine.

GLORY BEE: Are you sure you don't want me to sing, sir? I'd be glad to sing.

COLONEL: No singing. Nobody was born today.

GLORY BEE: Is there going to be anything else, sir?

COLONEL: Not right now.

GLORY BEE: More coffee?

COLONEL: Yes, maybe some more of that.

GLORY BEE: I'll be right back. Enjoy your dessert.

COLONEL: Thank you so very much. (COLONEL *keeps staring at the candles as* GLORY BEE *crosses back to right.* STUBBS *stays center.* WHITE WOMAN *stops* GLORY BEE *as she passes.*)

WHITE WOMAN: Oh, miss!

GLORY BEE: Your clam chowder will be up any second now.

WHITE MAN: I don't want it. It's too late for clam chowder.

WHITE WOMAN: I would like to tell you something, miss.

GLORY BEE: Shoot.

WHITE WOMAN: Did you know that those two men over there are drinking hard liquor in your restaurant? Your family restaurant. (*Pause.* GLORY BEE *turns and looks at the* COLONEL.)

GLORY BEE (*back to* WHITE WOMAN): No, I didn't know that.

WHITE WOMAN: Well, they are. I watched them sneak it into their coffee. They're very sneaky, those two. I'd like to speak to your manager.

GLORY BEE: The manager is dead. *(GLORY BEE exits.)*

WHITE MAN: What'd she say?

WHITE WOMAN: I hope she realizes that I still want my clam chowder even though you don't want yours.

WHITE MAN: She realizes nothing. *(Pause. STUBBS wheels himself extreme downstage center and parks there, staring out at audience. COLONEL remains in booth, staring at candles. White couple resume their trance state.)*

COLONEL *(staring at candles)*: Stubbs? The dessert is here. It's arrived. *(Pause. No response from STUBBS. He just stares at audience.)* She remembered the candles. God bless her. *(STUBBS blows his whistle and suddenly lifts his shirt again, exposing his chest wound to the audience.)* Stubbs? I sincerely hope there hasn't been a serious breach created between us. I wouldn't want something like that. Not today, anyhow. We must remember why we came here. We can't forget our purpose. Stubbs? *(Pause. STUBBS remains with his shirt up. No response.)* Are you with me on this? Look—I'll drop the whole business about the specific positions. I know it irritates you. I'll drop that. I promise you. Important as it may be for our— *(Pause. COLONEL stares at STUBBS who remains as before. No response.)* It was simply a means of finding some common ground, Stubbs. *(Pause. No response from STUBBS.)* All right, look—I'll put all the toys away. How's that suit you? If you're going to be a baby about it. *(COLONEL begins to clear the table of all the toys and puts them back in his bag. He keeps speaking through all this. STUBBS remains with his shirt up, facing front. Collecting toys.)* See? I'm putting the toys away, Stubbs! They're disappearing one by one. You don't have to worry about any of that. Out of sight, out of mind! All I want— All I've ever wanted was for us to toast the death of my son and have a nice dessert. That's all. Simple as that. Stubbs?

STUBBS *(still holding up his shirt)*: God bless the enemy!

COLONEL: There's no reason in this wide world to put a wall up between us. That's not going to get us anywhere. What was it I said, anyway? What was it, specifically, that I said that could have caused this cruel reaction? All I said was: "Don't talk foolishly." That's all. "Don't talk foolishly." I could have said that to anyone. I could have said it to myself. In fact, I may very well have been referring to myself when I said that. It wasn't even directed at you. It was directed at me. I heard how foolish I was sounding and I made that comment and then you went and took it personally, as though I were referring to something you said when, in fact, it was something I said. *(Pause.* STUBBS *remains with his shirt up. No response. Silence.)* I suppose now what we're going to do is forget all that time in the hospital. Is that it? All that long time when I nursed you. Changed your shitty sheets. Cleaned your fingernails? Emptied your bladder bag. You don't remember any of that, I suppose. That's all been long forgot. *(Pause. Slowly,* STUBBS *lowers his shirt and stares out at audience.)*

STUBBS *(quietly, facing out)*: I remember the moment you forsook me. The moment you gave me up.

COLONEL: That dog won't hunt, Stubbs. There was never anything like that and you know it. We've been through all this before. Now come and eat your dessert.

STUBBS: The moment you invented my death.

COLONEL: I'm going to start without you in a minute!

STUBBS: When you threw me away. *(COLONEL suddenly throws a fit and starts beating on the table with his fist, then, just as suddenly, he stops.)*

COLONEL *(slamming table)*: I NEVER, NEVER, NEVER, NEVER!!!!! *(Explosion with short burst of percussion.* STUBBS *keeps staring out at audience.)*

STUBBS *(facing front)*: When you left me it went straight through me and out the other side. It left a hole I can never fill. *(Pause. Silence.)*

COLONEL: Stubbs. Please. I don't want to eat alone. Not today. It makes no sense. Any other day I'd be glad to eat alone, even welcomed it. I've loved to eat alone. I've gone out of my way to eat alone. I've walked miles in search of empty restaurants. You know that. But not today. The purpose of all this was to honor my dead son. We have to do it together.

STUBBS *(facing out)*: Someone was killed. But it wasn't me. I'm not the one. *(STUBBS wheels himself over to the booth and parks in front of his banana split.)* I'm the lucky one.

COLONEL: Good. That's good. As long as we can always come back to our senses. That's the important thing. It's a blessing, Stubbs. It's a gift. An American virtue. As far out on a limb as circumstances might shove us we always have that possibility of returning to our common sense. Our fairness. Even in the midst of the most horrible devastation. Under the most terrible kind of duress. Torture. Barbarism of all sorts. Starvation. Chemical warfare. Public hangings. Mutilation of children. Raping of mothers. Raping of daughters. Raping of brothers and fathers. Executions of entire families. Entire generations of families. Amputation of private organs. Decapitation. Disembowelment. Dismemberment. Disinturnment. Eradication of wildlife. You name it. We can't forget that we were generated from the bravest stock. The Pioneer. The Mountain Man. The Plainsman. The Texas Ranger. The Lone Ranger. My son. These have not died in vain. These ones have not left us to wallow in various states of insanity and self-abuse. We have a legacy to continue, Stubbs. It's up to us. No one else is going to do it for us. Here's to them and to my son! A soldier for his nation! *(They toast and click their cups.)*

COLONEL *and* STUBBS: THE ENEMY HAS BROUGHT US TOGETHER! *(*COLONEL *blows out the candles.)*

COLONEL *(picking up spoon)*: Let's dig in, Stubbs. *(*COLONEL *begins to eat with gusto, but* STUBBS *just stares at his dessert.* GLORY BEE *enters from right, very slowly again, balancing two bowls of clam chowder on her tray, making her way carefully toward the white couple.)*

WHITE WOMAN: Here she comes.

WHITE MAN: Is that our order?

WHITE WOMAN: I think it's finally us.

WHITE MAN: But I don't want mine. Didn't she understand that?

WHITE WOMAN: She understands nothing.

WHITE MAN: It's too late for clam chowder. *(*GLORY BEE *reaches their table and sets a bowl down in front of each of them.)*

GLORY BEE: Here we go. Sorry for the delay, but the cook has been wounded.

WHITE WOMAN: There's no excuse.

WHITE MAN: Didn't you understand that I don't want mine?

GLORY BEE: I thought you were just saying that.

WHITE MAN: Saying what?

GLORY BEE: That you didn't want yours.

WHITE MAN: That's what I did say.

WHITE WOMAN: He did say that. I heard him.

GLORY BEE: I heard him too.

WHITE WOMAN: So why'd you bring it when you heard him say it?

WHITE MAN: It's too late for clam chowder. The time has passed.
(GLORY BEE *dumps bowl of clam chowder in* WHITE MAN'S *lap,
then throws the bowl offstage right. A loud crash of dishes follows.*
WHITE WOMAN *eats her clam chowder.*)

GLORY BEE: Will there be anything else, sir? (GLORY BEE *exits
right.*)

WHITE WOMAN *(eating)*: What'd she do?

COLONEL: Eat your banana split, Stubbs. It's going to get all
runny. (STUBBS *just stares at the dessert.* COLONEL *continues to
eat.* WHITE WOMAN *continues to eat.* WHITE MAN, *after staring
at his lap for a while, begins to wipe the mess up with his napkin.
As he eats.*) You're not still pouting, are you? Holding some
kind of secret grudge? (*Pause.* STUBBS *keeps staring at his
dessert.*) I don't know what ever gave you this idea that I
would have deliberately deceived you. Where did you come
up with a notion like that? Who put that in your noggin?
(*Pause.* STUBBS *keeps staring.* WHITE MAN *keeps cleaning. Still
eating.*) You don't think for a minute that if you actually
were my son that I would dream up this elaborate scheme,
do you? What would be the purpose of that? Where would
that get us? (*Suddenly* STUBBS *smashes his banana split with his
fist. Everyone else continues as usual.*)

STUBBS: I'M EIGHTY PERCENT MUTILATED!!!!!

COLONEL: Nothing to be done about that, Stubbs. All in the past.
Can't wallow in our miseries. Now you've gone and ruined
a perfectly good dessert. Suppose you think I'm going to
buy you another one. Well, you're dead wrong about that.
Just because you've burnt the bacon doesn't mean *I* drink
the grease. (*The* WHITE MAN'*s cleaning of his lap slowly turns
into masturbation as* WHITE WOMAN *continues eating, oblivious.*)
That's what comes from striking out blindly. Have to learn
to pay for your actions. Become a man.

STUBBS: Become a man.

COLONEL: Exactly. *(STUBBS turns his wheelchair toward WHITE MAN and moves toward him, then stops. He blows his whistle. WHITE MAN continues masturbating. WHITE WOMAN keeps eating.)*

STUBBS *(to WHITE MAN)*: Become a man!

COLONEL *(continuing to eat)*: Clean up your mess now, Stubbs. Don't leave it for someone else. *(STUBBS keeps staring at WHITE MAN who continues getting more worked up as WHITE WOMAN ignores him.)*

STUBBS *(to WHITE MAN)*: BECOME A MAN!

COLONEL: Stubbs! Get back over here and clean up your mess or I'm going to have to spank you! Do you want a good spanking? Is that what you want? A good solid thrashing. Maybe that's what you need.

STUBBS *(to WHITE MAN)*: BECOME A MAN! *(WHITE MAN continues, carrying himself to the verge of orgasm.)*

COLONEL *(standing)*: All right! All right! You leave me no alternative. *(COLONEL unbuckles his sword and lays it on the table. He crosses, downstage, opening his jacket and removing his belt as he goes. WHITE MAN keeps masturbating through this and gradually reaches a climax as WHITE WOMAN continues to eat. Circling STUBBS with belt.)* I do my damnedest to appeal to your good sense and reason. I bend over backward and where does it get me? You throw it all back in my face. You blatantly refuse me. Your arrogance is a slander on all that I stand for. All that I've slaved for. It's not just me, Stubbs. It's the principles. The codes. The entire infrastructure that you cast aspersions on. When I thrash you, you must remember this. You must hold it in your mind when you feel the sting of the whip. You must keep it at the most forefront of your consciousness. You must never forget that your punishment has a purpose. LONG LIVE THE ENEMY! *(COLONEL begins to savagely whip STUBBS with the belt. In the course of this, WHITE MAN reaches orgasm. STUBBS is beaten to the floor, but COLONEL continues, relentlessly.)*

STUBBS: LONG LIVE THE ENEMY! *(As the beating continues, the cyclorama is again lit up with the fireworks of war. The drummers erupt from backstage. STUBBS crawls around the stage on all fours as COLONEL pummels him with the belt. The WHITE WOMAN continues eating calmly through all this. WHITE MAN slumps in his chair, exhausted. STUBBS finally collapses in a heap with COLONEL standing over him. The war panorama subsides. Sounds and drums fade. Pause as COLONEL puts his belt back on but remains over STUBBS. GLORY BEE enters from right again with a pot of coffee on her tray, crossing very slowly toward the booth, completely focused on the coffeepot. Silence.)*

COLONEL *(to GLORY BEE as she passes behind him)*: If you stare at the pot, you're bound to spill. *(GLORY BEE keeps steadfastly making her way to the booth. When she gets there she refills the two cups.)* I'm going to give you another chance, Stubbs. One last chance. God knows I've given you enough already. We're going to go back in time. You and me. Back to the field of battle. We're going to fix ourselves there just as surely as though we were standing there today. Breathing the fire. Staring straight into the eyeballs of death itself. *(COLONEL stands and crosses back to the booth, leaving STUBBS on the floor.)*

STUBBS *(on floor)*: From here I can see their boots. *(COLONEL reaches the booth and picks up the toy infantrymen.)*

GLORY BEE *(to COLONEL)*: Did you make this mess?

COLONEL: No. He did. *(COLONEL crosses back to STUBBS with the toys and squats next to him on the floor. He sets the toys down. STUBBS stares at the toys.)*

STUBBS: From here, I can see their bodies mixed with ours.

COLONEL: Sit up now, Stubbs, and take stock of things.

STUBBS *(still lying on the floor)*: Their heads are blown off. *(COLONEL spanks STUBBS hard on his ass.)*

COLONEL: SIT UP, I SAID! *(STUBBS pulls himself to a sitting position, facing the toys.)*

STUBBS: Some of their heads have fallen on the bodies of our own men. It's a funny sight. *(COLONEL slaps STUBBS across the face.)*

COLONEL: SNAP OUT OF IT!

WHITE WOMAN: Give it to him! You should have done that when he was just a little boy. All of this could have been avoided. *(COLONEL crouches closer to STUBBS and becomes more confidential. GLORY BEE is cleaning up the banana split mess at the booth.)*

COLONEL: It's the loss, Stubbs. The loss. That's what puzzles me. How could we be so victorious and still suffer this terrible loss? How could that be? Was it an accident? A stray piece of shrapnel that broke off and tore through his chest? That doesn't seem fair, does it? Here you are, still alive. Living the lush life, having a dessert. And he's gone. Vanished. Blown to tiny pieces. There wasn't even enough left of him to bury a finger. I asked them to send me a finger. A toe. A strand of his hair. They couldn't find the slightest trace. Not even a scrap of flesh. *(GLORY BEE suddenly starts singing an old Billie Holiday song in full voice as she cleans up the banana split mess. She sings with real feeling, not trying to parody the lyrics. All the other characters are suspended.)*

GLORY BEE *(singing)*:
Good morning heart-ache
Here we go again
Good morning heart-ache
You're the one who knew me when

Might as well get used to you
Hangin' around
Good morning heart-ache
Sit down.
(She exits with tray and coffeepot, right. This time she moves quickly and freely with no concern about spilling. Pause. STUBBS and COLONEL are staring out at audience. Silence.)

COLONEL: What time is it? What am I thinking? *(COLONEL stands abruptly, digging an old railroad pocket watch out of his coat and checking the time. He turns around himself as though suddenly lost. STUBBS remains on the floor.)* What am I thinking, Stubbs? We have to get you back before the curfew. Where's my sword? What's become of my sword? *(He sees his sword lying on the table by the booth and moves toward it, then stops suddenly and turns back to STUBBS.)* Your pills! The pills! You haven't taken your pills! *(COLONEL starts patting all his coat pockets, searching for a bottle of pills as he moves back to STUBBS.)* You haven't taken them yet, have you, Stubbs? Try to remember. *(STUBBS is busy moving the toy soldiers around on the floor, placing them in positions. COLONEL keeps turning in small, nervous circles, patting and searching through his jacket.)* What am I thinking? What the hell am I thinking? I know I brought them with me. I remember picking them up off your side table. I remember having a sense of duty about it. *(COLONEL finally finds the bottle of pills in one of his pockets.)* Aha! I knew it! I knew I hadn't forgotten. Thank God! Thank Christ! Thank the Holy Ghost! I have them, Stubbs! I have them right here. *(COLONEL moves right and yells offstage for GLORY BEE. STUBBS keeps maneuvering the toys. Yelling off right.)* Oh, miss! Miss! What the hell was her name? "Bee" somebody? Miss! A glass of water, please! It's an emergency! *(COLONEL returns to STUBBS and brings the wheelchair over next to him.)* Come on now, Stubbs. We have to get you back before they lock the doors on us. We'll be up shit creek without a paddle.

STUBBS (*on floor with toys*): It's very clear what happened. We were back to back. Like this. (*He moves toys.*) Exactly like this.

COLONEL: Stubbs, get up off the floor now. You have to take your pills.

STUBBS: Caught in a cross fire.

COLONEL: STUBBS!

STUBBS: Don't yell at me. That'll get you nowhere.

COLONEL: Please, Stubbs. Take your pills now. We have to get you back or they'll suspend my visiting privileges. They're very strict about that. You know how they are.

STUBBS: I could feel his spine trembling on my spine. There was nothing we could do about fear. We couldn't bargain with fear. We couldn't talk ourselves out of it. Neither one of us knew how to pray. We had no idea who God was. Who was God? (COLONEL *picks up* STUBBS *and puts him back into the wheelchair.*)

COLONEL: We can reconstruct this later. At the hospital. We'll have all day tomorrow. We have all week.

STUBBS: It was friendly fire that took us out. That's what it was. You could see it heading at us from the mountain, not the sea. It was coming straight at us.

COLONEL: If they lock the doors on us, Stubbs, we'll be sitting ducks. We'll be on the street. Wide open to attack.

STUBBS: It was friendly fire. It smiled in my face. I could see its teeth when it hit us. I could see its tongue.

COLONEL: Pull yourself together now, Stubbs! We're going to have to make a sprint for it! If we're caught in the open they'll cut us to pieces! (STUBBS *faces audience in wheelchair as*

GLORY BEE *enters, from right, very slowly, balancing a glass of water on her tray and moving inch by inch toward* STUBBS.)

STUBBS: There was a face on the nose of the missile. They'd painted a face. You could see it coming. A lizard with smiling teeth. A friendly lizard. It was seeking us out. Hunting our warm bodies. It was glad it found us. You could tell. It was happy to receive us. It could care less who we were, but happy we were human. Happy we weren't just a concrete bunker or another stupid building. Overjoyed that we had skin and blood. We opened our arms to it. We couldn't resist its embrace. We were lovers when it hit us. We were in heaven. (COLONEL *crosses to* GLORY BEE *with the bottle of pills in his hand. He stops her.*)

COLONEL *(to* GLORY BEE*)*: Can't you remember the simplest thing! Don't stare at the glass! You're bound to spill if you stare at the glass. I've told you that a thousand times. Here, let me show you. (COLONEL *tries to take the tray and glass away from* GLORY BEE, *but she won't give it up. Pulling tray.*) Give it to me! Release your hold! (GLORY BEE *releases her grip and* COLONEL *takes it. He begins to move randomly around the stage, balancing the glass on the tray. He spins and turns, leaps in the air, making a ridiculous dance out of his demonstration as* GLORY BEE *watches.* STUBBS *stares straight out, ignoring the* COLONEL. *To* GLORY BEE.) Now watch me. Study it closely. (*He begins to dance.*) You have to pick a point in space. A specific point. Sometimes it's helpful to close one eye until you've found it. One eye may be more dominant than the other, in which case you have to experiment. You have to test them for accuracy and precision, always bearing in mind your ultimate objective. Your specific mission. Always reminding yourself that the human body is little more than a complex machine and, like all machines, can be trained and programmed to fulfill our every need. Through repetition and practice. Repetition and practice. Slowly, a pattern begins to emerge. Slowly, through my own diligence and perseverance, this pattern takes on a beauty and form that would have otherwise been incomprehensible to my random, chaotic laziness. Now I become a master of my own destiny. I can see the writing on the wall. I understand my purpose in the grand scheme of things. There's no longer any doubt. Fear takes a backseat to the certainty and confidence that now consumes my entire being. I am a God among men! I move in a different sphere. I fly on the wings of my own initiative! *(COLONEL spins to a stop and turns toward GLORY BEE. To GLORY BEE.)* You see? How simple? How pure? Now, you try it. *(COLONEL moves toward GLORY BEE, holding out the tray and glass of water to her. She refuses to take it.)* Here. Give it a whirl. It's your turn now. *(GLORY BEE refuses.)* You don't want a beating, do you?

WHITE WOMAN: You'd better try it. I've seen him when he comes apart and it's not a pretty sight.

COLONEL *(to GLORY BEE)*: Maybe you'd like a good beating. *(GLORY BEE takes the tray and glass reluctantly as COLONEL escorts her downstage left by the arm. STUBBS blows his whistle and lifts his shirt again, showing his scar to the audience. COLONEL grabs one side of GLORY'S tray so that the two of them are holding it between them, balancing the glass of water. To GLORY BEE.)* Now—simply let yourself go and allow your body to give itself up to the force of my superior momentum. Here we go. Cast your fate to the wind! *(COLONEL begins to propel GLORY BEE around the stage. They move like a dance team with GLORY BEE falling right into the rhythm. WHITE MAN begins to sing as COLONEL and GLORY BEE waltz to the melody, holding the tray and glass between them.)*

WHITE MAN *(singing)*:
Sometimes I live in the country
Sometimes I live in the town
Sometimes I have a great notion
To jump into the river and drown

Irene, good night
Irene, good night
Good night, Irene
Good night, Irene
I'll see you in my dreams.

WHITE MAN *and* WHITE WOMAN *(singing)*:
Last Saturday night I got married
Me and my wife settled down
Now me and my wife are parted
I'm gonna take another stroll downtown

Irene, good night
Irene, good night
Good night, Irene
Good night, Irene
I'll see you in my dreams.©

(COLONEL and GLORY BEE continue their dance all over the stage.)

COLONEL *(waltzing)*: Stubbs, I think I'm in love. Do you think that's possible? At my late age? *(STUBBS pulls his shirt back down and stares straight ahead as COLONEL and GLORY BEE continue to waltz.)*

STUBBS: No.

COLONEL: You're only jealous, Stubbs. You're maimed and jealous. It's a shame.

STUBBS: MY THING HANGS LIKE DEAD MEAT!

COLONEL *(dancing)*: Exactly. No son of mine has a "thing" like that. It's not possible.

STUBBS: If my "thing" comes back. If it grows straight and strong and tall— Will you take me back?

COLONEL: Too late for that, Stubbs. The time has passed. On the other hand, things are looking up for me.

STUBBS: You're in love.

COLONEL: Exactly.

STUBBS: Suddenly.

COLONEL: Right.

STUBBS: She's caused you to forget the curfew.

COLONEL: That's correct.

STUBBS: She's caused you to forget my pills.

COLONEL: We're running away to Mexico!

STUBBS: You're leaving me for good?

COLONEL: Exactly. It's a dead end, Stubbs. We did our best. Here. Take your pills. You might as well take them. (COLONEL *dances* GLORY BEE *over to* STUBBS *and sets the tray, glass, and pills down on* STUBBS's *lap, then dances off again with* GLORY BEE *in his arms.*)

STUBBS: IT'S TOO LATE FOR PILLS! (STUBBS *throws the tray, glass, and pills off right. A loud crash of dishes follows, off right, more like an explosion.*)

COLONEL (*still dancing*): That's not the attitude we try to engender, Stubbs. It's only the present that stinks. Try to remember that. The future holds bright promise. Acapulco! Marimbas under the full moon! A new name! I was thinking something along the lines of: "Mr. and Mrs. Domingo Chalupas." We'd be entirely incognito. A mystery surrounds us! We begin to spawn children. All boys! Each of them physically perfect in their own way. Each of them beyond reproach. It's not too late to begin again, and with a woman like this, the prospects are endless!

STUBBS: Will you miss me?

COLONEL: I may have moments, Stubbs. A moment here, a moment there. Fleeting moments.

STUBBS: But you'll try to forget me? To wipe me out?

COLONEL: I'll do my best.

STUBBS: You'll never erase me completely.

COLONEL: Don't be so sure about that.

STUBBS: You'll miss the Enemy.

COLONEL: I'll make a new one. I'm very adaptable.

STUBBS: You'll never replace me.

COLONEL (still dancing): It's already been done!

STUBBS: She'll never hold up to the punishment!

COLONEL: She's a woman of substance.

STUBBS: She'll bottom out!

COLONEL: Not a chance.

STUBBS: She'll wish she'd never been born!

COLONEL: Bitterness, Stubbs. Bitterness.

STUBBS: Why are you so determined to abandon me? Is it my HELPLESSNESS! (STUBBS suddenly stands on wobbly legs, trying desperately to keep his balance. COLONEL and GLORY BEE stop dancing and stare at him. Pause.)

COLONEL: Stubbs. Don't be an idiot! (STUBBS falls back into the wheelchair, breathing hard from the struggle to stand. Pause.)

STUBBS: Is it my IMPOTENCE! (STUBBS stands again, gripping an arm of the wheelchair, then letting go and tottering badly as though about to fall flat on his face.)

COLONEL: There are certain things that are irreversible, Stubbs. Irreversible. Now, sit down and stop trying to be a hero. You're less pathetic as a cripple. (STUBBS begins to fall forward. GLORY BEE rushes to him and props him up before he has a chance to fall. STUBBS remains standing at an angle with most of his weight being supported by GLORY BEE, who groans under the effort. COLO-

NEL *makes no move to help.)* This won't change anything, Stubbs. This sad little last-ditch attempt. It won't change a heartbeat. It certainly won't bring my son back, now, will it? *(STUBBS throws his arms around GLORY BEE'S shoulders and begins to stagger forward haphazardly toward left with GLORY BEE still trying to support him.)*

STUBBS: Your son. *Your* son. I remember him running. Crazy. Running toward the beach. Throwing his rifle in the green sea. Throwing his arms to the sky. Running to the mountain. Back to the beach. Screaming. I remember his eyes.

GLORY BEE *(supporting STUBBS)*: I can't keep this up forever, you know. I'm a waitress.

STUBBS: I remember his eyes. *(STUBBS and GLORY BEE stop, left, but she remains supporting his weight. COLONEL moves to the wheelchair.)*

COLONEL: We're bound to miss curfew now, Stubbs. I hope you're proud of yourself. I hope you're good and happy about that.

STUBBS: I remember him falling. Picking him up. Dragging him down the beach. Screaming his head off. Carrying him on my back. *(STUBBS staggers forward with GLORY BEE supporting him desperately.)*

GLORY BEE: Oh, my God.

STUBBS: He kept speaking your name in my ear. Whispering it. Chanting your name like a prayer. Calling to you as though you might appear out of nowhere.

GLORY BEE *(staggering under his weight)*: This is pure torture, you know. *(STUBBS continues to stagger, with GLORY BEE doing her best to keep him upright.)*

COLONEL: What're you going to do when she finds out about your "thing," Stubbs? How're you going to explain that one?

STUBBS: As though you might suddenly appear and save him. Transport him back across the green sea. Sweep him up in your arms and take him safely back home.

GLORY BEE: I can't hold you forever, you know.

STUBBS (*continuing to stagger*): Keep thinking of "home." That's the way to pull through this. Fix a picture in your mind. A backyard. A tree house. A better time. Truman, maybe. "Straight-Talkin' Harry." Think of station wagons! County Fairs! Ferris Wheels! Think of canned goods and cotton candy! Home Economics. Production lines! The Great Northern Railroad! Think of what we've achieved! The "Trail of Tears"! The Mississippi! Samuel Clemens! Little Richard! The Dust Bowl! The Gold Rush! The Natchez Trace! It's endless! A River of Victory in all directions! Flooding the Plains! Hold to an image! Lock onto a picture of glorious, unending expansion! DON'T LET YOUR-SELF SLIP INTO DOUBT!! Don't let it happen! You'll be swallowed whole!

GLORY BEE: I can't keep this up!

STUBBS (*staggering badly*): Lock onto an image or you'll be blown to KINGDOM COME!! (*STUBBS and GLORY BEE crash head-long onto the booth and lie there in a pile, exhausted and breathing hard. COLONEL pushes the wheelchair over near the booth, then slowly sits down in it. Pause.*)

COLONEL: All right, Stubbs. Have it your way. Looks like we've finally hit our crossroads here. I may just have to make a dash for the hospital on my own bat. Completely unassisted. Is that what it's come down to? A final split? An absolute parting of the ways? (*Pause. STUBBS and GLORY BEE just lie there, breathing hard. COLONEL turns the wheelchair and wheels himself away from the booth, very slowly, almost leisurely, toward downstage right. GLORY BEE props herself up and looks out into space. Pause.*)

GLORY BEE *(in booth)*: You know what I miss? You remember how we used to have those little "quiet times" just before the sirens? Way back when it first started? I think it's a shame we don't have those anymore.

WHITE MAN: I agree.

GLORY BEE: I miss those so much.

WHITE WOMAN: I don't remember any "quiet time." When was that?

WHITE MAN: You remember. *(COLONEL arrives downstage right in wheelchair and stops, staring out over audience. Pause.)*

COLONEL: Maybe you think you're breaking my heart with this desperate show of independence. But don't get excited. I was born in isolation. If I can't have companionship it won't kill me. Aggression is the only answer. A man needs a good hobby. Something he can sink his teeth into. *(STUBBS sits up, clutching at the booth for support. GLORY BEE stays seated in the booth. COLONEL remains sitting in wheelchair, facing audience.)*

STUBBS *(quietly, to COLONEL)*: I remember the moment you forsook me. The moment you invented my death. That moment has lasted all my life.

COLONEL *(facing front)*: Your imagination has done you in, Stubbs. If you think you're breaking my heart, you're sadly mistaken. I can easily do without. It's a question of training. Repetition and practice. Repetition and practice. All those days. All those horrible long days without the enemy. Longing out the window. Staring at the stupid boredom of peacetime. The dullness of it. The idiot deadness in everyone's eyes. Did you think I was just treading water back then? Spinning my wheels? I was gearing up, Stubbs. Silently stockpiling my secret arsenal for just such an occasion as this. Knowing full well that the enemy has the same hunger for me as I have for him. Never doubting for a second that he would reemerge. He would reemerge because I commanded it.

GLORY BEE *(from booth)*: The thing I can't get over is, it never occurred to me that "Danny's" could be invaded. I always thought we were invulnerable to attack. The landscaping. The lighting. The parking lot. All the pretty bushes. Who could touch us? Who would dare?

WHITE MAN: I absolutely agree.

GLORY BEE *(from booth)*: When the first wave of missiles hit us I kept studying the menu. I thought the menu would save me somehow. The pretty colored photographs of all our specials. The "Catfish Dinner." The "Chicken-Fried Steak." I worshipped the menu.

WHITE MAN: What was it we used to do in those "quiet times"?

WHITE WOMAN: You got me.

WHITE MAN: Didn't we dance or something? Weren't we on a pier? A dock of some kind? Watching lights in the distance?

WHITE WOMAN: Have you lost your mind?

WHITE MAN: Didn't we dance cheek to cheek?

WHITE WOMAN: COME TO YOUR SENSES! *(She whacks the WHITE MAN across the head with her purse. He doesn't react. An explosion in the distance.)*

COLONEL *(in wheelchair, facing front)*: If you think you can touch me in some way—fondle me—cajole me into your frame of reference— If you think you can make an appeal of some kind—maybe beg—maybe crawl and pray—maybe sacrifice your own blood or the blood of your children. You're sadly mistaken. *(Suddenly, from left, a metal busboy's wagon, loaded with gas masks, is rolled onstage. It arrives all by itself and stops centerstage. The characters ignore it. Pause.)*

GLORY BEE: I worshipped the menu. To me it held a life. An unthreatened life. Better than the Bible. I missed the Cold W. with all my heart.

WHITE: Me too.

COLONEL: I think she senses your weakness, Stubbs. She can smell it on you. How could she help but smell it? The hole through your middle. The rotting core. The limpness. There's no way you can disguise something like that. Your only hope is to throw yourself at my feet and beg for mercy. Imitate my every move. I'm your only chance now.

WHITE WOMAN: Shouldn't we be getting under the table by now? Shouldn't we be tucking our heads between our knees? *(STUBBS stands again, suddenly.)*

STUBBS: If we can make it to the mountain, they might realize we're on the same side! We'll wave every flag we can get our hands on. Every color. They've got to recognize us! *(STUBBS lurches forward, losing his balance as he heads upstage. GLORY BEE stays sitting in the booth and watches STUBBS as he crashes headlong into the metal wagon, upsetting all the gas masks. He falls and just lies there. COLONEL continues to sit in wheelchair, staring out over audience without turning back toward STUBBS and his accident. Pause.)*

COLONEL: A touching display. I still think Mexico is the ticket, when you get right down to it. *(GLORY BEE kneels down next to STUBBS and strokes his back softly but mechanically.)*

GLORY BEE: I missed the sounds of people clinking coffee cups. Spoons scraping on bowls. Knives and forks scratching plates. The rustle of napkins and money.

COLONEL *(still facing audience)*: She's playing you for a sucker, Stubbs. You can see right through it.

GLORY BEE: I missed the voices of conversations I couldn't make out. Just the sounds of humans temporarily stopping for breakfast, then moving on.

COLONEL: Tell her about your "thing," Stubbs! Don't forget about that. Best to get it out in the open. (STUBBS *rolls over on his back and embraces* GLORY BEE, *pulling her on top of him.*)

STUBBS (*rolling with* GLORY BEE, *holding her*): Lock onto a picture of "home."

COLONEL (*still facing front but getting worried*): Now, listen to me, Stubbs! Let's not fly off the handle here. The truth of it is that we may, in fact, be somehow remotely related. I'm not saying directly, now. I'm not at all suggesting first generation or anything like that. But possibly cousins. Second cousins at the very least. It's within the realm of possibility. There's certain evidence that I've withheld until I was sure I'd gathered all the facts. I didn't want you to become overexcited for no good reason. (STUBBS *rolls across the floor with* GLORY BEE *held in his grip.* COLONEL *spins the wheelchair around, facing* STUBBS. *Directly to* STUBBS.) Stubbs! Don't be a maniac! Give that up! Give it all up! Relinquish your self completely! If you promise me this— If you make a solemn oath—Scout's honor. Hope to die. Stick a needle in your eye. If you give me some sign of total, absolute, unconditional submission—then I might—I just might consider—*adopting* you. I'm serious, Stubbs. I'm absolutely serious. I'll fill out the necessary forms. I'll go through all the red tape. I don't mind a bit. But only if you swear on a stack of Bibles to submit!

STUBBS (*rolling on floor with* GLORY BEE): My thing is coming back!

GLORY BEE: Oh, great! (COLONEL *propels the wheelchair quickly toward* STUBBS *and* GLORY BEE *as they continue to roll back and forth as one body.*)

COLONEL: That's not possible, Stubbs! That's out of the question. You have no say in the matter. It's already been decided long ago. It's a question of destiny!

WHITE WOMAN: Well, I'm not waiting anymore. At a certain point you have to take things into your own hands. *(WHITE WOMAN gets up from her chair, crosses to one of the gas masks on the floor, and picks it up. She returns to the table and puts the gas mask on.)*

STUBBS: My thing is arising! I can feel it!

COLONEL: Stubbs! Stubbs, you have to listen now. Your "thing" is not the issue. Your "thing" is beside the point. It has little consequence. It's a selfish, stupid, little tiny concern. Listen up!

STUBBS: It's coming back! It's all coming back to me now!

COLONEL: You're dreaming, Stubbs! Wildly hallucinating again.

STUBBS: No—listen—here's how it was. Listen to me now! *(STUBBS stops rolling with GLORY BEE and tries to sit up from the floor. He gets GLORY BEE to help him. COLONEL stays in wheelchair. Struggling to sit.)* When I was hit. It went straight through me and out—

COLONEL: We've heard that old song a thousand times.

STUBBS *(blowing his whistle loudly)*: LISTEN TO ME! *(COLONEL stops and turns the wheelchair to face STUBBS from a distance. Pause. To GLORY BEE.)* Help me up. Help me get up! *(GLORY BEE pulls STUBBS up to his knees. Struggling to get to his knees.)* The part I remember— The part that's coming back—is this. *(To COLONEL, on his knees.)* Your face. Your face leaning over my face. Peering down.

COLONEL *(in wheelchair)*: I was there. It's true. Right by your side.

STUBBS: Your face, lying. Smiling and lying. Your bald face of denial. Peering down from a distance. Bombing me.

COLONEL: I brought you everything you asked for! Powdered donuts. I went blocks out of my way to find them. Cracker

Jacks! Did you think they had those things in the cafeteria?
Is that what you thought?

STUBBS: I remember your squirming silence.

COLONEL: I emptied your bladder bag!

STUBBS: You had my name changed! YOU INVENTED MY
DEATH!

COLONEL: That simply isn't true, Stubbs. There was some mix-
up. Some computer scramble. I don't know where you get
these ideas.

STUBBS: No "next of kin." No "next of kin." A "friend of the
family," they told me. That's what they told me!

COLONEL: It was simpler all the way around.

STUBBS: Some mysterious "friend of the family." A friend of a
friend of my father's friend.

COLONEL: I was there from dawn 'til dusk. I watched the sun rise
and fall on your stupid head! I listened to you babble. I read
you comic books. (Pause.)

STUBBS (on his knees): Your face of pure guilt. Squirming. Nothing to be done about that. No way of tracing it. Tracking
it down. No way of knowing the original moment. Abraham, maybe. Maybe Abraham. Judas. Eve. Maybe her. No
way of knowing for sure. Best way is to kill all the sons.
Wipe them off the face of the earth. Bleed them of all their
blood. Let it pour down into the soil. Let it fill every river.
Every hole in this earth. Let it pour through every valley.
Flood every town. Let us drown in the blood of our own.
Let us drown and drink it. Let us go down screaming in the
blood of our sons. (COLONEL slowly wheels himself to downstage
center, where he sits, facing out toward audience.)

COLONEL: We've got to keep our back to the mountain, Stubbs.
At all costs. You can see our position. We've got a perfect

vantage point from here. We're lucky in that respect. There are certain advantages to isolation. After all, we're not in exile. This is our domain. We've earned every inch of it. Surrounded by water. Engulfed by the prairies. Marooned. *(Pause.)* MAROOOOOOOOOONED!! *(Pause.* GLORY BEE *picks up a gas mask and puts it on* STUBBS, *then dons one herself and curls into fetal position upstage center. The* WHITE MAN *remains sitting in his chair, facing right without his gas mask on. The* COLONEL *remains in wheelchair, facing out and not looking back at* STUBBS.*)* It's the perfect situation. We couldn't have asked for a better deal. If they attack us on our flank, we've got them surrounded. If they come from air, sea, or land, we'll cut them off at the pass. We're invincible, Stubbs. There's no doubt about it. Invincible! *(*STUBBS *begins to rise to his feet.)* Stubbs? You're right behind me, aren't you? You're right where I imagine you to be? You're not turning tail? Burying your face in the sand? Crying for mother? Put your back up against me, Stubbs, so I can feel you. Press your spine into my spine. Give me the impression that you're with me to the bitter end. That's the spirit! *(Pause.* STUBBS *is now standing and facing the back of the wheelchair.)* Stubbs? We have to stick together in this. The sacrifice needs a partner. You understand that, don't you? *(*STUBBS *begins to slowly advance on the* COLONEL *from behind.)* The attack could come at any second now. Put your back up against me, Stubbs, so I can feel your spine. We're in this together. *(*STUBBS *stands behind the wheelchair, staring down at the* COLONEL'*s head, with his gas mask on.)* Stubbs? Are you there? Are you still there? Don't run out on me now. As soon as this is over, I'll take you back. I promise you. I will. I'll make it official. Lock, stock, and barrel. It's not too late for that. I'll proclaim it in public. *(Pause.)* Stubbs? Are you listening? You haven't left me yet? You haven't disappeared? STUBBS! *(Suddenly,* STUBBS *grabs the* COLONEL *around the neck in a stranglehold. Choking, in* STUBBS'*s stranglehold.)* If you're very good, Stubbs— If you're very, very good—I'll buy you two desserts. Anything you want. Hot fudge. Milky Ways. Anything your heart desires. I'll take you to the movies. How 'bout that? I'll take you to the park. We'll swing. We'll slide. Anything your heart desires. Stubbs? *(STUBBS releases his hold on COLONEL and grabs the sword with both hands. He steps one step back from the wheelchair and raises the sword in one quick and decisive movement, as though to decapitate the COLONEL, and then freezes in that posture. COLONEL stares straight ahead.)*

STUBBS *(through gas mask)*: GOD BLESS THE ENEMY!!!!!!!
(WHITE MAN, still sitting, facing right, starts singing.)

WHITE MAN *(singing)*:
Sometimes I live in the country
Sometimes I live in the town
Sometimes I have a great notion
To jump into the river and drown

Irene, good night
Irene, good night
Good night, Irene
Good night, Irene
I'll see you in my dreams.

WHITE MAN *and* GLORY BEE *(singing)*:
Last Saturday night I got married
Me and my wife settled down
Now me and my wife are parted
I'm gonna take another stroll downtown

Irene, good night
Irene, good night
Good night, Irene
Good night, Irene
I'll see you in my dreams.©

WHITE MAN, GLORY BEE, *and* WHITE WOMAN *(singing)*:
    Stop ramblin', stop your gamblin'
    Stop stayin' out late at night
    Go home to your wife and your family
    Sit down by the fireside bright

    Irene, good night
    Irene, good night
    Good night, Irene
    Good night, Irene
    I'll see you in my dreams.

WHITE MAN, GLORY BEE, WHITE WOMAN, *and* COLONEL *(singing)*:
    I love Irene, God knows I do
    Love her 'til the seas run dry
    And if Irene turns her back on me
    I'm gonna take morphine and die

    Irene, good night
    Irene, good night
    Good night, Irene
    Good night, Irene
    I'll see you in my dreams.©

(The stage lights dim slowly to black, leaving STUBBS *and the* COLONEL *frozen.)*

END

Simpatico

A PLAY IN THREE ACTS

Simpatico was first presented at the Joseph Papp Public Theater in New York, on 14 November 1994. The cast was as follows:

CARTER	Ed Harris
VINNIE	Fred Ward
CECILIA	Marcia Gay Harden
SIMMS	James Gammon
KELLY	Welker White
ROSIE	Beverly D'Angelo

Directed by Sam Shepard
Designed by Loy Arcenas
Lighting by Anne Militello
Music by Patrick O'Hearn
Sound by Tom Morse

Simpatico received its British première at the Royal Court Theatre London, on 6 April 1995. The cast was as follows:

CARTER	Sean McGinley
VINNIE	Ciaran Hinds
CECILIA	Janet McTeer
SIMMS	Tony Haygarth
KELLY	Miranda Pleasence
ROSIE	Diana Hardcastle

Directed by James Macdonald
Designed by Rob Howell
Lighting by Brian Harris
Music by Stephen Warbeck
Sound by Paul Arditti

ACT 1 Cucamonga, California
ACT 2 San Dimas, California; Midway, Kentucky;
Cucamonga, California
ACT 3 Lexington, Kentucky; Midway, Kentucky;
Cucamonga, California

Act One

Scene: Lights come up on—a cheap, ground-floor apartment on the outskirts of Cucamonga. A sign with this single place-name, "CUCAMONGA", hangs above the set. The apartment is very sparse. A sink piled with dirty dishes against the stage-right wall. A bed with one blanket against the left wall. A pile of dirty clothes at the foot of the bed, on the floor. Rough stucco walls in pale green, absolutely bare with no attempt to decorate. A window in each wall trimmed in pale Mexican orange with sun-bleached plastic curtains. The windows look out into black space. No trees. No buildings. No landscape of any kind. Just black.

Note: This set occupies most of the stage in Act One. In Acts Two and Three it takes up only part of the stage, on the stage-right side.

Actors have entered in the dark. Lights come up on VINNIE, *sitting on the edge of the bed, elbows on knees, staring at the floor. He's dressed in a dark blue long-sleeved shirt, dark slacks with no belt. Everything very rumpled as though he's been sleeping in his clothes for weeks. Bare feet.* CARTER *peruses the room, crossing from one window to the next, looking out, then moving to the sink. He's dressed in a very expensive beige suit, dark tie, brown overcoat slung over one arm and a briefcase containing his cellular phone. His shoes are alligator loafers with little tassels. Both men are well into their forties.*

CARTER: Well, this isn't bad, Vinnie. Cozy. Close to the

mall. Little sparse maybe. Picture I had was that you were much worse off.

VINNIE: What's sparse about it?

CARTER: Well—it could use a lady's touch. You know—a few throw-rugs or something. What do they call those? You know—throw-rugs.

VINNIE: All's I need is a bed.

CARTER: Sixties style, huh?

VINNIE: I didn't have a bed in the sixties.

Pause.

CARTER: Right. Well, you got someone looking after you? Someone to do the laundry? Dishes? I can get that arranged for you if you want. Local talent.

VINNIE: I'm fine.

CARTER: Okay. (*Moves to pile of laundry.*) But you shouldn't ought to let the laundry pile up on you, Vinnie. You let that happen, it starts to go sour. Gives you a bad impression of yourself.

VINNIE: I don't need the laundry for that.

Pause.

CARTER: You taking care of yourself otherwise? Not too much booze?

VINNIE: Not *too* much.

CARTER: Get out for a uh—stroll now and then? Fresh air. Blood pumping?

VINNIE: I walk everywhere.

CARTER: Good! That's good. Gotta keep your health up. Funny how the mind follows the body. Ever noticed that? You get sick, first thing you know the mind starts going straight to hell.

VINNIE: I walked clear to Glendora yesterday.

CARTER: Glendora?

VINNIE: Yeah. Clear to Glendora and back.

CARTER: That's quite a hike—Glendora. Out near where Shoemaker had his big wreck isn't it?

VINNIE: You know very well where Glendora is.

CARTER: What happened to that car I bought you?

VINNIE: Sold it.

CARTER: Why'd you do that?

VINNIE: Jap car.

CARTER: Well, you shoulda told me what you wanted, Vinnie. I could've got you an American car easy enough. Little Jeep Cherokee or something. All you gotta do is ask.

VINNIE: Cherokees flip. They're unstable.

CARTER: Well, a Mustang then or—

VINNIE: I don't need a car. I walk. Ever since I lost my Buick I walk.

Pause.

CARTER: Okay. Just seems like you might need some wheels to get around out here, that's all. We always used to.

VINNIE: I don't.

CARTER: All right. Good. Fair enough. I'm just trying to look out for you, Vinnie. (*Pause.*) Everything okay otherwise? Need some more cash? New shirts? You got that TV I sent you, didn't you?

VINNIE: Sold that too.

Small pause.

CARTER: They don't make American TVs anymore, Vinnie. They don't exist. They haven't made a purebred American TV for over forty years now.

VINNIE: I know that. "RCA".

CARTER: Whatever.

VINNIE: "His Master's Voice".

CARTER: Yeah—

VINNIE: Who was his Master anyway?

CARTER: Look—You wanted to talk to me, right? You called me. You've got some kind of a major crisis going on. Something that couldn't wait.

VINNIE: I do. Crisis is my middle name.

CARTER: I flew all the way out here just to talk to you, Vinnie. Do you wanna talk or do you wanna be cryptic and weird?

VINNIE: I appreciate that.

CARTER: What.

VINNIE: That you came all the way out here. Just to talk. I appreciate that.

CARTER: No problem. Our friendship always comes first. You know that. Always has.

VINNIE: If you say so.

CARTER: I do.

VINNIE: I haven't asked you for much special treatment over the years, have I Carter?

CARTER: No you haven't. You've been very understanding about this whole business.

VINNIE: Never called you collect in the middle of the night.

CARTER: Never.

VINNIE: Never interfered with your private life.

CARTER: No.

VINNIE: I've been extremely discreet.

CARTER: You have, Vinnie.

VINNIE: I've been a good boy.

CARTER: Yes.

VINNIE: Because I could really hurt you if I wanted to—

CARTER: All right, look Vinnie—let's—

VINNIE: I could demolish you if I really had a mind to. You haven't forgotten that have you?

CARTER: No! (*Pause.*) I haven't forgotten that.

VINNIE: Good. (*Pause.*) I still own all the negatives, you know. I still have them in my possession. All the early correspondence.

CARTER: Could we just get down to this problem you're having. This big problem that couldn't wait.

VINNIE: I'm not holding you up or anything am I?

CARTER: I've got to catch a return flight in about two hours.

VINNIE: Returning to the family?

CARTER: That's right.

VINNIE: Little wife? Little lady?

CARTER: Hey, don't think you can trot right across my head, pal! Just because you did me a couple a' crumby favors a long time ago.

VINNIE: Favors?

CARTER: A *long*, long time ago! (*Pause.*) There's certain
limits—certain parameters. I'm not gonna be black-
mailed, Vinnie.

VINNIE: Farthest thing from my mind.

CARTER: Good. Now, what's the problem?

Pause.

VINNIE: Uh—I got arrested about a week ago.

CARTER: Oh great! That's just wonderful! Arrested! Now
you've gotten yourself arrested!

VINNIE: Don't worry. Nothing showed up on the records.
No trace of you anywhere. No trace of Simms. You've
been very thorough about all that.

CARTER: What'd you get arrested for?

VINNIE: It was—kind of multiple charges.

CARTER: Terrific.

VINNIE: "Trespassing". "Invasion of Privacy". And uh—
"Harassment".

CARTER: Harassment?

VINNIE: Yeah. Harassment.

CARTER: You didn't assault anyone, did you?

VINNIE: No. I don't do that. That's not my specialty. You
know that.

CARTER: Who'd you harass then?

VINNIE: No one.

CARTER: All right—Who *charged* you with harassment?

VINNIE: A woman.

CARTER: Here we go—

VINNIE: But it won't stick. Told me to stay away from her house. Hysterical reaction on her part, is all it was. Petty-anti stuff.

CARTER: Hysterical reaction to what?

VINNIE: She felt I'd deceived her, I guess.

CARTER: Deception is not harassment.

VINNIE: Exactly *my* point.

CARTER: What else did you do to her?

VINNIE: Nothing. I didn't touch her. We never even kissed. Never hugged even.

CARTER: So, it's just a uh—"psychological" thing with her, I suppose. Same old, same old.

VINNIE: Must be. I can't figure it out.

CARTER: What's the "Trespassing" deal? The "Invasion of Privacy"?

VINNIE: Uh—See, I had her believing that I was a detective.

CARTER: Oh, Vinnie—

VINNIE: A real detective. She was absolutely convinced.

CARTER: That's the *deception* part. I'm talking about the—

VINNIE: She went right along with it. I showed her my badge, handcuffs, the gun, false ID. She got very excited about the whole thing.

CARTER: You're not carrying a weapon again are you?

VINNIE: Only on dates.

CARTER: You can't take chances like that, Vinnie. Walking around here with a weapon. Did they find it on you?

VINNIE: No. I ditched it. I'm very good at that. You know that. Went back two days later and picked it up, right where I'd left it.

CARTER: You can't take those kind of risks! I've told you that.

VINNIE: Not now anyway.

CARTER: That's right.

VINNIE: There was a time and place for risks and that time has passed.

CARTER: That's what *I've* said!

VINNIE: I was just repeating it. Just to reassure you that I've absorbed your instructions.

Pause.

CARTER (*with patience*): *Where* did you trespass and *whose* privacy did you invade?

VINNIE: I met this woman—

CARTER: We're going backwards, Vinnie.

VINNIE: You'll have to bear with me. You've got no choice.

Pause.

CARTER: All right.

VINNIE: I met this woman—like I said. Watched her walk into the bar.

CARTER: I thought you weren't drinking these days.

VINNIE (*sudden violent explosion*): NOT TOO MUCH, I SAID!! NOT TOO MUCH!! (*Pause into sudden calm.*) You're not listening.

CARTER: I am.

VINNIE (*calm*): You're interrupting. You've got to pay close attention to this. Try to grasp all the details.

CARTER: I am. Take it easy. I'm just asking.

VINNIE: I watched her. She had a movement to her. A kind of life. Like a dog caught in the headlights.

CARTER: A dog caught in the headlights?

VINNIE: Similar to that.

CARTER: You were *attracted* to her. In so many words.

VINNIE: I was. I admit that. I'm not ashamed to admit that. I had a thought. A thought came into my head as soon as I saw her and I'd never had this kind of thought before. I said to myself: "If I could have this woman—I would never ever ask for anything else again in my whole life." I said to myself: "Please, dear God in Heaven, deliver this woman to me and I will never pester you again for anything whatsoever. For all Eternity I will leave you alone." (*Pause.*) And a miraculous thing occurred.

CARTER: What was that?

VINNIE: She came straight over to me. As though I'd called her. As though I'd conjured her up. Sat down right next to me and smiled. Just like she was answering my little prayer.

CARTER: Congratulations. So, then what? You started the scam on her? The "detective" scam? I can't believe you're still doing this, Vinnie.

VINNIE: She asked me what I do for a living. Right off the bat. Very sincere eyes. Well, you know, that's the one question that always throws me.

CARTER: What's that?

VINNIE: The question of "occupation". What I *do* for a living.

CARTER: I've offered you all kinds of jobs over the years, Vinnie. All kinds of opportunities.

VINNIE: I worked for you once. Once was enough.

CARTER: That was a partnership! We were absolutely equal.

VINNIE: Could I continue my story? Please.

Pause.

CARTER: I thought you'd given all this up, Vinnie. You told me you'd stopped doing this.

VINNIE: What.

CARTER: All this business with women. Pretending.

VINNIE: It's not a business!

CARTER: How many times have you gotten yourself into a jam like this over a woman?

VINNIE: Never. Not like this.

CARTER: Oh, this one's different. I see.

VINNIE: Are you listening to me or scolding me!

CARTER: I'm *telling* you! This is *exactly* what I've been warning you about all these years. One little slip–up like this and the whole thing can come unraveled.

VINNIE: There's no way they can connect you to me.

CARTER: When you apply for a State Racing License what is the main prerequisite? Fingerprints! Right? Finger-prints, Vinnie! You've got no concept of how things are hooked up these days. How international files are kept. Information stored. Microchips. Fibre optics. Floppy discs. It's an art form now, Vinnie! An industry!

VINNIE (*sudden explosion again*): I AM TALKING ABOUT
A WOMAN!!

Pause.

CARTER: All right. Calm down. Jesus. We're just trying to
have a conversation.

VINNIE: I AM NOT TALKING ABOUT MICROCHIPS
AND INDUSTRIES!! I AM TALKING ABOUT A
WOMAN!!

CARTER: If you're going to scream, I'm going to leave.

VINNIE (*calmer*): You're not listening to me, I don't think.

CARTER: I am.

VINNIE: I don't think so.

CARTER: I am. It's just—

VINNIE: So, tell me what I'm saying then. Tell me back.

Pause.

CARTER: You wanna take a walk? Go out and have a drink
somewhere? Get some air?

VINNIE: Tell me what I'm saying. I'd like to hear it. Back.

CARTER: Let's have a drink.

VINNIE: *You* don't drink. Remember?

CARTER (*pause*): I've taken it up again.

VINNIE: Oh? Things not so hot back home?

CARTER: What?

VINNIE: I said: (*As though speaking to the deaf.*) "THINGS—
NOT—SO—HOT—BACK—AT—HOME?"

CARTER: Everything's fine. I just have an occasional highball to take the edge off. Just to relax. That's all.

VINNIE: Ah, the Occasional Highball!

CARTER: Whatever, Whiskey sour. Now and then.

VINNIE: No harm in that.

CARTER: None whatsoever.

VINNIE: Kids back in school are they?

CARTER: They start this week.

VINNIE: It's that time of year. PUMPKIN TIME!

CARTER: Yeah.

VINNIE: Rosie's happy?

CARTER: I'd just as soon not talk about Rosie, if you don't mind.

VINNIE: She still got those amazing tits that kinda sit up like little puppy dogs and bark at you?

CARTER *charges* VINNIE, *grabs him by the throat and throws him backwards onto the bed, then smashes him with the pillow.* VINNIE *smiles and lays there passively while* CARTER *stands over him. Long pause.* CARTER *backs off.*

VINNIE (*sitting up on bed, smiling*): So—You're back on the bottle my good man. I happen to have some of that Northern Irish stuff. "Black Bush". The best.

VINNIE *reaches under bed, pulls out bottle of bourbon and a short glass. Pours himself a drink as they continue.*

CARTER: No thanks.

VINNIE: Too rough? Black Bush can be pretty rough if all you've been used to is the "Occasional Highball".

CARTER: Are you going to finish telling me about this woman?

VINNIE: You're not listening, Carter. Your mind is elsewhere.

CARTER: Just don't talk about my wife, okay?

VINNIE: *Your* wife?

CARTER: That's right!

VINNIE: I was just curious is all. We go off in different directions. Lota time goes by. Lota water under the bridge. You can't help but wonder.

CARTER: Wonder to yourself.

VINNIE: Green swimming pool. White Mercedez. Blue car phone. Must have a phone in every car, right Carter? Every bathroom. Keep track a' things while you're taking a dump. Cellular business. How is business these days?

CARTER: Market's down. The Arabs have dropped out of the game.

VINNIE: But the Japs—the Japs are coming on strong.

CARTER: Not strong enough.

VINNIE: The rich are clamping down!

Pause.

CARTER: Look, Vinnie. I gave you all kinds of options. I mean—

VINNIE: Options!

CARTER: I did. At one point in time you could have—

VINNIE: The option to disappear, for instance. The option to perpetually change my name and address. The option to live like a ghost.

CARTER: Look—You're here, you're alive. You're not in jail. So far anyway.

VINNIE: Three pluses in your book!

CARTER: Better than dead, Vinnie. Better than being locked away.

VINNIE (*sudden quiet sincerity*): I *am* dead. I *am* locked away.

Pause.

CARTER: Maybe you'd be better off in Europe. What do you think? Did you ever think of Europe? We could set you up over there. Some little obscure village tucked away in Austria, maybe.

VINNIE: What am I gonna do tucked away in Austria? Ski? Yodel, maybe?

CARTER: I don't know—

VINNIE: I'll tell you what the option is. Here's an option. You turn yourself in, Carter.

CARTER: Hey!

VINNIE: You walk right into the FBI and confess the whole fandango. Lay all your cards on the table. Worst they'll give you is a slap on the wrist and a little fine. Man of your position.

CARTER: What the hell good is that gonna do? What're you saying?

VINNIE: Let me off the hook.

CARTER: Let yourself off the hook. I'm not your jailer.

VINNIE: Let me off the hook, Carter!

Pause.

CARTER: I'm—perfectly willing to help you out in any way I can. You know that, Vinnie. I always have been. That's why I'm here, now. But—

VINNIE: You're here, *now*, because you're scared and guilty. That's why you're here, *now*.

CARTER (*laughing*): Scared and guilty?

VINNIE: One or the other. Or both.

CARTER: Scared and guilty!

VINNIE: Neither one is the right motive.

CARTER: Oh, well, I apologize for that!

VINNIE: Neither one has to do with kinship or brotherhood or any sense of another man's suffering at the hands of a woman.

CARTER: Oh, so now we're suffering! We're suffering now!

VINNIE: One of us might be suffering!

CARTER: But the other one has no conception of it! Is that the idea!

VINNIE: That's the idea but the idea is a long way from the truth!

CARTER: Aah! The Truth! The Truth! And only one of us is able to have a handle on that I suppose!

VINNIE: One of us is a helluva lot closer to it than the other one!

CARTER: And the other one is just blindly staggering! Just bashing into walls, leaving carnage in his wake!

VINNIE (*pause*): One of us has forgotten.

Pause.

CARTER: What do you want me to do, Vinnie? You want me to talk to this girl? Straighten something out? What exactly do you want me to do?

VINNIE: It was just a uh—wild impulse.

CARTER: What was?

VINNIE: Calling you up. Thinking there was some remote possibility that you might—have an answer.

CARTER: I'm not any better at figuring out women than you are, Vinnie.

VINNIE: No, I suppose not. After all, look who you ended up marrying.

CARTER: Look—

VINNIE: Does she ever pull that on you, Carter? The cold-shoulder routine? She could make a rock cry.

CARTER: I am *not* going to get into a conversation about Rosie!

VINNIE: She used to pull that on me. All the time. 'Course she never went so far as to have me arrested. You've never been arrested have you, Carter?

CARTER: No. I never have.

VINNIE: There's plenty of good reasons why you *should* be arrested: extortion, kickbacks, third-party transfers, money laundering—

CARTER: Hey, goddammit!

VINNIE: But, for some reason, you never were. Call it luck. Let's call it luck, shall we?

CARTER: Luck had nothing to do with it. We were both well aware of the risks going into it.

VINNIE: Even Rosie—

CARTER: Leave her out of this!

VINNIE: Even Rosie was well aware.

CARTER: I'm walking out the door, Vinnie! I'm walking!

VINNIE: No you're not. You're in no position to threaten me. I'm the one holding all the cards, Carter. I'm the one and only one who can call you any time of the day or night and have you book your ass out here to the edge of nowhere. Who else can do that? Does anybody else have that kind of power in your "organization"?

CARTER: You're not going to expose me. You want me to believe that? You're tied into Simms' dismissal every bit as much as me.

VINNIE: You made sure of that, didn't you?

CARTER: It was *you* who took the photographs, for Christ's sake!

VINNIE: And *you* who set him up!

CARTER: He didn't need setting up! There was more corruption in his commission than anything we could've ever cooked up ourselves. All we did was document the truth. I've got no regrets about that, believe you me. No regrets whatsoever. Simms hung himself.

VINNIE: Document the truth?

CARTER: That's right!

VINNIE: *I* took the photographs, Carter. I saw what I was shooting!

CARTER: Nobody twisted your arm either.

VINNIE: Would you like to see them again to refresh your memory?

CARTER: No! I would *not* like to see them again!

VINNIE: I didn't think so.

CARTER: Nobody coerced you into taking those pictures, Vinnie. You were a free agent.

Pause.

VINNIE: What was in it for me? I forgot that part. There must have been something. Something rewarding.

CARTER: Is that what this is all about? Your reward? If you want me to increase your monthly deposit that can be arranged, Vinnie. That's easy. Just come out and say it and stop tap-dancing around.

Pause.

VINNIE: Are you a member of a country club out there?

CARTER: What?

VINNIE: Are you a member of a country club out there?

CARTER: Out where?

VINNIE: Out there in the "Blue Grass Country" where you've forged a brand new life for yourself and your cute little wife.

CARTER: A country club?

VINNIE: Yeah. Are you a member of one? It's a relatively straightforward question.

CARTER: What's that got to do with anything!

VINNIE: I bet you are, aren't you?

CARTER: Yeah! Yeah, I'm a member of a country club! So fuckin' what!

VINNIE: Well, that must be something new and different for you, huh? Being a member. Must've been difficult at first. Fitting in. Pretending you had something in common. Kissing ass with the gentry.

CARTER: I don't have time to screw around here, Vinnie.

VINNIE: But now it's become second nature, right? You've acquired an affinity. You stride right through the pro-shop on your way to the bar, laughing and slapping all your divorced buddies on the butt. Cracking inane jokes about pussy you've never had. Collecting football pools and swapping putters. Like your seedy past is long forgot. Might never have really even taken place. Might have actually belonged to another man. A man so remote and dead to you that you've lost all connection. A man completely sacrificed in honor of your bogus membership in the High Life.

CARTER: Nobody forced you into a hole, Vinnie! Nobody!

VINNIE: Nobody did! It must've been DESTINY!

CARTER: Nobody demanded you screw yourself up with women and booze and lying and pretending—

VINNIE: LYING!

Long pause.

CARTER: I've gotta go.

VINNIE: You should. The kids'll be late for school!

Pause.

CARTER: I can't keep this up, Vinnie. It's a dead end. Every time it's a dead end.

VINNIE: Kinda like marriage, isn't it?

CARTER: Worse.

VINNIE: Well—

CARTER: I get this—sickening feeling that it'll never end.

VINNIE: It's a *lot* like marriage.

CARTER: We just go around and around and around—

VINNIE: It *has* been going on for a spell, hasn't it? Old pal, old buddy, old friend of mine.

Pause.

CARTER: What do you want from me, Vinnie? I've tried to take care of you. I really have.

VINNIE: Yeah. I guess you have.

CARTER: I mean, I don't know what else to do except give you more money. Buy you stuff. Move you to a different place. What else do you want me to do?

VINNIE: Come clean, Carter. It's real simple.

Pause.

CARTER: Look—I've got a proposition to make you.

VINNIE: A proposition!

CARTER: I'm prepared to make you an offer. You name me a price. Just name me a price—a *realistic* price and I'll pay you *cash* for all the stuff you've got on me. All the negatives, letters, tapes, whatever you've got. We'll clean this whole mess up, once and for all, and be done with it.

VINNIE: But then we'd never see each other again, Carter.

CARTER: I'm serious, Vinnie! I want to end this thing!

Pause.

VINNIE: You're the only friend I've got, Carter. I mean— this girl—This girl isn't gonna work out. I can tell she's not gonna work out.

CARTER: You don't know that. All you've got to do is go talk to her. I mean if you've got that much feeling for her—

VINNIE: SHE WON'T TALK TO ME! She had me arrested! It wasn't any fun being arrested. I mean I'm not a criminal!

CARTER: No, you're not.

VINNIE: I'm not a criminal in the common sense!

CARTER: Of course not.

VINNIE: Not like you. I mean, I'm basically innocent. I'm an intrinsically innocent person, Carter!

CARTER: Try to calm down.

VINNIE: All I was doing was trying to impress her. That's all. I might have gone a little overboard with the gun and the handcuffs but I wasn't trying to hurt her. She had no reason to arrest me, Carter!

CARTER: No, she didn't.

Pause.

VINNIE: It's a terrible thing—trying to replace someone— You know? Trying to find someone to take the place—I mean—see, after Rosie ran off I just kinda—(*Takes a drink.*)

CARTER: She didn't "run off".

VINNIE: She didn't?

CARTER: No.

VINNIE: What would you call it?

CARTER: She—eloped.

VINNIE: Oh! "Eloped"! *That's* what you call it. That's right. "Eloped"!

CARTER: Well, she didn't "run off". That makes her sound sneaky and deceitful. That just wasn't the case.

VINNIE: "Eloped". (*Offers* CARTER *a drink*.) Drink?

CARTER *refuses drink*.

VINNIE: Takes two to elope, I guess. That must be the difference. If it's only just one person eloping then you might call it "running off".

CARTER: You might.

Pause.

VINNIE: Where—did you elope *to* when you both "eloped"?

CARTER: You're bound and determined to get it around to Rosie, aren't you. You can't help yourself.

VINNIE: Well, it's the main thing we share in common these days, isn't it, Carter?

CARTER: I didn't come here to talk about Rosie.

VINNIE: I'm just curious. Again. In a state of wonder. I used to wonder about it all the time. It was my constant obsession. I'd wake up with it heavy on my mind. The two of you alone in the Buick. Highway 40 East. Driving through the night with her neck on your shoulder. Tucumcari. Amarillo. The smell of cattle in the feedlots. Oil on the wind. The lights of Memphis twinkling across the placid Mississippi.

CARTER: It wasn't that poetic. Believe me.

VINNIE: No?

CARTER: No! It wasn't. I mean—it may have started off that way—

VINNIE: That was *my* Buick too. You realize that, don't you? *My* Buick and *my* wife.

CARTER: It was *her* choice, Vinnie. I never—(*Stops himself.*)

Pause.

VINNIE: What? You never what?

CARTER: One thing—just led to another. It was *her* idea to run away together, not mine.

VINNIE: "Elope".

Pause.

CARTER: Yes.

VINNIE: You were a victim of circumstance?

CARTER: Well—

VINNIE: And it all just happened to coincide with our little scam on Simms, I guess. That was convenient.

CARTER: It had nothing to do with that!

VINNIE: My forced exile!

CARTER: She had made it up in her mind a long time before that!

Pause.

VINNIE: Oh. Is that right?

CARTER: Yes. That's right.

VINNIE: How long before?

CARTER: Look—

VINNIE: How long!

CARTER: I don't know how long! Months maybe.

VINNIE: Months? For months you were both sneaking around! Boffing each other in the back seat of my Buick while I was out steadfastly hustling your dirty work! Preparing the ground for your Big Success!

CARTER: No! It was nothing like that. It came out of nowhere.

VINNIE: One day she just woke up and realized she was with the wrong man? That must've been it, huh? A sudden revelation. That happens sometimes. That happened to me once. A sudden revelation.

Pause. CARTER *goes to* VINNIE, *takes bottle from him and takes a belt straight from the bottle.*

VINNIE: Would you like a glass?

CARTER: No.

CARTER *hands bottle back to* VINNIE.

VINNIE: I don't blame her a bit, actually, Carter. Tell you the truth. You were on a roll. Unstoppable. I thought you might even end up running for Congress. Smooching babies and waving from cabooses. You had that aura about you. A kind of uh—yuppie Protestant aura, that's become so popular these days.

CARTER: It caught me by surprise, Vinnie. I was as shocked by it as you were.

VINNIE: I doubt it.

CARTER: I didn't even realize I had any feelings for her until—she just—opened up to me, I guess. She seemed so—

VINNIE: Desperate?

CARTER: Yeah. She did. Desperate and vulnerable at the same time.

VINNIE: A deadly combination.

CARTER: It just caught me completely off-guard.

VINNIE: Yeah. She pulled that on me too. In the beginning. All wide-eyed and bushy-tailed.

CARTER: But it wasn't like a game with her or anything—not like *you* pretending to be a detective. She—

VINNIE: I never pretended with Rosie.

CARTER: No, but you know what I mean.

VINNIE: I know what you mean but I never pretended with her. I never *had* to pretend with Rosie.

CARTER: All right—

VINNIE: You're not trying to imply that me and her had some superficial thing going, are you?

CARTER: No, I'm just saying—

VINNIE: That suddenly *you* came along and she saw the light?

CARTER: No! She seemed to have this idea in her head. And I don't know where it came from.

VINNIE: What idea?

CARTER: That I was her—ticket—out. I guess.

VINNIE: Well, you were, weren't you? She got what she wanted.

CARTER: No. No, she didn't.

VINNIE: Oh. Well, what happened, Carter? Come on. You can tell me. We're old buddies. Confidants. We've been through the wars together.

CARTER: I don't know what happened.

VINNIE: Things went sour?

CARTER: Yeah. Very suddenly.

VINNIE: Things went a little limp in the sack, did they?

CARTER: No. She—(*Stops himself.*)

VINNIE: What?

CARTER: I've gotta get going, Vinnie. I really do.

VINNIE: Hang on, hang on. She found someone else. Is that it?

CARTER: No!

VINNIE: Here, take another pull.

> VINNIE *offers* CARTER *the bottle.* CARTER *takes it and drinks, hands it back.*

CARTER: I didn't want to get into this!

VINNIE: Well, I didn't realize there was any big trauma. I thought you and Rosie were—

CARTER: We're not!

VINNIE: You wanna—sit down and talk about it?

CARTER: No! I do *not* want to sit down and talk about it! I've got no business here! I've gotta get back. I don't have time to fuck around here with your personal problems, Vinnie!

VINNIE: *My* personal problems?

CARTER: That's right. That's why I'm out here, in case you forgot.

VINNIE: Well, maybe I could help you out, Carter.

CARTER: You?

VINNIE: Yeah. Maybe I could help you out with Rosie. I don't know.

CARTER: *You* could help *me* out with Rosie? What is wrong with you, Vinnie?

VINNIE: I don't know. Seems like it'd be a fair exchange. I help you out with Rosie, you could help me out with Cecilia.

CARTER: Cecilia?

VINNIE: This girl.

CARTER: The one who had you popped?

VINNIE: Yeah. That one.

CARTER: I don't know how your mind operates, Vinnie. You don't give two shits about this girl, do you? You're just looking for a way to sabotage me.

VINNIE: Sabotage you?

CARTER: Yeah! Plotting behind my back. What else have you got to do, laying around here with your bottle and your bullshit detective paraphernalia? Dream up ways stab me in the back!

VINNIE: I was just making an offer, Carter. That's all I was doing. A friendly gesture. I know how—painful it can be, see—When things—fall apart.

Pause.

CARTER: I am leaving, Vinnie! I am walking out this door and you can take all the junk you've supposedly got on me and turn it in.

VINNIE: You don't want me to do that.

CARTER: Gather it all up and trundle it down to the local PD! Tell them your amazing tale! Tell them how come you've waited fifteen years before you revealed all the slimey facts! Tell them how much you want to go to prison right along with me! I'm sure they'll be more than willing to re-open the case. There's such a scarcity of dramatic crime these days!

VINNIE: I'll make you a deal.

CARTER: Oh, now you're gonna make *me* a deal? Stick it where it fits, Vinnie!

VINNIE: Just listen to me.

CARTER: I made you an offer but all you wanna do is jerk me around! Play this little psycho-game of how you're really the big dog pushing all the buttons. All you are is a scumbag fugitive from the law, Vinnie! A fleeing felon! That's all you are. A low-life punk who gets busted for harassing women. Good luck, pal.

VINNIE: No wait! Just hang on a second.

CARTER: You can't hurt me, Vinnie. You've hurt yourself too much.

VINNIE: Just do me one favor, okay? One last favor. I haven't asked you for many favors over the years, have I?

CARTER: Are you begging now?

VINNIE: Yeah. Yeah, I guess I am.

CARTER: You're begging. That's better.

VINNIE: Yeah.

CARTER: That's more in line with how it should be.

VINNIE: Yeah. Yeah, I guess you're right.

CARTER: What kinda favor do you want, Vinnie?

VINNIE: I got—used to talking to this girl. I liked talking to her. She's—nice, ya know. She's not Rosie but she's—nice.

CARTER: A *nice* girl.

VINNIE: Yeah.

CARTER: And you want me to tell her what a nice guy *you* are, right? What a sweetheart you are, deep down.

VINNIE: You don't have to lie. Just—

CARTER: Make up a story.

VINNIE: Tell her—how I used to be.

CARTER: When was that?

VINNIE: Back—you know—When we were runnin' claimers. In the old days, you know.

CARTER: Oh yeah. You were pretty nice back then.

VINNIE: We had some laughs.

CARTER: We did.

VINNIE: Tell her how we used to swap those two geldings around—you know. How the money was flying.

CARTER: Back before Simms got wind of it, you mean?

VINNIE: Don't mention anything about him. There's no reason to.

CARTER: He's changed his name, you know.

VINNIE: Simms?

CARTER: Yeah. I set him up with a bloodstock agency back there. Selling seasons and shares. Dabbling in pedigrees. He's doing all right for himself.

VINNIE: Changed his name?

CARTER: Calls himself "Ames" or something. Ryan Ames, I think it is.

VINNIE: Seasons and shares? Simms?

CARTER: Yeah. What's so surprising about that? He was always very industrious.

VINNIE: So that means there's two of us collecting hush money off you?

CARTER: It's not hush money! I just thought it was the least I could do for him, after he—stepped aside.

VINNIE: Well, he must've been very grateful. How much do you give *him* a month?

CARTER: I don't *give* him anything! He's got a job. He's independent.

VINNIE: Does he get more than I do?

CARTER: He's got nothing but a job, Vinnie! That's all. An opportunity to put himself back on track. The difference is that *he* took advantage of it.

VINNIE: The difference?

CARTER: Between you and him.

VINNIE: Oh, yeah.

CARTER: Now what's this big favor?

VINNIE: What?

CARTER: With the girl—Cynthia or whatever her name is.

VINNIE: Cecilia.

CARTER: Cecilia, yeah.

VINNIE: I can't believe Simms is back in the mainstream, selling seasons and shares. Doesn't anybody recognize him?

CARTER: He changed his name.

VINNIE: "Ames"? "Ryan Ames"? What is he, impersonating an Irishman or something? Right in the middle of Lexington?

CARTER: Midway.

VINNIE: Ah. Midway. So you've got him tucked away too.

CARTER: Some people have the capacity to take their knocks and keep on going, Vinnie.

VINNIE: I guess—Midway. That's quaint.

CARTER: Some people even get stronger from it.

VINNIE: I tried, Carter. It wasn't from a lack of trying. I've changed my name a dozen times and nothing came of it. I've moved all over the place. I was in Texas for a while, remember? Arizona. Nothing came from any of it. I just got—further and further—removed.

CARTER: Well, let me try to talk to this girl for you.

VINNIE: I don't know. I don't know if she's the answer. I mean—

CARTER: Let me just talk to her. She might come around.

VINNIE: I was thinking, you know—What I was going to tell you was that if you could get her to change her mind about me—Maybe get her to come over here and talk to me about the whole business—What I was thinking was—

CARTER: What?

VINNIE: That I'd hand over all—the stuff. Let you have it.

CARTER: All the negatives?

VINNIE: Everything.

CARTER: You've still got it all?

VINNIE: Yeah. It's all in a shoe-box. It's all stacked very neatly in there. Not a speck of dust on anything. I check it all on a regular basis.

CARTER: Good.

VINNIE: I check it every night before I go to bed. Some of— the letters—kinda take me back.

CARTER: You still have them? All the letters?

VINNIE: Every one.

CARTER: All the pictures?

VINNIE: Yeah. All but a couple.

CARTER: There's a couple missing?

VINNIE: Two. Yeah. But I know where they are.

CARTER: You *gave* them to someone?

VINNIE: It's all right.

CARTER: Who'd you give them to, Vinnie?

VINNIE: It's all right.

CARTER: WHO'D YOU GIVE THEM TO!

VINNIE: Cecilia. She has them. She's got them in a safe place.

CARTER: Why'd you give them to Cecilia, Vinnie!

VINNIE: Just—I loaned them to her as proof.

CARTER: Proof of what?

VINNIE: That I actually *am* a detective.

Pause.

CARTER: Give me her address.

VINNIE: You're gonna talk to her?

CARTER: Just—give me the address, Vinnie!

VINNIE: You're gonna talk to her about me or are you gonna ask her for the pictures back?

CARTER: I'm going to talk to her about you. I'm going to, very calmly, explain to her the roots of your particular insanity.

VINNIE: No, don't tell her that. She already thinks I'm crazy.

CARTER: She's right.

VINNIE: That's not gonna help! I don't want her coming over here out of pity!

CARTER: What difference does it make why she comes? Once she's here you can line things out with her. Vindicate yourself.

VINNIE: *I AM NOT GUILTY*!!

Pause.

CARTER: No. No, you're not, Vinnie. And I'll make sure she understands that. I'll make sure she sees that your downfall was the result of bad company. Nothing else. Just plain old bad company.

Pause. CARTER *moves downstage, then suddenly remembers something and turns to* VINNIE.

CARTER: What year was that Buick, anyway? You remember?

VINNIE: '58.

CARTER: '58. Well, maybe I'll try to find you another one, Vinnie.

Blackout.

Act Two

SCENE ONE

Stage is divided in half. Stage-right half is occupied by CECILIA's *house. Above this set is another place-name card that reads—* "SAN DIMAS". *The interior is very simple, 1940s style with a few plants and a "woman's touch" about it. Sofa and chair with coffee table between them. Curtained windows, again looking out into black. Stage-left set is in blackness and should "disappear" as much as possible. Lights up stage right on* CECILIA *in action, serving tea on a tray to* CARTER *who is seated on sofa facing her.* CECILIA *is a very attractive yet slightly eccentric dark-haired woman in her mid-thirties. She wears a brightly flowered Japanese silk robe. Her hair up off her neck but unruly strands are dangling free.*

CECILIA (*serving tea on coffee table*): So, you and Vinnie go back a long way, huh?

CARTER: Yeah, that's right. We do. Clear back to the fifties in fact.

CECILIA: That far?

CARTER: Back to the days of "I LIKE IKE".

CECILIA: That's hard to believe.

CARTER: Why's that?

CECILIA: I don't know. It's hard to believe he's ever known anyone for any length of time. He's such a loner.

CARTER: Well, he wasn't always like that, you know.

CECILIA: Like what?

CARTER: Separate. I mean—remote, like he is.

CECILIA (*offering tea*): Milk and honey?

CARTER: Oh, no thanks. Just black or—whatever you call it.

CECILIA: Tea. I call it tea.

CARTER: Yes. I'm used to drinking coffee, I guess. You know—black coffee. Force of habit.

CECILIA: Oh, I'm sorry. I should have asked. I'm strictly a tea drinker myself. Don't even keep coffee in the house. It gets me rattled.

CARTER: That's all right. This is fine.

CECILIA: Are you sure? I've got hot chocolate if you want. Ovaltine.

CARTER: No. This is great.

CECILIA: I've got little miniature marshmallows.

CARTER: No, really.

   Pause.

CECILIA: I got into it in London. Back in the seventies.

CARTER: What?

CECILIA: Tea.

CARTER: Oh. I see. But you're not English, are you?

CECILIA: No, no. Missouri. Independence, Missouri. "Home of Harry Truman". "Plain-Talkin' Harry".

CARTER: Right. Independence. Mark Twain's from there too, isn't he?

CECILIA: No, that's Hannibal. Hannibal, Missouri.

CARTER: Oh, that's right! Hannibal. I get them confused.

CECILIA: They just had the flood.

CARTER: Right.

CECILIA: Haven't been back there since I left.

CARTER (*glancing at his watch*): I'll be darned.

CECILIA: I've got no nostalgia about the place. "Americana" bores the shit out of me. Tom Sawyer and Huckleberry Finn. Who are they kidding? I went straight to London and never looked back.

CARTER: Well—That must've been kind of a shock, huh?

CECILIA: It was, but I loved it. London. Sipping tea and reading Byron, you know. I still think of it as home actually.

CARTER: Is that right.

CECILIA: It's the dampness I think. The moisture in the air. Something haunting about it. All that history.

CARTER: Right.

CECILIA: Hounds.

CARTER: What?

CECILIA: Hunting to hounds.

CARTER: Oh, right. Look—Vinnie was wondering—

CECILIA: But you and Vinnie are from around here originally?

CARTER: Yes. Yes, we are as a matter of fact. Only about ten miles away. Cucamonga. Pretty boring. "Home of Grapes".

CECILIA: Grapes?

CARTER: Yeah. Used to be nothing but vineyards as far as the eye could see. Cheap grapes—you know. "Ripple". "Thunderbird". Nothing fancy. Headache wine.

CECILIA: Hard to think of anybody being actually *from* this area.

CARTER: It is, isn't it. But it's true. Born and raised.

CECILIA: You went to school together?

CARTER: Yes, we did. From the sixth grade on.

CECILIA: Sixth grade? So you must have been through a lot then, huh? Lots of ups and downs.

CARTER: We have.

CECILIA: There's something nice about that—Having an on-going friendship. Must give you a real sense of conti-nuity.

CARTER: Well—

CECILIA: I miss that myself.

CARTER: What.

CECILIA: Continuity. Everything seems so busted up to me. Like I've lived a dozen different lives. But a long-lasting friendship—That must be a very nice thing to have.

CARTER: Well—yes and no.

CECILIA: Oh, I suppose there's times when you'd just as soon throw in the towel. Go your separate ways.

CARTER: There are. Yes.

CECILIA: But then you must just see yourself through those rough spots because you realize the value of continuity. "Perseverance Furthers". Remember that?

CARTER: What?

CECILIA: The I-Ching. "Perseverance Furthers". I don't know how many times I used to roll the coins and it came up "Perseverance Furthers". Must've been trying to tell me something, I guess.

CARTER: I don't know uh—anything about that.

CECILIA: Oh, it was just a fad for a while. Everybody used to do it so I did it. I don't do it anymore.

CARTER: What'. that?

CECILIA: Roll the coins. It was just a fad. You know—but then there's lots of things that just kind of fall by the wayside as you get older. Don't you think?

CARTER: I guess—I was—

CECILIA: Like cheating on your partner. I gave that up too.

Pause. She sips tea.

CARTER: Uh—I wanted to talk to you about Vinnie—

CECILIA: Never used to bother me at all. That's what's so amazing. No guilt. No remorse. No nothing. Then one day it just stopped. Why do you suppose that is?

CARTER: I have no idea.

CECILIA: It had nothing to do with conscience or will-power or anything like that. It just suddenly came to an end. I knew it was over.

CARTER: What.

CECILIA: Cheating.

CARTER (*trying to make a joke out of tension*): Yeah. Remember the days when sex was safe and racing was dangerous?

CARTER *laughs nervously.* CECILIA *doesn't. Pause.*

CECILIA: That's not the reason I stopped.

CARTER: Oh, I didn't mean—You're not with a uh— "partner" now, are you?

CECILIA: Oh, no! Not now. I was talking about the past. The distant past. That's why it was so great meeting up with someone like Vinnie. He kind of reminded me of myself.

CARTER: How's that?

CECILIA: Just the way he was fishing in the dark, I guess. Experimenting.

CARTER: Oh, you mean the "detective" routine? Well see, that's what he wanted me to try to explain to you.

CECILIA: You don't have to explain.

CARTER: No, but see—

CECILIA: I don't need you to explain him to me. In fact I wish you wouldn't. I understand exactly what he's going through.

CARTER: You do?

CECILIA: Yes. Of course.

CARTER: So, you've uh—dropped the charges then, I guess, huh?

CECILIA: What charges? (*Pause.*) Who *are* you exactly?

CARTER: I told you. I'm an old friend of Vinnie's.

CECILIA: Anybody could say that, just to get in the door. Have you been observing me or something? Stalking me?

CARTER: No, look—I'm perfectly legitimate. I have full identification and everything. References if you want. I'm licensed to race in six states.

CECILIA: How can you identify your friendship? How is that possible? Do you have pictures of it or something? The two of you holding hands? Displaying strings of trout?

CARTER: No, I don't carry pictures with me—Look—call him up if you don't believe me. Go ahead and call him. Better yet, we could both go over there and meet him face to face.

CECILIA: You're not getting me in a car alone, buster, if that's what you think. I'm young but I wasn't born yesterday.

CARTER: Whoa! Hang on a second. Let's just slow down here, all right? I have no intention of harming you or molesting you or anything else. Let's be very clear about that.

CECILIA: I suppose you're a detective too, huh? Is that it? Partners in crime?

CARTER: No! I am *not* a detective and neither is Vinnie! That's what I'm trying to get at here. Vinnie is a very sick individual and he needs serious medical attention, in case you didn't know it.

CECILIA: Sick?

CARTER: Well—

CECILIA: He's not a rapist or anything?

CARTER: No. Nothing like that.

CECILIA: I didn't think so. I can usually tell when someone's potentially harmful. I've developed a keen sense of that over the years. I got a sense of you too. Right off the bat. Soon as I saw you through my little window. A man in trouble.

CARTER: *I'm* not in trouble. Vinnie's in trouble.

CECILIA: Soon as I saw you step up on my porch and arch your neck back like you were trying to relieve yourself of serious pain.

CARTER: I came here to talk about my friend, Vinnie! That's the only reason I came. I'm not here to be psychoanalyzed.

CECILIA: As though the pain in your neck was only a symptom of something much bigger. A much bigger pain.

CARTER: Look—I have a plane to catch. I'm only here for a very short time. I would like to keep the conversation on Vinnie, if you don't mind. Do you think that's possible?

CECILIA: I don't see why not. More tea?

CARTER: No, thank you.

Pause.

CECILIA: Where are you flying off to?

CARTER: Kentucky.

CECILIA: Aah, my favorite state!

CARTER: Is that right.

CECILIA: "Home of the Derby"!

CARTER: Exactly.

CECILIA: The "Blue Grass State".

CARTER: Yes.

CECILIA: "My Old Kentucky Home"!

CARTER: Look—Could we—

CECILIA: I used to dream about the Derby.

CARTER: Is that a fact.

CECILIA: One of the last bastions of true American aristocracy, don't you think?

CARTER: Yeah, sure.

CECILIA: The closest thing we have to English royalty. Pomp and circumstance!

CARTER: I don't know.

CECILIA: Have you ever been?

CARTER: Where?

CECILIA: To the Kentucky Derby?

CARTER: Many times.

CECILIA: No, really? And you say it so casually, as though you've almost become bored with it. I would die to go to the Derby!

CARTER: It's part of my business.

CECILIA: What business?

CARTER: The horse business. Thoroughbreds.

CECILIA: You're kidding! Vinnie was involved in that too, wasn't he? A long time ago. Seems like he told me something about that. Of course it wasn't on the same scale as the Derby.

CARTER: He may have been. I don't know. Could we please—

CECILIA: You two must have a *lot* in common.

CARTER: We used to.

CECILIA: But now you've drifted. That's too bad. It's sad actually. It's the one thing that breaks my heart.

CARTER: What's that.

CECILIA: People drifting apart. It's worse than death, I think. Worse than dying alone, like a dog. Don't you think?

CARTER: I don't know. I don't know anything about that stuff. All I want to do is just try to explain something to you here and then I'll be on my way. I don't want to take up any more of your time.

CECILIA: I'm not a busy woman. I've got all the time in the world.

CARTER: Fine. That's fine. I'd just like to—I'm not sure you realize exactly how much you mean to Vinnie.

CECILIA: No, I'm sure I don't. We've only known each other a short while.

CARTER: He told me—now this could just be another one of his bizarre delusions—but he told me that you had become a little bit miffed at him over some incident or other. That you had filed certain charges against him. Criminal charges.

CECILIA: Charged him? You mean gone to the police?

CARTER: That's right. That's what he claims. He says he was arrested.

CECILIA: Now why would I do something like that? We were having an affair, for Christ's sake.

CARTER: You were?

CECILIA: Yes. We were. We *are* as far as I'm concerned. Unless he's changed his mind. Is that what this is all about? He couldn't bring himself to face me directly so he sent *you* with the bad news? His old "buddy"?

CARTER: What bad news? No, look—

CECILIA (*standing suddenly*): If it's over, it's over! He doesn't have to send a middleman. Tell him that for *me*!

CARTER: It's *not* over! He wants to see you. He's desperate about it in fact. He called me all the way out here.

CECILIA: Yeah, he's so desperate he's got to send somebody else to take his place!

CARTER: I'm not—He was under the impression that you were pissed off at him!

CECILIA: I *am* pissed off at him!

CARTER: Not *now*! Then!

CECILIA: When?

CARTER: At the time you made the charges against him!

CECILIA: I never made any crumby charges!! I might have called the police but I—

Pause.

CARTER: Oh. Then—

CECILIA: Why don't you just get the hell on outa here, mister, and tell your old pal to take a hike for me. Go on! Get outa here!

CARTER (*standing awkwardly*): Now wait a second—Just wait a second. This whole thing has gotten outa hand. I'm very, very sorry if I gave you the wrong idea here. Vinnie's crazy about you. He really is. I've never seen him act this way before. He talks about you like you were sent from heaven or something.

CECILIA: Heaven?

CARTER: Yeah. He said you answered this little prayer of his.

CECILIA: What prayer? Get outa here. This is too weird.

CARTER: All he wants is to see you and talk to you. That's all he wants. He misses you terribly.

CECILIA: Then why doesn't he come over here himself? Why does he send you?

CARTER: He didn't "send" me. I volunteered.

CECILIA: There's something very fishy about this.

CARTER: I guess he thought you weren't going to be very receptive to him. I mean, assuming he was telling the truth.

CECILIA: About what?

CARTER: ABOUT BEING ARRESTED!

Pause.

CECILIA: Don't raise your voice in my home, mister.

CARTER: I'm sorry. It's just—that I'm worried about him.

CECILIA: You're worried?

CARTER: I am. I've seen this pattern of his before.

CECILIA: What pattern?

CARTER: This—despair he gets into. This—anguish.

CECILIA: Anguish and despair.

CARTER: It's no joke. He's liable to do something very serious to himself.

CECILIA: Oh. I see.

CARTER: If you could just come with me over there and have a talk with him—

CECILIA: I'm *not* getting into your car, pal. So just give it up.

CARTER: No, I didn't mean that! You can go there any way you want. Walk, drive, take the bus! It makes no difference to me *how* you get there! I just think that it would do him a world of good if he could see you and— talk things out.

Pause.

CECILIA: He told you that *I* had him arrested? For what?

CARTER: Trespassing. Invasion of Privacy and uh—Harassment.

CECILIA: That's amazing.

CARTER: He could have been making it all up. It's possible.

CECILIA: I really liked him, you know. Right from the get-go. He seemed like such a sweet man, underneath. Innocent. A man like that has no business being in such a seedy occupation as that. It's bound to pull him down sooner or later.

CARTER: What occupation?

CECILIA: A private investigator. It just doesn't suit him at all.

CARTER: No, see, that's exactly what I'm trying—

CECILIA: He has all kinds of potential, but you can't continue to rub up against that kind of low-rent world he lives in without feeling the effects.

CARTER: He is *not* a private investigator! He's not a detective or anything like that! That's what I've been trying to get through to you, here!

CECILIA: He showed me his badge and his gun. He took me on surveillance with him. He even showed me pictures from a case he'd worked on.

Pause.

CARTER: What case?

CECILIA: Some case involving a racing official or something. He said it was years ago.

CARTER: He talked to you about that?

CECILIA: He talks to me about everything.

CARTER: What'd he tell you?

CECILIA: I can't remember all the details of it. But he wasn't lying.

CARTER: He lies about everything! It's all part of this illness of his. This sickness! He's a professional liar.

CECILIA: Well, the pictures didn't lie. I can tell you that much.

CARTER: What pictures?

CECILIA: He showed me a couple of pictures of this guy that were presented as evidence against him.

CARTER: What were the pictures of?

CECILIA: What difference does it make to you?

CARTER: I am trying to figure out what's going on in his head. That's all.

CECILIA: They were very, very filthy pictures. That's about all I can say. I've never seen anything like it, in fact.

And, believe me, I've been around the block. I may not
look it but I have.

CARTER: Was there a woman involved?

CECILIA: A woman?

CARTER: In the pictures!

CECILIA: What's your interest in this, anyway?

CARTER: Let me see them.

CECILIA: What?

CARTER: THE PICTURES! THE PHOTOGRAPHS! Do
you still have them?

Pause.

CECILIA: You're a very strange man, mister. You don't
come into somebody's home, a total stranger, and start
raising your voice and making demands. Where were
you brought up?

CARTER: I'm sorry.

CECILIA: I don't care who you are but you don't start acting
like a cop in my own house. Unless you are a cop?

CARTER: I'm *not* a cop. I'm not a detective. I'm just worried
about my friend, that's all. This business with the
pictures is quite a surprise. I mean if he's actually gone
so far as to set somebody up—or put someone's
personal integrity in jeopardy then—well, he's in trouble. Big trouble. I don't know if I can bail him out of this
kind of a mess.

CECILIA: Someone's personal integrity?

CARTER: Yes, that's right.

CECILIA: He told me this case happened years ago.

CARTER: It doesn't matter!

CECILIA: He said everything about the case had probably been long forgotten.

CARTER: Something like that is never forgotten! Never. Believe me. It could loom its ugly head at any given moment and destroy an innocent man's life.

CECILIA: Well he couldn't have been all *that* innocent. This commissioner guy. Some of those postures I've never even seen in the animal kingdom.

CARTER: Let me see them.

CECILIA: I didn't save them or anything. I'm not a pervert.

CARTER: What'd you do with them?

CECILIA: I don't have a clue. I might have given them back to Vinnie.

CARTER: He said *you* had them! Did you destroy them?

CECILIA: No.

CARTER: Did you let them out of the house?

Pause.

CECILIA: Oh. So he already told you about it then?

CARTER: What?

CECILIA: The pictures. You already know.

CARTER: He mentioned something—

CECILIA: So why are you acting so surprised?

CARTER: Look, I can't stress how important it is to locate these photographs. Vinnie could go to jail for a very long time.

CECILIA: Vinnie could?

CARTER: Yes. He could. He certainly could. I mean—I'm
just trying to keep him out of trouble. That's all I've
been doing for the last fifteen years.

Pause. CARTER *moves to window and stares out as* CECILIA
watches him.

CARTER: There's a lot of other things I'd rather have been
doing. Believe me. I'm a busy man but—I figured I
owed it to Vinnie. He just never seemed to get the same
breaks, you know. So—Anyhow, I thought I'd just
make a quick trip out here and get him fixed up. You
know—whatever he needed—and then get right back
home. It's always been like that in the past. I've always
taken care of him. And I don't mind. I mean—I figured I
kinda owed it to him, you know. It's my responsibility.
I can't just—get rid of him. (*Pause, checks his watch.*)
Shit, I've already missed my flight I think. (*Turns to*
CECILIA.) Look, would you just consider meeting me
over there at his place—in an hour or so. Please, just
consider it. We could get all this straightened out. It
would do him a world of good. We could all get back to
normal.

Pause. She stares at him.

CECILIA: More tea?

She pours as lights dim into cross-fade.

SCENE TWO

Night. Place-name card above stage-left set reads—"MIDWAY.
KY. 'RED EYE' ". Cross-fade. Lights up on SIMMS' *bloodstock*
office in Kentucky. SIMMS *is bent over his desk, absorbed in*
paperwork, surrounded by reference books, stacks of magazines,
etc. A small window directly behind him, looking out into

blackness. A leather armchair in faded green across from SIMMS'
desk. Racing pictures and genealogy charts on walls. SIMMS, *in his
mid-sixties, wears a grey vest over a white shirt with sleeves rolled
up. Dark slacks. Everything rumpled and worn. A green visor-
cap to shade his eyes from the overhead lamp.* VINNIE *enters out of
darkness left with a "Redwing" shoebox tucked under his arm.*
SIMMS *continues his paperwork, oblivious. Pause.*

VINNIE: Uh—Mr Ames? Ryan Ames?

SIMMS: What'd they do, leave the hallway unlocked? Man
  could be murdered this time a' night.

VINNIE: I'm sorry. The door was open. I'm Vincent Webb.
  Vincent T. Webb. From California.

  VINNIE *crosses to desk.* SIMMS *remains seated. They shake
  hands across desk.*

SIMMS: Vincent T. Webb.

VINNIE: Sorry to interrupt—

SIMMS: Nothin' to it. Just the usual obsessive perusal of
  charts: Sire lists; auction reports. Can't study enough on
  the Blood Horse these days.

VINNIE: No, I suppose not.

SIMMS: Most boys have all this modern software nonsense—
  computer read-outs and what-have-you. Fax machines.
  Electronic mail. Me, I still prefer to stumble around
  with the old-fashioned dirty paper. I like to fondle it.
  Gives me a feeble sense of something tangible in the
  midst of all the abstract frenzy.

VINNIE: Yeah. I know what you mean.

SIMMS: So, you're a Western man, huh? Out in the Golden
  Land of high purses and racial conflict?

VINNIE: That's right.

SIMMS: Still run *live* horse-racing out there, do ya, or is it all on the TV monitor now like it is across the rest of wide America?

VINNIE: Oh no, they uh—still have live racing. They sure do. Santa Anita. Del Mar. You know—they're institutions.

SIMMS: "Off-Track Betting"! Who invented that one?

VINNIE: I'm not sure.

SIMMS: Bandits! Bandits and cuff-snappers. You don't belong to either of those two sub-species, do you?

VINNIE: No, sir. I'm—

SIMMS: Bushwhackers and Backstabbers. Snakes. Whole damn industry's full a' snakes now. Thoroughbred's gonna be an obsolete animal before you know it. They'll find some way to turn the whole damn thing into a Pac-Man Game. You wait and see.

VINNIE: I suppose so.

SIMMS: No question about it. All the icons are dead and buried—"Sonny-Jim" Fitzsimmons, "Bull" Hancock, Mr Madden—This is the very last generation of honest-to-God true horsemen. Once they're gone, the game's up.

VINNIE: That'll be a sad day in hell, won't it.

SIMMS: You got that right. (*Pause.*) What line a' work do you follow, Mr Webb?

VINNIE: Uh—well I—I dabble somewhat. I mean—

SIMMS: A dabbler! Good thing to be. Little a' this, little a' that. Not enough "dabblers" these days, I'd say. Too many experts.

VINNIE: Well—I don't know.

SIMMS: In what area do you do the most "dabbling", Mr Webb?

VINNIE: Well, I—fool around with pedigrees and—

SIMMS: A pedigree man! There ya go. My line exactly.

VINNIE: But only as a sideline.

SIMMS: Aha.

VINNIE: A hobby—kind of.

SIMMS: A hobby.

VINNIE: I used to be very involved—I mean I was in the horse business some time ago. I've kinda—lost touch.

SIMMS: Helps to keep abreast of things, that's for sure. A stallion can move up and down the lists in a matter of days. Requires constant scrutiny. That is, if you want to stay in the game.

VINNIE: Yeah, I can see where it would.

SIMMS: Used to be no such a thing as a "bloodstock agent". Now you've got owners dumber than dirt. Don't know "Native Dancer" from "Nasrullah". Couldn't tell a sesamoid from a cannon-bone and couldn't care less about it.

VINNIE: Yeah—

SIMMS: So what's your main line, Mr Webb?

VINNIE: Excuse me?

SIMMS: You said pedigrees was a sideline. What's your *main* line?

VINNIE: Oh, uh—well, actually I've been working as a private investigator for the past five years.

SIMMS: A "sleuth"! A "gumshoe", as we used to call 'em.

VINNIE: That's right.

SIMMS: How 'bout that. Used to love those old detective movies. Raymond Chandler. Dashiel Hammett. Don't make enough a' those kinda movies anymore, do they?

VINNIE: No, they sure don't.

SIMMS: Don't make *any* of 'em, as a matter of fact.

VINNIE: I guess not.

SIMMS: *Double Endemnity*, *Maltese Falcon*. Pictures with a plot you could sink your teeth into.

VINNIE: Right.

SIMMS: Who was it decided to do away with all the plots?

VINNIE: What?

SIMMS: They must've had a meeting somewhere. Behind closed doors.

VINNIE: I don't know. I—stopped going to the movies.

SIMMS: Wise decision, Mr Webb. Very wise. (*Pause.*) So— you're an authentic detective, is that it?

VINNIE: It's—a way to make a living.

SIMMS: Must come across some dyed-in-the-wool characters, in the course of things.

VINNIE: Yeah. You do. You sure do.

SIMMS: Some real scumbags too, I suppose.

VINNIE: Yup. Plenty of those.

SIMMS: So, what do you need from me? All the low-down on somebody's sleazy past? Oh, I've seen 'em all roll through this little murky office, believe you me. The whole wide spectrum.

VINNIE: I'll bet you have.

SIMMS: It's the spotless ones you gotta watch out for. The "lawyer-types". The ones who've got beepers hung on their hips and tassled loafers free of manure. They can't go to the bathroom without carrying their carphones with 'em. They're the ones who'll kill a horse to collect the insurance. Pay a groom to cut their air off in the middle of the night. Ruthless and clean as a whistle.

VINNIE: No, uh—I'm actually on a search for a man who used to hold a very high position out West.

SIMMS: Oh, I see. A kingpin, huh?

VINNIE: A man—who fell from grace.

SIMMS: Well, that includes just about everybody on my Christmas card list, Mr Webb. Have a seat.

VINNIE: "Vinnie". You can call me "Vinnie".

VINNIE sits in armchair as SIMMS gets up, moves to a liquor cabinet tucked into bookshelves, takes out a bottle of bourbon and glasses.

SIMMS: "Vinnie"? Sounds more New Jersey than California.

VINNIE: Yeah. I know. Friends always called me "Vinnie". Short for Vincent, you know—

SIMMS: Bourbon, Vinnie?

VINNIE: Uh—no thanks.

SIMMS: *Kentucky* bourbon? Maker's Mark, Fighting Cock?

VINNIE: No. That's all right. I'm on the wagon.

SIMMS: Yeah, I was on that for a while myself but the wheels broke off. (*Pours himself a drink.*) So—you're on a manhunt, is that it?

VINNIE: More, less. I happened to accidentally come across some material in the course of an entirely different investigation. This uh—material was so shocking, in a way, that I got sidetracked.

SIMMS: I see. And what type of "material" would that be?

VINNIE: Well, it was of a pornographic nature.

SIMMS: Aha! Pornographic! Now we're talkin' modern language. It's just about all pornographic these days, isn't it, Mr Webb? Not much left that isn't.

VINNIE: Well, I suppose. If you look at it that way.

SIMMS: That's exactly the way I look at it. Music, news, politics—pornography personified. Wouldn't you say?

VINNIE: Um—This stuff I came across is so specifically amoral that, unfortunately, it became incriminating to the party in question.

SIMMS: So, he must've paid the piper then, huh? This "party"?

VINNIE: Yes. He did.

SIMMS: Probably paid ten times over. Didn't he?

VINNIE: Well—

SIMMS: Must've suffered very dearly for his little transgression. Maybe suffered far more than any of his revilers could've imagined. That's the way it usually goes.

VINNIE: I don't know.

SIMMS: No. Of course not. How could you? You'd have to be inside the man's skin, wouldn't you?

Pause.

VINNIE: My point is—What I'm trying to get at, is that I've uncovered some very interesting evidence along with this material.

SIMMS: And what would that be?

VINNIE: Well, on closer examination and following a few crazy leads that I had, it would appear that this man was framed.

SIMMS: Is that right? And what led you to that conclusion, Mr Webb?

VINNIE: Well, I started to delve into it a little bit and—

SIMMS: "Dabble."

VINNIE: Excuse me?

SIMMS: Never mind. You started to "delve" and . . . ?

VINNIE: Yes. I traced the photographs right back to their source. There were dates on the negatives, see—

SIMMS: Photographs?

VINNIE: Right. That's the "material" I was referring to.

SIMMS: I see.

VINNIE: I've got them right here.

SIMMS: In the shoebox.

VINNIE: Yes. I've got all of them. The negatives.

SIMMS: The originals.

VINNIE: That's right.

SIMMS: Dirty pictures.

VINNIE: They are. No question about it.

SIMMS: Are you a Puritan, Mr Webb?

VINNIE: Am I—what?

SIMMS: A Puritan. A "Founding Father"?

VINNIE: No, I—

SIMMS: Does sex trouble you?

VINNIE: No. I've got no problem with that.

SIMMS: Are you terrified by a beautiful woman?

VINNIE: No!

SIMMS: You indulge in the odd blow-job from time to time?

VINNIE: What? Look—

SIMMS: No?

VINNIE: I'm not here to—

SIMMS: Never?

VINNIE: Maybe once—or twice—in the past.

SIMMS: In the past?

VINNIE: A long time ago. I can't remember. A long, long time ago.

SIMMS: Did you enjoy it?

VINNIE: What?

SIMMS: The blow-job in the past. Did you enjoy it?

VINNIE: I can't remember. I was very, very young—

SIMMS: Did you wish it would last forever or did you just take it in your stride, like a man, and go on about your business? Go on "living your life", as they say? Realizing there's no such thing as eternal ecstasy?

VINNIE: I'm trying to explain something here!

SIMMS: That you were shocked.

VINNIE: No! I mean about the origin of the photographs!

SIMMS: You are shocked even though you yourself had debauched in the very same activity. Probably worse.

VINNIE: Worse?

SIMMS: No?

VINNIE: No. Never like this stuff. I mean this is really—

SIMMS: Really what?

VINNIE: Barbaric. I mean—Primitive.

Pause.

SIMMS: I see. Barbaric. Carries an edge of violence, does it?

VINNIE: What I'm trying to say is that—this man was set up and I happen to know the party responsible. I have letters. Correspondence. Absolute proof.

Pause.

SIMMS: How many lives do you think a man can live, Mr Webb? How many lives within this *one*?

VINNIE: I'm not sure I understand you, sir.

SIMMS: Well, say for instance, you could put the past to death and start over. Right now. You look like you might be a candidate for that.

VINNIE: That's not possible. I mean—

SIMMS: No? Vengeance appeals to you more.

VINNIE: Vengeance?

SIMMS: Yes. Blood. Now why is that? Why is blood more appealing than re-birth? Is it the color? The satisfaction of seeing it out in the open? Bursting free of its fleshy boundaries?

VINNIE: I'm not—I'm just trying to help out an innocent man, that's all.

SIMMS: Ah, so it's *innocence* that attracts you! Justice!

VINNIE: I'm a detective! That's my job. I'm paid to get to the bottom of things.

SIMMS: And who's paying you now?

VINNIE: Well, that's the thing—I've struck out on my own because I believe I could help this condemned man reinstate himself.

SIMMS: Vindication!

VINNIE: Yes. Exactly.

SIMMS: And he would, most likely, be very grateful for that. This poor man. This fallen soul. Most likely he would pay you a great deal of money.

VINNIE: I'm not interested in money.

SIMMS: No?

VINNIE: No.

SIMMS: Did you know this sinner? Is he a personal friend of yours?

VINNIE: No, he's not.

SIMMS: Then it *is* blood. Am I right?

VINNIE: Not exactly.

SIMMS: Well, if it's not blood or money then it must be drugs or sex.

VINNIE: No. It's not any of that.

SIMMS: Don't tell me you're a man of honor? The last of a dying breed? Is that possible, Mr Webb?

VINNIE: The man I'm looking for went under the name of "Simms". "Darrel P. Simms". Does that ring any kind of a bell with you, Mr "Ames"?

Pause.

SIMMS: "Simms"? "Darrel P." Nope. Can't say that it does.

VINNIE: Commissioner of Racing in Southern California, nineteen fifty-nine through seventy-eight. Approximately.

SIMMS: Ah! California. Now that's a whole different ballpark. Tough for us old Kentucky Hardboots to keep pace with the West Coast, ya know. Hard for us to consider it legitimate when we're straddling the apex right here.

VINNIE: You're not from Kentucky originally though, are you?

SIMMS: Bourbon County. Born and bred.

VINNIE: Oh. I didn't realize that.

SIMMS: No. How could you? You don't know me from Adam. Do you, Mr Webb?

Pause.

VINNIE: If I could find this man—If you could help me track him down, I'm sure he'd be very interested in what I've uncovered.

SIMMS: Why are you so sure?

VINNIE: He can't help but be interested! He's been living in the shadow of blackmail now for fifteen years! Look—there's a very powerful figure here, in the racing industry, who's gotten away with murder at Mr Simms' expense.

SIMMS: I'm not in the muckraking business, Mr Webb. I'm
in the horse business. You're either buying gold or
mining for gold but you'll never find a diamond up a
goat's ass. I don't give two shits about these festering
souls and all their dirty laundry. I'm obsessed with my
work. Can you understand that?

VINNIE: Yes, but I have *inside* information—

SIMMS: I'm so completely absorbed in my work that the
outside world has disappeared. It's vanished, Mr Webb.
I'm no longer seduced by its moaning and fanfare. I'm
busy with the "Sport of Kings".

VINNIE: But I could turn this whole thing around for Simms!
He could be completely exonerated and Carter would
end up crawling on his knees like a lizard.

SIMMS: Carter? Lyle Carter?

Pause.

VINNIE: Yes. That's right.

SIMMS: You're kinda plowin' in high cotton, aren't ya boy?
You need to go see the powers that be. I'm just a little
ole bloodstock agent. That's all I am. Seasons and
shares. Small potatoes. And I like it that way.

VINNIE: But you—

SIMMS: What?

VINNIE: You must have heard of this man, "Simms",
somewhere along the line. I mean—over the years.

SIMMS: As a matter of fact, I *did* hear of him. Quite a while
back. Out West somewhere. I suppose it could've been
California. I think maybe you're right about that.

Vilified in the press, as I remember. Slandered. Railroaded outa town.

VINNIE: That's him! It was all over the news.

SIMMS: They had a field-day.

VINNIE: That's the man!

SIMMS: Lost his family too, I believe.

Pause.

VINNIE: Oh. I didn't know that.

SIMMS: Yes. Wife and kids packed it up on him. I believe that's right. Bankrupt. Lost everything in fact. Bottomed out completely.

VINNIE: I'm sorry to hear that.

SIMMS: Why should you be sorry? Loss can be a powerful elixir.

VINNIE: I mean—in general. It's uh—a sad thing.

SIMMS: That's just something to say, Mr Webb. That's just something lame to say.

VINNIE: Yes, but—

SIMMS: You have no way of knowing. Do you?

VINNIE: No—but—What became of him?

SIMMS: "Simms"? Disappeared I think.

VINNIE: He never showed up under a pseudonym—an alias of some kind?

SIMMS: Not to my knowledge, no. 'Course you're free to snoop around town. Do your "dabbling". After all,

gossip happens to be Lexington's second biggest industry. My guess though, if you *do* happen to find him, is
that he's willing to let sleeping dogs lay. That's just my
hunch.

VINNIE: Why would you suppose that? He's got everything
to gain.

SIMMS: I'm a gambler, Mr Webb. We go on hunches.

VINNIE: But if I was him—if I was this man and I had this
kind of an opportunity—to come out of hiding—to live
out in the open again and regain my—my self-esteem—
my good standing in the public eye—To move freely. It
just seems to me—

SIMMS: You're not.

VINNIE: What?

SIMMS: You're *not* this man.

Lights dim into cross-fade.

SCENE THREE

*Night. Cross-fade back to stage-right split set. Place-name card
above reads—"CUCAMONGA". Lights up on* VINNIE'S *room
from Act One.* CARTER *is sitting on bed, sifting through contents
of cardboard boxes he's pulled out from underneath* VINNIE'S
bed: letters, photographs etc. and VINNIE'S *detective paraphernalia.* CARTER *in shirtsleeves now with cuffs rolled up, collar open,
tie hanging loose. He drinks from* VINNIE'S *bottle. His suit jacket
and overcoat are thrown on foot of bed. His briefcase containing
cellular phone is on the floor, center stage.* CECILIA *moves through
the room, pausing at dirty dishes and* VINNIE'S *pile of dirty
laundry.*

CECILIA (*examining laundry*): I can't believe he lives like this. Gives you a whole different impression of someone when you see how they actually live.

CARTER: Yes, it does doesn't it. He's basically a pig.

CECILIA: Well, I wouldn't go that far.

CARTER: He's always been a pig.

CECILIA: It's just so stark and—

CARTER: I told him he needed a few throw-rugs to liven the place up, but he wouldn't listen.

CECILIA: Do you think you ought to be going through his private things like that? I mean, what if you come across something personal?

CARTER: I'll ignore it.

Pause. She moves to the sink as CARTER *keeps sorting through papers, etc.*

CECILIA: Look at these dishes! There's ants all over the place. Trails of ants.

CARTER: You don't have any idea where he may have stashed them, do you? The photographs?

CECILIA *begins rinsing dishes and washing them as* CARTER *continues.*

CECILIA: No, I never ask him things like that. It's none of my business.

CARTER: I thought you and him were having some big flaming affair.

CECILIA: Well, I don't know how big and flaming it was— but I don't pry into his private life.

CARTER: So, you've never even been in this place, evidently?

CECILIA (*washing dishes*): No. I never have.

CARTER: So all the uh—"trysting" must've been done at *your* house, huh?

CECILIA: Trysting?

CARTER: Screwing around. Heavy petting.

CECILIA: We never did that.

CARTER: Oh.

CECILIA: He comes over to my place and we have tea and talk.

CARTER: Tea and talk. Sounds great.

CECILIA: It was. It—*is*.

CARTER: He enthralled you with detective trivia, I suppose.

CECILIA: I was interested in his latest case.

CARTER (*drinking*): Oh yeah? Which one was that? The time he almost toppled the Heads of IT&T?

CECILIA: It was a divorce settlement.

CARTER: Ah! Juicy.

CECILIA: We were working on it together. In fact, it might've been *that* woman who had him arrested. I'll bet it was.

CARTER: I see. Some *other* woman.

CECILIA: She might've felt we were getting too close to the heart of the matter.

CARTER: Poor thing.

CECILIA: It was very exciting. I'd never been on surveillance before.

CARTER: It never occurred to you that the whole deal might be an elaborate game to get you in the sack?

CECILIA: I've told you, we never did that.

CARTER: Never kissed? Never hugged even?

CECILIA *turns to him at the sink.*

CARTER: Just a little peck on the neck?

CECILIA: What's it to you?

CARTER: Just curious.

Pause. CECILIA *resumes washing dishes.*

CECILIA: So, where's he gone to? Your best friend. You said he was going to be here. He was "dying to see me".

CARTER: Probably down at the mall or hiking to Glendora. He takes long walks these days. Long, aimless walks.

CECILIA: You make him sound so desperate.

CARTER: Well, there's nothing like heartbreak to drive a man insane. He didn't have that far to go anyway.

CECILIA: He's not crazy. Just lonesome.

CARTER: He's a madman. Didn't you recognize that? Couldn't you see that in his eyeballs when you first slid up next to him at the bar?

CECILIA: What bar?

CARTER: Wherever you met him!

CECILIA: I don't drink.

CARTER: No, of course not! You're a teatotaller.

CECILIA: I met him at the Safeway. That's where I work. I was bagging groceries for him and—

CARTER: Fine! It doesn't matter *where* you met him. My point is that he's nuts! Anyone with half a brain could figure that one out. He's a lunatic!

CECILIA: So now you've suddenly shifted to insults. Is this a tactic of yours or are you just a grumpy drunk?

CARTER: I'm not drunk! I'll let you know when I'm drunk.

CECILIA: That's considerate of you.

CARTER: I just don't see how it's possible for a full-grown woman to fall for that kind of lame, adolescent bullshit. I mean I used to pretend I was the Lone Ranger but I grew out of it.

CECILIA: Did you wear a mask?

CARTER: What?

CECILIA: When you were the Lone Ranger—did you wear a mask?

CARTER: I didn't say I *was* the Lone Ranger, I said I was *pretending* to be the Lone Ranger.

CECILIA: Did you wear a mask?

CARTER: No! I didn't wear a mask! I didn't *need* a mask!

CECILIA: You were that good?

CARTER: Yes! I was.

CECILIA: Did you pull the wool over everyone's eyes?

CARTER: What?

CECILIA: You and Vinnie—the "Detective" and the "Lone Ranger". Did you fool everyone or just each other?

CARTER: Look—"Miss Priss"—Did he ever talk to you about these photographs? Did he ever mention where he might have hid them?

CECILIA: I don't think they were as vital to him as they are to you. The only reason he showed them to me was to share something about his past.

CARTER: Sure.

CECILIA: What?

CARTER: You don't actually believe that, do you? A man shows you a bunch of obscene pictures in order to "share something about his past"? Are you kidding?

CECILIA: He showed them to me as examples of his work. That's all.

CARTER: Why are you so thick, Cecilia? Missouri's raised some very shrewd citizens over the decades. Why aren't you one of them?

CECILIA: You must be quite ruthless in business too, I suppose.

CARTER: Oh yeah, I'm a regular cut-throat.

CARTER's *cellular phone starts buzzing, inside his briefcase. Pause. They both stare at the briefcase.*

CECILIA: Your briefcase is buzzing.

CARTER *stands up and staggers slightly from the booze, then pulls himself together and moves to the briefcase. He stands over it and stares at it. Pause.*

CECILIA: Maybe it's your buddy.

CARTER *squats down, opens briefcase and answers phone. As he does this, lights come up in a dim pool on* SIMMS, *seated at his desk, on the phone, stage left. No card.*

CARTER (*on phone*): Yeah.

SIMMS (*on phone, stage left*): We've got a little problem here, Carter.

CARTER: Who is this?

CARTER *stands slowly.* CECILIA *continues with dishes.*

SIMMS: "Ames". Your man in the Blue Grass.

CARTER: What're you doing calling me here!

SIMMS: Seems your boy has jumped clean across the line. State lines, to be exact.

CARTER: What boy? I've told you never to try to get ahold of me! How'd you get this number?

SIMMS: Your boy, "Vincent T. Webb". He's peddling some very classified material here. Thought you might be interested.

CARTER: What material? What're you talking about? He's out *here*! I just saw him!

SIMMS: Well, he's got a very convincing double then.

CARTER: He came to you?

SIMMS: In the flesh.

CARTER: What's he want?

SIMMS: Three guesses.

CARTER: Don't try to pull anything on me, Simms!

SIMMS: I just thought maybe you'd like to know what's on the open market. I might be able to sell you a share.

SIMMS *hangs up softly. Lights dim on him.* CARTER *stays on phone.*

CARTER: SIMMS! HEY! HELLO! SIMMS! (*He slams phone back into briefcase.*) Lousy, goddamn scummy bastard!

CARTER *moves back to bottle and drinks.*

CECILIA (*at sink*): Who was it?

CARTER: Just—a client. Business.

CECILIA: Simms?

CARTER: What?

CECILIA: Who's Simms?

CARTER: Why don't you just leave now. There's no point in you being here anymore. Vinnie's not here and—

CECILIA: He might come back.

CARTER: He's *not* coming back!

CECILIA: He skipped town?

CARTER: Yes! That's exactly what he did. He skipped town.

CECILIA: Something to do with these photographs?

CARTER: None of this is any of your business! The only reason you're here is because I thought you could bring Vinnie out of this slump he was in.

CECILIA: But now he's run off.

CARTER: That's right.

CECILIA: With all your dirty pictures.

CARTER: They're not *my* dirty pictures!

CECILIA: But you want them. You want them very badly.

CARTER: Will you please leave! Will you go now? Get lost! Vamoose.

CECILIA: You were so eager to get me here. Now you want me gone. It's very confusing.

CARTER *moves back to briefcase, takes phone out and dials.*

CARTER (*as he deals with phone*): I've got things to arrange here. I've already missed my plane. I'm supposed to be back with my family, getting the kids ready for school. Buying notebooks and lunchpails. Halloween's coming up. Little League. There's—

CARTER listens on phone. As it begins to ring in SIMMS' office, lights come up softly on SIMMS again, seated at his desk, hovering over his work. SIMMS looks at the phone ringing on his desk but doesn't answer. He goes back to his work and lets it ring.

CECILIA: Little League?

CECILIA finishes dishes, then moves to VINNIE's dirty laundry and starts gathering it up.

CECILIA: I thought it was football.

CARTER (*still waiting on phone*): Answer the phone, you slimy shithead! ANSWER THE GODDAMN PHONE!!

CARTER slams the phone back into the briefcase.

CECILIA (*gathering laundry*): Nobody home?

Pause. CARTER watches her.

CARTER: What're you doing?

CECILIA: Laundry.

CARTER: Leave it? He doesn't deserve clean laundry. You're not his maid. Just leave it and get out of here.

CECILIA: Little League?

CARTER: What?

CECILIA: Little League in the Fall?

CARTER: I was thinking about the future!

CECILIA: I thought it was football in the Fall.

CARTER: I am *not* in the mood for domestic chit-chat about sports right now! Thank you very much. I'm in the midst of a crisis, in case you didn't notice. Suddenly I'm in the midst of a crisis!

CECILIA: That's the thing about crisis.

CARTER: What?

CECILIA: It happens suddenly.

CARTER: Will you please get the hell out of here!

CECILIA (*continuing to gather laundry*): I'm waiting for Vinnie.

CARTER: Vinnie is *gone*! Understand? He's double-crossed me. Sold me out! Down the river!

CECILIA: That's no way to talk about your best and oldest friend.

CARTER: Vinnie is a weasel! He's a low-down, treacherous, diabolical little man. The scum of the earth. He's systematically trying to crucify me!

CECILIA: For what?

CARTER: Exactly! For what? For something deeply buried in his sick imagination. That's "for what".

CECILIA: What could that be?

CARTER: Excuse me?

CECILIA: Deeply buried?

CARTER: I AM TRYING TO THINK HERE! I AM TRYING TO THINK!!

Pause. CARTER *drinks and wanders.* CECILIA *collects laundry.*

CECILIA: Maybe it's a woman.

CARTER: Will you get out! What in the world is the matter with you? You're like a termite or something, boring away. Why do you persist in staying when you know you're not welcome?

CECILIA: You invited me.

CARTER: I know that!

CECILIA: Sometimes, if you just lay all your cards on the table, miraculous things begin to occur. Things you could never foresee.

CARTER: I don't need any half-baked philosophical notions from you. Things are falling apart! THE SKY IS FALLING! THE SKY IS FALLING!

Pause. CECILIA *stares at him.*

CECILIA: "Chicken Little", isn't it?

CARTER: Look, smart ass!

CECILIA: You shouldn't be so hard on Vinnie, just because he's a detective and you're not.

CARTER: He's *not* a detective!

CECILIA: Where is he now?

CARTER: Kentucky! He's in Kentucky!

CECILIA: That was fast.

CARTER: He couldn't wait to double-cross me.

CECILIA: That's where you're from.

CARTER: Brilliant.

CECILIA: Are you going back out there? Track him down?

CARTER: I just came from there!

CECILIA: "What goes around, comes around." You ever heard that one? A musician I knew used to say that all the time.

CARTER: I am going to hit you in a minute. I am going to strike you!

CECILIA: You're not on the verge of a nervous breakdown, are you, Mr Carter?

CARTER: I'm being squeezed! Do you know what that's like? Have you got any idea what that's like? It's almost as though he's planned it or something. Set me up. (*Pause.*) You're not in on this with him, are you? The two of you in cahoots?

CECILIA: Vinnie's mind doesn't work like that.

CARTER: His mind? Now we're going to talk about his mind? He *has* no mind! He's brainless!

CECILIA: You're just jealous is all.

CARTER: Jealous?

CECILIA: I think so. There's that tone about it.

CARTER: A jealous tone.

CECILIA: Yes.

CARTER: What is it, exactly, that you find so fascinating about him? It's unbelievable. I mean, I don't get it. You're not a half bad-looking woman, Cecilia.

CECILIA: Gee, thanks.

CARTER: No, I mean really—You're a very attractive young lady, in your own way. It would seem to me that you'd

have a lot bigger fish to fry than some down-and-out
loser with a detective complex.

CECILIA: Maybe you should lie down.

CARTER: I'm not lying down!

CECILIA: You might be able to think better.

CARTER: I am *not* lying down! I'm not playing into your
hand. That's it, isn't it? You get me into the sack and
keep me here, while he goes off to knife me in the back.

CECILIA: I'm not a slut Mr Carter.

CARTER: I didn't say that.

CECILIA: Those might be the kind of women you've dealt
with in the past but I'm not one of them.

CARTER: What women?

CECILIA: Any woman.

CARTER: Did Vinnie talk to you about women in the past?

CECILIA: Don't get paranoid on me, Mr Carter. Panic is a
terrible thing. It's in the air. But there's no reason to
succumb to it.

CARTER: I'm not panicked!

CECILIA: I've known panic, myself. You can pick it up from
the TV, radio. The telephone. It's like a disease.

CARTER: I AM *NOT* PANICKED!!

CECILIA: It can take over your whole body. Your mind. This
sense of impending doom.

Pause. He stares at her.

CARTER: You've felt that kind of thing before? Why would
you feel something like that? Someone like you. Work-

ing in the Safeway. What do you know about "impending doom"? You've never—*done* anything have you? I mean—

CECILIA: Done anything? Like what?

CARTER: Nothing.

CECILIA: No—like what, for instance? I've done lots of things you might never suspect me of.

CARTER: Betrayed—something. Someone.

CECILIA: Oh—Betrayed. I don't know about that. Have you?

CARTER: What?

CECILIA: Betrayed someone?

CARTER: No.

CECILIA: Well, there you are then—both of us must be completely innocent on that score and yet we've both felt impending doom. Isn't that something.

CARTER: Well, maybe not *completely* innocent—

CECILIA: No. Maybe not.

CARTER: I mean little things, here and there. Things that couldn't be helped.

CECILIA: Right.

CARTER: Things—beyond your control.

CECILIA: Well, those things you can't blame yourself for.

CARTER: No.

CECILIA: Those things are just—

CARTER: Accidental, almost.

CECILIA: That's right.

CARTER: Circumstance.

Pause. CARTER *stares at her.*

CARTER: How did he find you exactly? He just strolled into
the Safeway one day and there you were—bagging his
groceries?

CECILIA: Coincidence, I guess.

CARTER: And he never even kissed you? Never tried? I—I
don't understand that.

CECILIA: He kissed me once.

Pause.

CARTER: He did?

CECILIA: Yes. Just once.

CARTER: Where?

CECILIA: In my kitchen.

CARTER: I mean on your body! Where on your body!

Pause.

CECILIA: That's private, Mr Carter.

Pause.

CARTER: I'm going to lay down.

CECILIA: Yes. I think you should.

CARTER *goes to bed, takes a long drink of whiskey and lies
down.*

CARTER: I have no idea what to do now. I can't go back
there, I can't stay here. I can't—face.it. I can't—It's like
everything's going backwards! I came out here to fix
things up! Why is he doing this to me?

CECILIA: Would you like a neck rub?

CARTER: No! Don't touch me!

CECILIA: You should try to rest now.

CARTER: I *am* resting! I'm supposed to be home but I'm
resting. I'm supposed to be taking care of business! I'm

the backbone of the whole operation and I'm laying here in Vinnie's bed.

CECILIA: Just breathe softly through your nose. Try to relax.

CARTER: Don't tell me how to breathe! I know how to breathe.

CECILIA: You'll be all right.

CARTER: Why did you let him kiss you! Why'd you let him do that?

CECILIA: Mr Carter—

She reaches out and touches his back softly. CARTER *jerks up and sits on bed.*

CARTER: DON'T TOUCH ME!

CECILIA *backs off.*

CECILIA: All right. Take it easy. I was just going to—

CARTER: He wants me to crawl, see. That's what it is. He wants me to suffer. It's not enough that I pay through the nose—that I cater to each and every little need of his—that I send him T-shirts and socks and see that all his bills are paid—HE WANTS ME TO SUFFER!! It's a vendetta!

CARTER *takes another belt from the bottle, gets up and starts to move through the room.*

CECILIA: You should really try to calm yourself down. It's not good for your blood.

CARTER (*on the move*): He was the one, see—That's what everybody forgets. He was the one with the big ideas. Right from the get-go. "All we'll do is switch a couple a' racehorses. That's all." That's what he said. "Happens all the time. Nobody'll know. They're both bay. Both geldings. Two white socks. Doctor the lip tattoos.

They're identical. Who's gonna know? Public always loses anyway!" That's what he said. "The track's robbing them ten times worse than we are. It's not like it's murder or rape or something monumental. It's nothing monumental! It's just deception! Just plain old-fashioned deception, that's all. Happens all the time. It's going on right now."

CECILIA: Mr Carter?

CARTER (*drinks and rants*): We almost pulled it off too. If it hadn't been for Simms, we woulda pulled it off. Simms could've closed one eye and no one would've been the wiser. We even offered him a piece of the action but he wouldn't take it.

CECILIA: Simms?

CARTER: Vinnie took the pictures, see. I had nothing to do with it. Vinnie set the whole thing up. Him and—this chippie he hired. It was him who rented the motel room. I told him it was going to backfire on him. Sooner or later. I told him that. Way back when he first got the idea.

CECILIA: Do you want me to call your wife for you?

CARTER: My wife?

CECILIA: Maybe you could talk to her.

CARTER: My wife?

Pause.

CECILIA: Yes. Don't you want to go back home, Mr Carter?

Pause. CARTER *is good and drunk by now, disoriented. He looks around the room, then stares at the window. He crosses to one of the windows and stares out.*

CECILIA: Is something wrong?

CARTER *opens the window, staring out.*

CECILIA: Mr Carter, you're starting to scare me. I'd be more than willing to call somebody for you. Is there anybody you would like to talk to?

CARTER (*staring out open window*): There's still a smell about the place. You know? Alfalfa. Dirt. A distant, vague smell of cut alfalfa. I noticed that when we were walking from the car. Did you notice that?

CECILIA: No. I'm not sure what alfalfa smells like.

CARTER (*stays at window*): Amazing. Alfalfa. Smells just like the earth. Me and Vinnie used to buck three wire bales right down the road there where the thrifty is. Right past there. Used to watch a horse named "Swaps" trot down the fence line with his neck bowed and his tail cocked high. You remember Swaps?

CECILIA: No.

CARTER: Never heard of Swaps? One tough racehorse. In his day.

CECILIA: Are you all right?

CARTER (*still at window*): You're on my side, aren't you Cecilia? When we get right down to it? You're not going to—betray me? Even though you might've kissed him. That's—forgivable. That's understandable. But you're not—deceiving me now, are you? You're not hiding something?

CECILIA: I'm from Missouri, Mr Carter. There's nowhere to hide in Missouri.

CARTER: I could trust you—I mean if I asked you to do something for me, you wouldn't double-cross me? You wouldn't go to Vinnie—You're not like the rest of them are you?

CECILIA: I'm not going to do anything illegal, if that's what you mean.

CARTER: No. None of us are. Nothing like that. I'd never ask you to break the law. I'm not a criminal.

CECILIA: I think you should try to get some sleep and think things over. Maybe in the morning—

CARTER *breaks away from window, back toward the bed and begins to wander again, drinking.*

CARTER: It's too late for that! It's too late for sleeping and waking and sleeping and waking. I've been doing that all my life and it hasn't helped.

CECILIA: I don't really want to get involved. I mean, Vinnie and me were just friends—

CARTER: This is strictly on the up-and-up, Cecilia. Best way to be in this business. Gotta protect your reputation. People find out sooner or later anyway.

CECILIA: I don't know anything about business or—

CARTER: I could get you box seats at the Derby, Cecilia. Free access to the Clubhouse. The Paddock. Mint juleps. The Inner Circle. You could meet the Governor!

CECILIA: The Derby?

CARTER: Yes. First class all the way. Deluxe. Understand? Wined and dined.

CECILIA: The Kentucky Derby?

CARTER: That's the one. Churchill Downs.

CECILIA: I've got nothing to wear.

CARTER: I'll take care of that. Don't worry about that.

CECILIA: But, I've got a job here—

CARTER: This is the chance of a lifetime, Cecilia! It's like no other horse race in the world. Impressions are stamped on you for life. Branded. The Twin Spires. The icy eyes of Laffit Pincay. The hands of Eddie Arcaro. The rippling muscle of Seattle Slew. These are things that never leave you, Cecilia. Things beyond seduction. Beyond lust!

CECILIA: I don't know, I've never—

CARTER: "My Old Kentucky Home"? They sing that, you know. They all sing that. The masses. Even the ones who don't know the words. Even the ones from Illinois and Wisconsin. They all want to be part of it. They're all dying to belong to something old and rooted in American earth. They're swept up in the frenzy. Have you ever felt that, Cecilia? Have you ever felt like throwing yourself to the dogs?

CECILIA: I've dreamed about it.

CARTER: Yes. But the dream is nothing. Wait 'til you see it in the flesh and blood.

Pause.

CECILIA: What do you want me to do?

CARTER *goes to cellular phone and dials* SIMMS' *number. Lights come up dimly on* SIMMS *again.*

CARTER *(as he dials)*: I want you to talk to this man. Tell him you're coming. Tell him you're bringing him something. He'll know what it is.

CECILIA: What man?

CARTER: Tell him you're working for me. My personal representative. He'll understand. Here—Tell him.

CARTER *hands her the phone, once he's dialed the number.* CECILIA *takes it and stands there, waiting for* SIMMS *to answer but he doesn't.* CARTER *crosses to* VINNIE's *bed, takes another drink and lies down on his back. Phone keeps ringing.* SIMMS *stares at it and goes back to his work.*

CARTER (*lying on bed*): You make a move like this, Cecilia. A radical move. Just one little move and everything shifts. Everything falls into place behind it. It carries its own momentum. It's a frightening thing but it pays off in the end. You'll see. It pays big dividends. It has a power all its own. Like a force of nature.

CECILIA *stands there waiting for* SIMMS *to answer phone but he never does. Lights fade slowly to black on both sides as phone keeps ringing in* SIMMS' *office.*

Act Three

SCENE ONE

Day. Place-name card that reads—"LEXINGTON". Split-stage right. Living room of CARTER's Kentucky mansion, very simple set with the impression of wealth. A sofa, glass table and carpet. VINNIE is standing in the room with his box tucked under his arm, facing a young and very attractice nanny named KELLY. She is dressed in a dark skirt, white blouse, short black heels and her hair done up in a bun. Lights up.

KELLY: Did you uh—have an appointment with Mrs Carter or anything?

VINNIE: Does she take appointments now?

KELLY: Well, I mean—was she expecting you?

VINNIE: No, I don't think she was.

KELLY: How did you get in, exactly?

VINNIE: Through the back door.

ROSIE'S VOICE (*off stage*): Who is it, Kelly? Is someone there?

KELLY (*to* ROSIE): It's—I don't—

ROSIE'S VOICE (*off*): Don't send them away! Kelly?

KELLY: Yes, mam?

ROSIE'S VOICE: Don't send them away, all right? I'm in the mood for company! I can feel it coming on me!

KELLY: He's—(*To* VINNIE.) What's your name?

VINNIE: Webb. Vincent T. Webb.

KELLY (*to* ROSIE): It's a Mr Vincent T. Webb!

ROSIE'S VOICE: Vincent T. Webb?

KELLY: That's what he says!

ROSIE'S VOICE: Who in the world is that? Sounds like a lawyer! He's not a lawyer is he?

KELLY (*to* VINNIE): Are you a lawyer?

VINNIE: No. I'm a detective.

KELLY (*to* ROSIE): He's a detective!

ROSIE'S VOICE: A what!

KELLY (*to* ROSIE): A detective!

ROSIE'S VOICE: A detective?

KELLY: That's what he says.

ROSIE'S VOICE: Is something wrong? Has something happened?

KELLY (*to* VINNIE): Has something happened?

VINNIE: No. Nothing's happened.

KELLY: Nothing's happened!

ROSIE'S VOICE (*off*): I can't take any excitement, Kelly! My pills haven't kicked in!

KELLY (*to* VINNIE): She doesn't know you. I think you should just—

VINNIE: She knows me.

ROSIE'S VOICE: Has something happened to Carter! Is that it?

KELLY (*to* VINNIE): She says she doesn't know you.

ROSIE'S VOICE: Kelly!

KELLY: Mam?

ROSIE'S VOICE: Has something happened to Carter! Where's he from anyway? This detective.

KELLY (*to* VINNIE): Where are you from?

VINNIE: California.

KELLY (*to* ROSIE): California!

VINNIE (*to* KELLY): Cucamonga, California.

KELLY (*to* ROSIE): Cucamonga, California!

ROSIE'S VOICE: Cucamonga?

KELLY (*to* ROSIE): That's what he says!

ROSIE'S VOICE: Nobody's from Cucamonga! That's where Carter's from!

KELLY (*to* VINNIE): She says her husband's from there but nobody else is.

VINNIE: I *am* her husband.

Pause. KELLY *stares at him.*

KELLY (*to* VINNIE): You'd better leave.

ROSIE'S VOICE (*off*): Don't let him leave, Kelly!

ROSIE *enters upstage, slightly hung over and rumpled, pulling the sash of her robe together, pulling a slipper on. She spots* VINNIE *and smiles.*

ROSIE (*to* VINNIE): Oh—I'm sorry. So *you're* the detective. I uh—slept in. I heard the taxi in the driveway. It was in my dream in fact. I love taxis. I don't know why. They remind me of town, I guess. So colorful. All that—local advertising. We get so—disconnected sometimes—out here. Don't we, Kelly?

KELLY: Yes, mam. Um—this gentleman came in through the back door.

ROSIE: I know. Isn't that something. A Backdoor Man! We have such a disregard for crime out here. We leave doors open. Keys in the car. It's disgusting. It's a wonder we're not all raped and murdered.

KELLY: He says he knows you.

ROSIE: Oh. He does? (*To* VINNIE.) I'm sorry. Mr—Webb, was it?

VINNIE: Yes.

They shake hands. VINNIE *is reluctant to let her hand go.*

ROSIE: From—Cucamonga?

VINNIE: That's right.

ROSIE: That's amazing. My husband's from Cucamonga. Originally. In the beginning.

VINNIE: Yes. I know.

ROSIE: This isn't *about* my husband, is it?

VINNIE: No.

ROSIE: He hasn't done something?

VINNIE: Not that I know of.

ROSIE: That's a relief. You never know these days. Even the most intimate relationships are full of surprises. I'm from Glendora, myself. You know Glendora?

VINNIE: Yes. I walk there every day.

ROSIE: You do?

VINNIE: When I'm there.

ROSIE: Oh, that makes me so homesick! You have no idea. Just the sound of it—"Glendora". Like a Spanish woman's hair or something! Grapefruit trees! Orange blossoms on the wind! The snow-capped San Gabriels! I suppose it's changed though. Over the years.

VINNIE: Yes. It has.

ROSIE: Lost its splendor.

VINNIE: Yes.

ROSIE: Oh, would you—Kelly, did you offer Mr Webb a drink?

KELLY: No, mam. I was—

ROSIE (to VINNIE): What would you like? Coffee? Coca-Cola? Iced tea?

VINNIE: Bourbon please.

ROSIE: Ah, good choice. I like an early jump-start myself. What kind?

VINNIE: Black Bush.

ROSIE: I'm not sure we have that particular one in stock, do we Kelly?

KELLY: Mam—

ROSIE: What is it, Kelly?

KELLY: This man says—he knows you.

ROSIE: Yes, I know that. You already told me that. We're repeating ourselves, aren't we, Kelly?

KELLY: He says he—

ROSIE: Would you please go see if we have any of that—(*To* VINNIE.) What was the name, Mr Webb?

VINNIE: Black Bush. Irish.

ROSIE: That's it. "Black Bush". Those Irish have a way with words, don't they? Go see if we have that, Kelly.

KELLY: Mam. He says he's your husband.

ROSIE: Go find the Black Bush, Kelly! Do it, now!

Pause. KELLY *exits.* ROSIE *watches her.* ROSIE *turns to* VINNIE. *They stare at each other. Pause.*

ROSIE: Would you like me to take your coat and uh—your package?

VINNIE: No thanks.

ROSIE: If you're wearing a sidearm under there it doesn't matter. We've seen that before around here. Kelly's seen it. It's old hat.

VINNIE: I'm not.

ROSIE: So, you haven't come to do me in then? Splatter my brains all over the carpet in a fit of jealous rage? (*Pause.*) You're a long way from home, Vinnie.

VINNIE: Yeah. I am.

ROSIE: Carter just went out to see you. Did you know that? That's what he said he was up to anyway. You didn't somehow miss him did you? "Ships in the night"?

VINNIE: No. I saw him.

ROSIE: Oh, good. Did you work things out? I know it's been a long and bitter negotiation.

VINNIE: He said you two were on the outs.

ROSIE: Who?

VINNIE: You and him.

ROSIE (*laughs*): Is that what he said? Just like that? "On the outs"! Those were *his* words?

Pause.

VINNIE: Is it okay if I—sit down?

ROSIE: Help yourself! *Mi casa es su casa*, Vinnie. You know that. Just like the old days. Nothing's changed.

VINNIE *sits on edge of sofa, clutching shoebox under his arm.*

ROSIE: So, what've you got, a bomb in the box or something? Gonna blow us all to Kingdom Come?

VINNIE: I'm not going to hurt you.

ROSIE: You're not still harboring something, are you Vinnie? That's not healthy. That's the kind of thing that leads to cancer and insanity.

VINNIE: I just wanted to see you.

ROSIE: Well, here I am! Still in the bloom of things. I never would've recognized *you* though, Vinnie. You've let yourself go. I was watching you from the window and I was asking myself, "Now who is this? Who in the world could this be, arriving by taxi, with a package under his arm?" It's not roses, is it Vinnie? Roses for Rosie?

VINNIE: No.

ROSIE: I didn't think so. Too short for roses. Too compact. Unless you've cut the stems off. Out of spite or something. Wouldn't that be a shame.

VINNIE: So, how did you know?

ROSIE: What.

VINNIE: How did you recognize me?

ROSIE: Oh. The voice. Something in the voice rang a bell. A kind of apologetic menace. I don't know how else to describe it.

VINNIE: I'm not going to hurt you.

ROSIE: I'd feel a lot more reassured if you didn't keep repeating that.

VINNIE: I just want you to know. I didn't come here for that.

ROSIE: Good. That's good news. Now we don't have to talk about it anymore, do we? (Pause.) So you met up with Carter then? How did that go?

VINNIE: All right.

ROSIE: He said you were in some kind of an emergency again. He left here in a big rush.

VINNIE: I am.

ROSIE: Still?

VINNIE: Yes. I'm at the end of my rope. I may not look like it but I am.

ROSIE: Well, actually, you *are* looking a little rough around the edges, Vinnie. I didn't want to say anything—

VINNIE: I got arrested.

ROSIE: Oh. That's too bad. When was that?

VINNIE: A while back. Couple weeks ago.

ROSIE: Well, I'm sorry to hear that, Vinnie. What was it this time?

VINNIE: Assault with a deadly weapon. Attempted manslaughter.

ROSIE: You've escalated.

VINNIE: It won't stick. Just—hysterical reaction, is all it was.

ROSIE: It wasn't Carter, was it?

VINNIE: What.

ROSIE: Did you assault Carter?

VINNIE: No. He's safe.

ROSIE: Where is he?

VINNIE: Out there. My place.

ROSIE: How come he's out there and you're here? What's going on, Vinnie?

VINNIE: He's—He took up with a woman out there.

Pause. ROSIE *stares at him.* KELLY *re-enters with a tray and drinks. Pause, as she sets the drinks down on glass table then turns to go.* ROSIE *stops her.*

ROSIE: Kelly?

KELLY (*stops*): Yes, mam?

ROSIE: What time are you picking up the kids today?

KELLY: Three o'clock. The usual time.

ROSIE: Doesn't Simon have band practice?

KELLY: No, not today. That's Thursdays.

ROSIE: Oh. Right. Well, look Kelly, why don't you take them to have ice cream and then go to Toys 'R' Us or something. All right? Just find something to do with them for a little while.

KELLY (*looks at* VINNIE): Okay.

ROSIE: I need to talk with Mr Webb here.

KELLY: All right.

> KELLY *starts to go, then stops. She eyes* VINNIE *then turns to* ROSIE.

KELLY (*to* ROSIE): Is everything—Are you sure you'll be all right, Mrs Carter?

ROSIE: I'm fine, Kelly. Just go get the kids now. Do as you're told.

> KELLY *eyes* VINNIE *again, then exits. Pause as* ROSIE *and* VINNIE *sip their drinks.*

ROSIE: So—he's run off with a woman. Not that I'm shocked or anything. He's been carrying on behind my back since day one.

VINNIE: When *was* that?

ROSIE: What?

VINNIE: "Day One".

ROSIE: We're not going to drag that back up out of the dirt, are we Vinnie? Things happened. One thing led to another. I don't know. It was a long time ago.

VINNIE: But now it's over, right?

ROSIE: What.

VINNIE: You and him?

ROSIE: Apparently so! What're you trying to tell me? He's shacked up with a woman at *your* place and you've come all the way out here to give me the good news?

VINNIE: He met this girl—

ROSIE: A girl! A girl! It's always a girl. Never a woman.

VINNIE: He met this girl in a bar out there.

ROSIE: What a surprise!

VINNIE: I guess she got infatuated with him.

ROSIE: Oh, *she* got infatuated with *him*!

VINNIE: I guess.

ROSIE: And you, very generously, donated your bed to the cause!

VINNIE: No—

ROSIE: And now you've gone out of your way, as a friend, to make sure I understand all the sordid details!

VINNIE (*sudden burst*): HE STOLE MY BUICK, ROSIE! HE STOLE MY BUICK AND HE STOLE MY WIFE!

Pause. ROSIE *stares at him.*

ROSIE: You know, for a long time I kept dreading this confrontation. I had little nightmares about it. But now that it's here, it seems dull actually. Stupid.

VINNIE: You could've left me a note or something.

ROSIE: A note!

VINNIE: Something.

ROSIE: Oh you mean like: "Gone to the 7–11 to get a six-pack. Be right back"?

VINNIE: Something. Not just—disappeared.

ROSIE: We were *all* checking out of there, Vinnie! *All* of us. That was the plan. Remember?

VINNIE: Yeah. I remember.

ROSIE: No contact. No trace of any connection between us.

VINNIE: That was the plan.

ROSIE: It's a little late for regrets.

VINNIE: I just thought maybe you'd—

ROSIE: What?

Pause.

VINNIE: Come back.

ROSIE: To what? Life on the backstretch? Fifteen-hundred-dollar claimers? I could've set up house in the back of a horse trailer, maybe?

VINNIE: We had fun. We had some fun.

ROSIE: Fun!

VINNIE: Read the Form 'til two in the morning sometimes. Picking long-shots. Clocking works.

ROSIE: Fun.

VINNIE: Slept in the truck bed. Listened to the tin roof flap on the shedrow.

ROSIE: Fun, fun, fun!

VINNIE: You could've called me or something.

ROSIE: What about *you*? Where have you been all this time?

VINNIE: I had no idea where you went.

ROSIE: Come on. You knew where the checks were coming from. You knew the phone number well enough.

VINNIE: I didn't want to—interrupt your life.

ROSIE: Get outa here.

VINNIE: I thought you and Carter were—

ROSIE: What.

VINNIE: Getting along. I mean—

ROSIE: *You're* the one who disappeared, Vinnie. *You're* the one who vanished.

VINNIE: I'm here, now.

ROSIE: Well, isn't that great! Isn't that dandy! Fifteen years later you sneak through my back door with a dumb box and a hang-dog look on your face.

VINNIE: I wasn't sneaking.

ROSIE: What'd you come here for?

Pause.

VINNIE: I thought maybe I could set things straight.

ROSIE: What *things*?

VINNIE: I uh—found Simms. I went and talked to him.

ROSIE: Who?

VINNIE: Simms. "Ames", as he's called now.

ROSIE: I don't know who you're talking about.

VINNIE: He seems to have reconciled something with himself. No malice. He lives in his own little world. Studies bloodlines and stays out of trouble.

ROSIE: What're we talking about here?

VINNIE: He's the kind of man who was able to rebound from terrible shock and pull himself back together. He had no interest whatsoever in what I had to offer.

ROSIE: And what was that?

VINNIE: These.

VINNIE *holds out the shoebox to her. She doesn't take it from him.*

ROSIE: What's in there? Dead puppies?

VINNIE: Take it.

ROSIE *slowly takes the box and puts her hand on the lid but doesn't open it.*

ROSIE: Is a snake going to jump out at me or something? A tiny nightmare?

VINNIE: Open it.

Pause.

ROSIE: I just love surprises.

She slowly lifts the lid and stares at the contents, then suddenly drops the box, spilling photos, letters etc. and starts yelling for the nanny. She moves nervously around the room.

ROSIE (*yelling to off stage*): KELLY! KELLY, ARE YOU STILL THERE! KELLY GET BACK HERE! KELLY!!

VINNIE *drops to his hands and knees and starts quickly collecting the fallen articles and putting them back in the box.*

VINNIE (*on hands and knees collecting photos*): Now don't get excited. I was going to *give* them to you. I was going to give them all to you. Simms doesn't want them so I was going to just hand them over to you.

ROSIE: Who is Simms! I don't know this man! I have never heard of this man! (*To off-stage.*) KELLY!

VINNIE: Not on a long-term basis maybe.

ROSIE: Not on any kinda basis! Now get outa here!

VINNIE: Just a fling. Just a one-night stand in a Motel 6 on the edge of Azusa!

Long pause.

ROSIE: Now who is going to believe that? Who in the world is going to believe something like that? After all this time.

VINNIE: It's all right here. Pictures don't lie.

ROSIE: Take a look. Take a long hard look at that face. (*Referring to photo.*) Does that even remotely resemble someone we know?

VINNIE (*looking at photo*): It was a long time ago.

ROSIE: Pick all this shit up and get outa here. Now!

VINNIE *slowly rises with shoebox and contents.*

VINNIE: I was going to give it all back to you. You can burn it if you want to. I was gonna trade you straight across.

ROSIE: Trade me? Trade me for what?

VINNIE: I had this idea in my head. I had it all cooked up. I was gonna get another Buick. Just like the one I had. You remember that Buick?

ROSIE: No.

VINNIE: You remember me driving with one hand on the wheel and the other one on your knee?

ROSIE: No, I don't.

VINNIE: I was thinking maybe we could still run off together.

ROSIE: Run off? I'm a married woman, Vinnie! Where're we gonna run off to now?

VINNIE: I don't know. Mexico maybe.

ROSIE: Oh Jesus, Vinnie. Give it up! Everything has already happened! It's already taken place. This is it. There's no "running off" anymore. It's a done deal. You're in your little hell and I'm in mine.

VINNIE: It's not done!

VINNIE suddenly grabs her and pulls her violently to him. He tries to kiss her but she pushes him away. They stand apart. Pause.

ROSIE (*low, menacing*): You touch me—You so much as touch me again and I'll have you killed. This is *my* house. I'm the wife of someone. Someone of tremendous power and influence. He could have you done in from a distance and you wouldn't even know what hit you. I don't care who he's sleeping with—all it would take is a call from me. One little phone call and you'd be history, Vincent T. Webb. He'd do anything for me, Vinnie. Anything at all. And do you know why that is? Do you have any kind of clue, Vinnie? Because he *owes* me. He's deeply in debt to me. All from that one little brainstorm of mine, way back then. That one little night on the edge of Azusa.

VINNIE: Oh, so now you're suddenly gonna take all the credit.

ROSIE: Yeah, sure. Why not? It was a brilliant little notion. It paid off in spades too, didn't it? I probably shoulda just gone professional.

VINNIE: I took the pictures!

ROSIE: You certainly did. But *I* turned the trick. It was me who caused the heads to roll and don't you ever forget it.

VINNIE: I won't. I won't ever forget it.

Pause.

ROSIE: Did you actually think—You didn't actually think that—

VINNIE: What?

ROSIE: That's unbelievable—after all this time. Mexico?

VINNIE: It was just an idea.

ROSIE: Mexico?

VINNIE *hands her the shoebox as the lights fade.*

SCENE TWO

Midway, Ky. Split-stage left. SIMMS' *office again.* SIMMS *habitually hovering over his desk, pouring through papers and drinking. He's already had several drinks and is much more well-oiled than the first time he was seen.* CECILIA *stands nervously across the desk from him, dressed in her crisp new "Derby" outfit—brightly flowered dress, straw hat, white high heels, white gloves and a large purse stuffed with cash. Pause, as she watches* SIMMS *at work, mumbling, scratching notes with his pen and seemingly oblivious to her presence.*

CECILIA: I can come back, if you like. I didn't realize you were going to be so busy.

SIMMS (*staying with his work, not looking up at her*): No, no, no. Why come back when you're already here. Don't you worry. Everything's an interruption when you're working on bloodlines. It's an endless chain. Never get to the bottom of it. Just when you think you've discovered the key to the most mysterious breeding nick in the history of racing, the glaring truth of it all reaches up and slaps you right in the face.

CECILIA: I see.

SIMMS: No you don't.

CECILIA: Well, I was just wondering if—

SIMMS (*not looking up at her*): The glaring truth is that every single solitary thoroughbred horse in the world—living or dead—and all those foals yet to be born are, in one way or another, related by blood. From the glue factory to the winner's circle—each and every one of them carries some common factor, miniscule as it may be. So it's somewhat futile, don't you think, to try and factor out this elusive element of speed in the midst of such a vast genetic ocean. Even worse folly to attempt to identify what gives a thoroughbred heart.

CECILIA: Heart?

SIMMS: Yes. The guts to run. The guts to win. Courage—to put it plain.

CECILIA: That's amazing.

SIMMS: It is.

CECILIA: I never realized it was so—complex.

SIMMS (*finally looks up at her*): It's not. It's our vain efforts that make it that way.

SIMMS *stares at her. Pause.*

CECILIA: I—

Pause. SIMMS *keeps staring.*

CECILIA: I—don't know exactly how to put this but—

SIMMS: You're stunning.

CECILIA: What?

SIMMS: You're absolutely stunning.

CECILIA (*blushing*): Well, thank you. That's very kind.

SIMMS: Where did you come from?

CECILIA: I'm—You know—

SIMMS: Have you been standing there long? I'm very sorry. I tend to get absorbed. I didn't mean to be rude.

CECILIA: No, no—That's quite all right. It's fascinating stuff. I don't know anything about horses, myself.

SIMMS: Do you uh—Would you like a drink or—

CECILIA: No, thank you. I don't drink.

SIMMS *gets up and stumbles slightly, heading for his liquor cabinet.*

SIMMS: Oh. Well—You won't mind if I—

He fixes himself a fresh bourbon on ice.

CECILIA: No, please. Go right ahead.

SIMMS: Helps to keep the wheels churning. A little lubrication.

CECILIA: Yes.

SIMMS: You uh—You're in the horse business, I take it?

CECILIA: No, I'm not. I'm—an associate of Mr Carter's. I thought he talked to you about me. He was going to call and—

SIMMS: An associate?

CECILIA: Yes. We tried to call you but your phone was off the hook or something and he said he was going to let you know I was coming.

SIMMS: I despise the phone. Don't you?

CECILIA: Well—

SIMMS: The cloning of the phone. Another disease, don't you think?

CECILIA: I don't really—

SIMMS: Another desperate measure.

CECILIA: Didn't Mr Carter tell you I was coming?

SIMMS: Carter? Carter. That's funny. Another acquaintance of his popped in just the other morning.

CECILIA: Vinnie?

SIMMS: Oh, you know him then? Very disturbed individual, I thought. Very agitated. Lying through his teeth.

CECILIA: He's high strung.

SIMMS: Is that what it is?

CECILIA: He's had a string of bad luck.

SIMMS: Oh—well, that'll do it all right.

Pause. SIMMS *stares at her again.* CECILIA *squirms, nervously.*

SIMMS: You're absolutely gorgeous. I can't get over it.

CECILIA: Well, thank you very much.

SIMMS: You don't understand what kind of a storm you've begun to arouse inside me. I mean—I must be visibly shaking. Am I shaking? Can you see me shaking?

CECILIA: No, I—

SIMMS: You're just being polite.

CECILIA: I really, just want to—

SIMMS: If you knew—if you had the slightest clue as to the pounding that's going on in my cardiovascular system, you'd be able to manipulate me to your heart's content.

CECILIA: I don't—

SIMMS: That must've been Carter's intention, right?

CECILIA: No! He just—

SIMMS: You'd be able to have me groveling at your feet. Is that what he wants?

CECILIA: No!

SIMMS: Would you like to see me grovel?

SIMMS goes down on one knee, holding his drink.

CECILIA: No, please! Please don't do that!

SIMMS: Beg? Lick your boots? Kiss the ground you walk on?

SIMMS crawls toward her with his tongue lapping out. CECILIA *backs up fast.*

CECILIA (*backing up*): DON'T DO THAT! STAY AWAY!

SIMMS stops, then slowly rises to his feet and returns to his desk with his drink.

SIMMS: I'm sorry. I didn't mean to alarm you. It's been a long day.

CECILIA: I'm very flattered that you think I'm—attractive. But it's got nothing to do with why I came.

SIMMS (*suddenly curious*): This isn't Sunday, is it?

He turns and looks out the window, then looks back at CECILIA.

CECILIA: Sunday? No, I don't—I don't think so. Why?

SIMMS: Your outfit smacks of Sunday. Church. Spanking clean. Very Protestant.

CECILIA: Oh. It's my new Derby dress.

SIMMS: Derby?

CECILIA: Yes. My Kentucky Derby dress. I—I just bought it.

SIMMS: This is October, isn't it? Aren't we in October now?

CECILIA: We are?

SIMMS: Yes. I'm sure of it. (*Turns to window again.*) Look— the trees are turning gold. There's a chill in the air. Jack o' lanterns in every window. They wouldn't do that if it wasn't October.

CECILIA: Who?

SIMMS: Citizens. Those who play the game.

CECILIA: Oh, that's right.

SIMMS: The Derby's in May. First Saturday in May, to be exact.

CECILIA: I know but—

SIMMS: You're early. Or late, as the case may be.

CECILIA: I know. I was just trying it out.

SIMMS: Trying it out on *me*?

CECILIA: Mr Carter bought it for me and I thought I'd—

SIMMS: Carter.

CECILIA: It was his money.

SIMMS: He's a generous man.

CECILIA: He is.

Pause. SIMMS *stares at her.*

SIMMS: Have a seat, Miss—

CECILIA: Pontz. Cecilia Pontz. From Missouri.

CECILIA *remains tensely standing.* SIMMS *sits in his chair.*

SIMMS: A prairie flower!

CECILIA: I don't want to take up a lot of your time, Mr Ames.

SIMMS: Neither did the other man. But he did.

CECILIA: Excuse me?

SIMMS: Webb. He consumed a good half hour trying to convince me that vengeance was the best row to hoe. How do you feel about it, Miss Ponds? An eye for an eye?

CECILIA: Pontz. With a "z".

SIMMS: Pontz, with a "z". How do you feel about it?

CECILIA: What?

SIMMS: Vengeance.

CECILIA: I don't—I haven't thought about it much.

SIMMS: No. And why should you? You're in the Spring of life.

CARTER: Well, thank you.

SIMMS: Not your fault. It's genetics. All in the genes. We've got nothing to do with it. It was all decided generations ago. Faceless ancestors. The curvature of your hips. You can't possibily take credit for that now, can you?

CECILIA: Um—

SIMMS: The turn of your lips. Who first sculpted that in your far-away past?

CECILIA: I really—

SIMMS: Please, have a seat. You're looking flustered.

CECILIA: Oh. Thank you. Thank you very much.

She sits nervously in chair across from desk, clutching her bag.
SIMMS reaches across desk to relieve her of the bag.

SIMMS (*reaching*): Would you like me to take your bag?

CECILIA: No!

She whips the bag away from him and protects it.

CECILIA: No, thank you. I've got some private things in there.

SIMMS (*standing, stretched across desk*): Underpants?

CECILIA: Excuse me?

SIMMS (*sitting back in his chair*): Never mind. Sure you won't have a little tipple? Might loosen you up some.

CECILIA: No, I'm fine.

SIMMS: You certainly are, Miss Pontz. You certainly are that.

CECILIA: Um—Mr Webb—the other man—The man who paid you a visit—

SIMMS: The idiot. Yes?

CECILIA: Did he—Did he sell you something?

SIMMS: He sold me a bill of goods, if that's what you mean.

CECILIA: No, I mean—

SIMMS: Yes. That's what you're here for. Isn't it?

CECILIA: Well—

SIMMS: How did you get mixed up with those two knot-heads, Miss Ponds? A bright-eyed gal from Missouri.

CECILIA: Well, Mr Carter's an old friend of Vinnie's and I'd known Vinnie from before.

SIMMS: I see.

CECILIA: They've known each other since childhood.

SIMMS: Thick as flies.

CECILIA: But—they've gone separate ways. Something happened, I guess. Some—schism.

SIMMS: Separate ways?

CECILIA: Yes. They're like opposites now.

SIMMS: The right and left hand.

CECILIA: Excuse me?

SIMMS: Nothing. Your innocence is almost as shocking as your beauty.

CECILIA: I've—I'm sorry—I've never heard anyone talk like that. I just don't know what to say. I'm—

SIMMS: Speechless.

CECILIA: I'm trying to present something to you but you're making it very, very difficult! I came as a messenger from Mr Carter. He wants you to know—He wants to give you an alternative to the deal you've struck with Mr Webb. A better deal.

SIMMS: Have you laid down with him, Miss Ponds?

CECILIA: What!

SIMMS: Your Mr Carter—Have you done the down and dirty deed with him? Spread your magnificent thighs?

CECILIA *stands abruptly, drops her bag and fumbles to retrieve it.*

CECILIA: No! Of course not. I've only recently met him. Now listen, you have no right to—

SIMMS: You're not a high-paid chippie then? A Class Act? Something found in the Yellow Pages under "Executive Escorts"?

CECILIA: I don't need to be insulted, Mr Ames!

SIMMS: Nobody does, but you evidently, haven't got the full picture, Miss Cecilia from Missouri. Either that or you're dumber than a fence post.

CECILIA: Mr Carter simply wanted me to ask if you'd consider selling the negatives—the material—for a slightly higher price than you paid for them. That's all. Now I'd appreciate it if you were as straightforward with me as I'm attempting to be with you. He's offering a good deal of money. I've got it right here. (*She pats her bag.*) Cash. It's all present and accounted for.

SIMMS (*smiling*): Cash.

CECILIA: That's right. You *did* call him, didn't you? You *did* make some kind of an—overture. I was right there when you called.

SIMMS: You took a hot shower and shampoo; put on your crisp "Derby" dress; filled your purse with a "good deal of cash" and flew all the way out here, just to see me?

CECILIA: Yes. That's exactly right.

SIMMS: That's so sweet. It makes my skin tingle to think of you doing all that just for me.

CECILIA: I don't think you understand.

SIMMS: You're making me a proposition.

CECILIA: Yes, but it's got nothing to do with—

SIMMS: How 'bout Vinnie? Mr Vinnie. Have you laid down with him?

CECILIA: Do you want to sell the negatives or not, Mr Ames! Yes or no!

SIMMS (*chuckles*): The "negatives", the "negatives". What are these mysterious negatives?

CECILIA: You bought them, didn't you! You know very well what they are.

SIMMS: I heard they were of a libidinous nature. Is that true?

CECILIA: I don't know what that means.

SIMMS: "Off-color". "Lewd". "Racy". "Ruttish".

CECILIA: Yes. They are.

SIMMS: How "ruttish", Miss Cecilia?

CECILIA: Look—I don't have to explain to you—

SIMMS: Did they arouse your prurient interest? Did you get excited when you first saw them? You *have* seen them, haven't you?

CECILIA: Yes! I've seen them.

SIMMS: You've examined them closely?

CECILIA: I've seen them!

SIMMS: Well?

CECILIA: I can only say that anyone who would allow themselves to be photographed in those positions—

SIMMS: "Allowed"? Let me just explain something to you, Miss Pontz with a "z", that these two bandits, Webb and Carter, may have neglected to tell you—

CECILIA *begins to move around very nervously, clutching at her chest and having difficulty breathing. Like a sudden asthma attack.*

CECILIA: Would you—Would you mind opening up a window? I'm suddenly—short of breath. I feel like I'm suffocating or something.

SIMMS: Of course. (*Goes to window and opens it.*) Sure you wouldn't like to have a drink? It helps sometimes in moments like this.

CECILIA: No, I—I don't know what it is. My chest—It'll pass.

SIMMS: Hot flashes?

CECILIA: No!

SIMMS: Do you live alone, Miss Pontz?

CECILIA: WOULD YOU BE INTERESTED IN SELLING THE NEGATIVES, MR SIMMS! Or not. Please—just—I can't take much more of this. I'm not cut out for this. I work in the Safeway!

SIMMS: "Simms"? Is that what you called me?

CECILIA: I mean—Ames. Mr Ames. You know who you are! I've seen you! I've seen who you are! Don't pretend with me.

SIMMS (*moving back to desk*): You're a little mixed up, aren't you, Cecilia? A little bit scrambled.

CECILIA: I shouldn't have come here at all. I didn't want to be doing this. I've never done anything like this before in my life!

SIMMS: But your pals talked you into it?

CECILIA: They're not my "pals"! I hardly even know them.

SIMMS: They're snakes, Cecilia. That's exactly what they are. They crawl on their bellies.

Pause.

CECILIA: I just—All I really wanted to do was go to the Kentucky Derby. That's all. And Mr Carter offered me free tickets. The Clubhouse. I don't know.

SIMMS: The Derby.

CECILIA: Yes. It was foolish to get suckered in by something like that but—I love the Derby. I've always—I—I remember being in London. It rained all the time. Always raining. And I—I would stay in and watch the races. I remember watching that big red horse—That magnificent red horse. What was his name? He was on the news. Everybody knew his name.

SIMMS: Secretariat.

CECILIA: Yes! That's the one. Secretariat. And he won by miles that day. Twenty lengths or something.

SIMMS: Thirty-one.

CECILIA: Yes. Thirty-one lengths. It was incredible. I've never seen an animal like that. As though he was flying.

SIMMS: He was.

CECILIA: He was like that winged horse they used to have on the gas stations, you know—That red, winged horse.

SIMMS: Pegasus.

CECILIA: Yes! Just like Pegasus. Ever since then I've dreamed of going to the Derby.

SIMMS: That wasn't the Derby you were watching. That was the Belmont.

CECILIA: Oh. It was?

SIMMS: Yes. It was. New York: 1973. He smashed the world record for a mile and a half. Demolished it.

CECILIA: He did? I don't know. I just remember him, flying. He was on the news.

SIMMS: There'll never be another one like him. Do you know what his heart weighed, Miss Pontz?

CECILIA: His heart? They weighed his heart? How horrible.

SIMMS: Twenty-two pounds.

CECILIA: They actually weighed his heart?

SIMMS: Twenty-two pounds. Do you know what the weight of an average thoroughbred's heart is? Just an average, run-of-the-mill, thoroughbred horse that can't pay his own feed bill?

CECILIA: I don't know a thing about horses.

SIMMS: Eight pounds.

CECILIA: I can't believe they weighed his heart. That means they—cut him open? Dug inside?

SIMMS: That's a difference of fourteen pounds.

CECILIA: How could they do that to such a wonderful animal? Cut his heart out.

SIMMS: Treachery, Miss Pontz. Pure and simple, treachery.

Pause.

CECILIA: Well—

SIMMS: Sure you won't have a drink?

CECILIA: I should be going. I don't know what ever made me think I could go through with something like this. I'm from the Mid-West.

SIMMS: Why don't you have a drink? Just a smidgeon.

Pause.

CECILIA: All right. That might be—

SIMMS: There ya go! Are you breathing easier now?

SIMMS *moves to liquor cabinet and fixes her a bourbon.*

CECILIA: What?

SIMMS: You said you were suffocating.

CECILIA: Oh—Yes—I don't know what happened. It just suddenly came over me. A panic of some kind. I've had it before but—not for a long time. A pressure on the chest.

SIMMS: And it suddenly returned?

CECILIA: I guess so. Has that ever happened to you? As though you've lost track of everything. I was standing there and all of a sudden, I didn't recognize myself at all. I had no idea what I was doing here. This dress—

SIMMS: You're so unbelievably beautiful, it makes my mouth dry.

CECILIA: Why do you—Why do you keep saying things like that? Are you trying to—

SIMMS (*crosses to her with drink*): Seduce you? No. I'm past that, Miss Pontz. Way past that. This dog can't hunt anymore but he still gets "birdie". Bourbon?

Pause. He holds drink out to her. She takes it.

CECILIA: Thank you.

SIMMS: My pleasure.

Pause. She sips.

CECILIA: How could you—have done something like that?

SIMMS: Like what?

CECILIA: Like what you did in those pictures. You don't seem like the kind of man—

SIMMS: Well, some of us get caught with our pants down and some don't. I was one of the lucky ones.

CECILIA: Lucky?

SIMMS: I got over it.

CECILIA: But you must have—suffered.

SIMMS: It's all in the past. Now it's their turn.

CECILIA: They—set you up, then?

SIMMS: Bingo!

CECILIA: The two of them? I can't believe it. I feel so foolish.

He clicks glasses with hers and drinks.

SIMMS: At least you got a new dress outa the deal.

Pause.

CECILIA: Well, I should get back. I should take this money back to him.

SIMMS: How much money *is* there, in your—purse, Miss Pontz?

CECILIA: What? Oh—I don't really know. I never counted it.

SIMMS: A great deal.

CECILIA: Yes. I suppose. I've never seen so much money in my whole life, in fact. Last night—last night I did a funny thing. I was in my motel room. I was alone in there and—I was naked. And—I don't know why, but I laid all the money out on the bed. All of it. I covered the whole bed with it. And I—laid down on top of it and—fell asleep. It was funny. I've never done anything like that before. When I woke up I thought I was laying on leaves. Wet leaves.

SIMMS: Well, we all do strange things in the face of sudden fortune.

CECILIA: I should really get going. Thanks for the drink.

She moves to his desk and sets the glass of bourbon down on it, then turns to leave.

SIMMS: Miss Pontz—

She stops and turns to him.

CECILIA: What?

SIMMS: I was just wondering—since you've got the new dress and everything—if maybe you'd consider going to the Derby with *me*?

CECILIA: The Derby?

SIMMS: Yes.

CECILIA: That's in May, isn't it?

SIMMS: Yes. It is.

CECILIA: But we're in October.

SIMMS: That's right.

CECILIA: There's all those months in between.

SIMMS: We could—There's all that cash.

Pause.

CECILIA: No, I couldn't do that. That's not right.

SIMMS: We could travel.

CECILIA: No. I've got to get back.

SIMMS: We could take a ship.

CECILIA (*smiles*): No. Thanks anyway.

Pause.

SIMMS: If you change your mind—I'll meet you at the Clubhouse Turn.

CECILIA: That's in May?

SIMMS: Yes. First Saturday.

Lights dim. Cross-fade to Scene Three.

SCENE THREE

Cucamonga. Split-stage right—VINNIE's room. CARTER is lying in VINNIE's bed in T-shirt, boxer shorts, socks on, wrapped up tightly in blankets with the shakes. His teeth are chattering and he rolls slightly from side to side. His clothes are tossed in a heap on the foot of the bed. His cellular phone is on the floor in the briefcase. VINNIE is slowly perusing the room, checking out the sink and the absence of his dirty laundry. Pause as CARTER softly moans and rocks himself in the blankets.

VINNIE: Somebody, uh—did the laundry, I guess, huh? Dishes?

CARTER: Yeah.

VINNIE: You—hired somebody? I told you I didn't want that.

CARTER: No. Your girl. You know—Cecilia.

VINNIE: *She* did the laundry?

CARTER: Yeah.

VINNIE: She shouldn't of done that. Why'd you let her do that?

CARTER: She—wanted to.

VINNIE: So you brought her over here, I guess.

CARTER: Yeah. That was the plan. That's what you asked me to do. Remember?

VINNIE: We had a plan?

CARTER: You said you needed to talk to her! You were desperate.

VINNIE: That's right. I was. Desperate.

CARTER: What happened? Where were you?

VINNIE: I was—called away on business.

CARTER: Right.

Pause. VINNIE *moves over to him and stops.*

VINNIE: Why are you shaking, Carter? What's the deal? What is the problem here. Why are you in my bed?

CARTER: I'm—I don't know. At first I thought it was—the booze. You know—The—general shock to the system. I mean I'm not used to straight bourbon I guess, after all those years of nothing but cocktails.

VINNIE: You drank all my bourbon?

VINNIE *checks under bed, finds bourbon gone.*

CARTER: I'll get you another bottle.

VINNIE: Where? They don't carry Black Bush down at the 7–11, Carter. Where are you going to get me another bottle of Black Bush?

VINNIE *stands over* CARTER.

CARTER: Where did *you* get it?

VINNIE: I'll have to go a long way now. A long way out of my way.

CARTER: I'll find it for you. Don't worry.

VINNIE: I'll have to go on foot.

CARTER: I'll find it, all right! Don't worry about that!

Pause. VINNIE *moves around the space.*

VINNIE: You were messing with my stuff, too, weren't you?

CARTER: What stuff?

VINNIE: My boxes. They've been moved around. I can tell by the dust marks.

CARTER: No.

VINNIE: I can tell, Carter. (*Pause.*) Were you looking for something?

CARTER: No.

Pause.

VINNIE: So, where's Cecilia now? Where's she gone to?

CARTER: She—left. I don't know.

VINNIE: She came and left.

CARTER: Yeah.

VINNIE: She washed the dishes, did the laundry and left?

CARTER: Yeah.

VINNIE: What a gal.

CARTER: We waited for you. We waited for hours and then—

VINNIE: Drinking my bourbon.

CARTER: Well, she doesn't drink, you know—

VINNIE: Yes! I know that. I'm well aware of that!

CARTER: She wouldn't touch it.

VINNIE: Did you try to get her to?

CARTER: What?

VINNIE: Touch it?

CARTER: Look—

VINNIE: Get out of my bed, Carter.

CARTER: I'm—not sure I can.

VINNIE: Have you tried? Have you made a stab at it?

CARTER: My legs gave out.

> VINNIE *crosses to him. Stops at bed.*

VINNIE: What's going on with you?

CARTER: I don't know—I keep breaking out in cold sweats. My spine—

VINNIE: Your spine?

CARTER: My whole back gets frozen.

VINNIE: You want some uh—Alka-Seltzer Plus maybe? I've got some of that. Advil?

CARTER: No.

VINNIE: Tylenol? Extra-Strength.

CARTER: No.

VINNIE: Well, what, exactly, do you need, Carter? An ambulance?

CARTER: You went to Simms! Didn't you? You sold the stuff to Simms. Am I right? He called me, you know. Trying to deal behind your back. He told me the whole story.

> *Pause.*

VINNIE: I am exhausted. Every part of me is wiped out. I need my bed. Do you understand that? I need my bed now! This is *my* bed!

CARTER: And then you went to see Rosie. Didn't you? I know you did. I know you, Vinnie.

Pause.

VINNIE: Are you going to get out of my bed or am I going to have to get ugly?

Pause.

CARTER: I'll give it a try.

VINNIE: Ata boy! What a trooper.

CARTER *sits up slowly, shaking. He makes a great effort to swing his legs over the side and stand.* VINNIE *just watches him but makes no attempt to help.*

CARTER (*as he struggles*): What'd she say when she saw you! That must've been something, huh? Quite a little shock. Did she recognize you?

VINNIE: Yeah. She did.

CARTER: After all these years?

VINNIE: She knew, right off the bat.

CARTER: Just like old times, huh?

VINNIE: Nothing's changed.

CARTER: She's—still looking pretty good, isn't she? For a woman her age.

VINNIE: In the pink.

CARTER (*struggling to stand*): And she—She was glad to see you, I guess.

VINNIE: She was thrilled.

CARTER (*shaky, trying to remain standing*): Did she—throw her arms around you?

VINNIE: Yes. She did.

CARTER: Squeeze you?

VINNIE: She couldn't get enough of me.

CARTER (*still standing*): But you didn't—I mean, the kids were there. The nanny.

VINNIE: The kids were in school.

CARTER: But the nanny—Kelly.

VINNIE: She was there.

CARTER: So you didn't—I mean you just *hugged*, right? You and Rosie—You just—

CARTER *collapses back into the bed.* VINNIE *stands over him.*

VINNIE: Are you going to get out of my bed or not?

CARTER: I can't.

Pause. VINNIE *suddenly grabs* CARTER *by the ankles and jerks him off the bed, onto the floor.* CARTER *just lies there in a heap. Pause.* VINNIE *takes his coat off and lies down on the bed. He stretches and clasps his hands behind his head, stares at the ceiling. Pause.* CARTER *is shivering.*

CARTER (*from floor*): Could I—have a blanket?

VINNIE: No!

CARTER: I'm freezing.

VINNIE: You're pathetic.

CARTER: I don't know what it is—

VINNIE: You shouldn't fool with bourbon, Carter. It needs respect. You've got no respect.

CARTER: It's not that. It's not *just* that.

VINNIE: Oh. What is it then? Are you having a breakdown? A general crack-up? Is that it?

CARTER: I'm freezing.

VINNIE *snatches up one of the blankets and tosses it to* CARTER. CARTER *wraps himself up tightly in it and begins to roll slowly from side to side, lying on the floor.*

CARTER: Thanks.

Pause. CARTER *continues to rock slowly.* VINNIE *stares at the ceiling.*

VINNIE: How long do you expect these symptoms to continue?

CARTER: I don't know. It's never happened to me before. If I—should suddenly die, Vinnie—

VINNIE: You're not gonna die.

CARTER: I'm just saying—if I do.

VINNIE: You're not gonna suddenly die! You're not gonna get out of it that easy.

CARTER: No. I'm just saying—It happens all the time. Out of the blue. People—keel over with no prior indications. No symptoms whatsoever. It just—happens.

VINNIE: There's usually some hint of something. Some history.

CARTER: NOT IN MY CASE!!

Pause. CARTER *keeps rocking slowly, on the floor.* VINNIE *keeps staring at the ceiling.*

VINNIE: Could you stop that rolling around please. It's irritating. I'm trying to get some rest. I need rest now.

CARTER *stops rocking but keeps shaking. Pause.*

CARTER: So—What'd you and Rosie talk about?

VINNIE: The past.

CARTER: High school? The racetrack?

VINNIE: Just the past. In general.

CARTER: Did she—mention me at all?

VINNIE: No.

CARTER: Didn't she ask about me? I mean—she knew I was coming out here to see you and then you show up out *there*. Didn't she wonder about that?

VINNIE: I guess not.

Pause. CARTER *starts to rock back and forth again in the blanket.* VINNIE *stays on bed.*

CARTER: So—You must've made a killing off of Simms, huh? How much did he give you?

VINNIE: Bookoos.

CARTER: Well, it couldn't have been *that* much.

VINNIE: It was plenty.

CARTER: I know how much he makes a month so it couldn't have been all that much.

VINNIE: He cut me in on some shares. "Danzig". "Mr Prospector". Stuff like that. Big shares.

Pause.

CARTER: Do you think he's going to—

VINNIE: What?

CARTER: Get vindictive?

VINNIE: I wouldn't be at all surprised.

CARTER: You don't think he'll—go to the press or anything? Try to take it back to court?

VINNIE: I wouldn't be a bit surprised.

CARTER: He wouldn't go to the press. He'd never let those pictures out. They'd never print them anyway.

VINNIE: So, what're you worried about?

CARTER: I don't know. I just feel like—my number's up.

Pause. CARTER *keeps rocking slowly.*

VINNIE: When do you think you might *feel* like getting my bourbon?

CARTER: I can't walk.

VINNIE: Have you tried?

CARTER: I can hardly stand up.

VINNIE *sits up fast on bed.*

VINNIE: WILL YOU STOP THAT ROCKING BACK AND FORTH! STOP IT!

CARTER *stops.*

VINNIE (*from bed*): Now, sit up. Sit up, Carter!

CARTER *struggles to a sitting position. Very shaky.*

VINNIE: Now stand.

CARTER *struggles, but can't stand.* VINNIE *lunges off the bed, grabs* CARTER *by the chest and yanks him up to his feet, ripping the blanket away.*

VINNIE (*as he grabs* CARTER): STAND UP!

VINNIE *slaps him hard across the face. Just once. He holds him there.*

VINNIE: Now what in the hell's going on with you? I want you to put your clothes on. Pull yourself together and go out and buy me a bottle of bourbon! You *owe* me a bottle of bourbon.

CARTER: Where?

VINNIE: Just get dressed! I'll tell you *where* when you get your clothes back on.

CARTER *stumbles towards his clothes and starts trying to put them on but can't manage it.*

VINNIE: I have never seen anybody make such a big deal out of a hangover.

CARTER: It's not just that.

VINNIE: That's all it is! Amateur drinking! That's all it is!

CARTER: I'm completely cut off, Vinnie! I'm dying.

Pause.

VINNIE: What the fuck are you talking about? You weren't *dying* a couple a' days ago. You were full of yourself. You were strutting around here like a Banty rooster.

CARTER: I'm dying now.

VINNIE: Have you caught something? Have you found out that you *have* something?

CARTER: That would be easy, wouldn't it?

VINNIE: Easy?

CARTER: That would be understandable.

VINNIE: Do you want me to take you to the Emergency Room?

CARTER: You don't drive. Remember?

VINNIE: You can drive yourself. I'll go along with you. I'll ride shotgun.

CARTER: No.

VINNIE: No, what?

CARTER: I'm not going to the Emergency Room! It's past that.

VINNIE: You're giving up the ghost?

CARTER (*still struggling to dress*): I'm dying.

VINNIE: Stop saying that! (*Pause, mocks him.*) "I'm dying! I'm dying!" Good God—what a maudlin son-of-a-bitch you've turned out to be. What's happened to you? Have you been laying around here, feeling sorry for yourself? Moping in the dark? In *my* bed!

Pause.

CARTER: I can't get my pants on.

VINNIE: Jesus Christ!

CARTER: I can't.

VINNIE: Here—let me help you.

VINNIE *goes to him and holds his pants while* CARTER *attempts to put his legs in.*

VINNIE: Stop shaking and lift your leg! Just stop all that shaking and chattering.

CARTER (*as he tries to lift his leg*): I'm not going back there, you know.

VINNIE: Just lift your leg up!

CARTER: I'm not.

VINNIE: All right, you're not going back there. That's fine. You need to get dressed first.

CARTER: I'm not going back, Vinnie.

VINNIE: Will you lift your goddamn leg!

CARTER: I'm staying here.

> VINNIE *grabs his leg and forces it into the pants as* CARTER *hangs onto his shoulder. They struggle for balance, with the pants, going in small circles.*

CARTER: I'm going to change my name.

VINNIE: Good.

CARTER: I'm going to disappear.

VINNIE: That's great.

CARTER: I'm going to stay here with you.

VINNIE: No, you're not.

CARTER: I'll pay half the rent.

VINNIE: You're paying *all* of it now.

CARTER: I'll pay half.

VINNIE: Pull your pants up! Pull them up!

> VINNIE *turns loose of him and lets* CARTER *crash to the floor with his pants half way up. Pause.* VINNIE *watches him as* CARTER *crawls towards the blanket and reaches for it.*

VINNIE: You're not staying here, Carter. You're not staying here with me, if that's what you think. Where'd you ever get an idea like that?

CARTER (*pulling blanket around him*): We could maybe start up with the claimers again. Start brand new.

VINNIE: Those days are over, Carter. Long gone. Give it up.

CARTER: We made a couple a' mistakes. A couple a' bad mistakes.

VINNIE: Mistakes?

CARTER: Yeah. I admit that.

VINNIE: That's big of you.

CARTER: But we had a—partnership going there for a while. A real parternship. We were like—a team. We had a feeling between us. Didn't we, Vinnie? A real feeling.

Pause. VINNIE *moves toward bed, unbuttoning his shirt.*

VINNIE: I'm gonna lay down, Carter. I'm gonna lay down and I'm gonna fall asleep. I'm not gonna dream, I'm just gonna sleep. And when I wake up, I want you gone.

CARTER: I'll make you a deal then.

VINNIE: Sure. A deal. Another deal.

CARTER: I'll swap you straight across the board.

VINNIE: Swap me? Swap me for what?

CARTER: I'll take your place and you can have mine.

VINNIE: You're delirious. Why are you acting like this? It's time for you to go home, Carter!

VINNIE *sits on bed and starts taking off his shoes.*

CARTER: You can have it all. Even Rosie.

VINNIE: I don't want it all. I don't want anything you've got. You can stop sending me all your bullshit. All your TVs and Jap cars and corny golf shirts. All your guilt money. You can keep all that. Now if you don't get up off my floor, I'm gonna drag your ass out into the road and leave you there. I'm just gonna leave you laying out there, rolling and shaking and frothing at the mouth.

You can die with your tongue hanging out. I don't give a shit. Just get up off my floor! NOW!!

VINNIE *leaps at him from the bed and rips the blanket off* CARTER. *Pause as* VINNIE *hovers menacingly over him then returns to bed. He pulls the cardboard boxes out from under bed and starts taking out all his detective gear and putting it on: his shoulder holster and pistol, his badge, handcuffs, sneakers and overcoat.* CARTER *watches him from the floor.*

CARTER: What're you doing?

VINNIE: I'm going out to get a bottle.

CARTER: Now? You're not going to just leave me here, are you?

VINNIE: Yeah. That's what I'm gonna do.

CARTER: Wait a minute, Vinnie—

VINNIE: If you're not gone when I get back, I'm going to put you on the highway. In your underwear.

CARTER: Wait a second. Wait a second, Vinnie. This thing's bound to pass. I just need a little recovery time.

VINNIE: Time's up, partner.

CARTER: Let me stay here with you, Vinnie.

VINNIE: There's only one bed. And that's mine.

CARTER: I'll get a cot. A mattress, or something.

VINNIE: There's no room.

CARTER: I'll stay out of your way. I promise. I'll keep to myself. I'll stay completely—separate. If—If you have a girlfriend come over or something—If that Cecilia girl comes over, I'll—I'll go out on the lawn. I'll sleep out there. On the front lawn. I promise, Vinnie. I'll disappear. It'll be like—you won't even know I'm around.

VINNIE *has all his detective gear on by now. He moves to* CARTER *and stops, standing over him. Pause.*

VINNIE: I'll know.

CARTER: You're not gonna go out now, are you? I thought you were tired.

VINNIE: I'm suddenly inspired.

CARTER: What're you gonna do out there?

VINNIE: Surveillance. I'm working on a new case. It's a great feeling to embark on a case. It fills me with purpose. I'm my own man again. I move wherever I want to. I answer to no one. I cut through backyards and they never even know I'm there. I see it all, Carter. I'm a witness to it all. I see it through their windows. I see how helpless they all are. How they're all in the grips of something. And the great thing about this business is there's no end to it. It's bottomless. Just imagine that. Right now, right this very second, someone is cutting someone else's throat. It's amazing.

CARTER: Let me stay here just for a little while, Vinnie.

VINNIE: Go back home, Carter. The kids are waiting. It's Halloween.

VINNIE *exits, leaving* CARTER *alone on the floor. Pause as* CARTER *looks around the space. His chills intensify. He scrambles toward the blanket and wraps it around his shoulders. He holds himself across the chest and rocks slowly back and forth.*

CECILIA *enters from stage right with her purse still stuffed with* CARTER's *money and* VINNIE's *laundry all clean and folded. She's still wearing her Derby dress. She stops and stares at* CARTER. *He turns quickly toward her, shaking. Pause.*

CECILIA crosses to the bed and sets VINNIE's clean laundry on it. She turns towards CARTER with purse. She goes to CARTER and begins to take fistfuls of money out of purse and drops the money in front of CARTER in a pile.

CECILIA: Your money's all here. You can count it if you want to. I only used a little bit for sandwiches and tea. I'll pay you back, I promise. You should have told me the Derby was in May, Mr Carter. Why would you lie about something as simple as that?

CARTER's phone begins to ring. They both stare at it.

CECILIA: Do you want me to answer that?

Pause. CARTER just stares at phone. CECILIA moves to exit, stops and turns back to CARTER. Pause.

CECILIA: Somebody ought to answer that.

She exits. Phone keeps ringing. CARTER keeps staring at it without moving to answer. He shakes in his blanket as lights dim slowly. Phone rings into the blackness then stops.

Methuen World Classics *and*
Methuen Contemporary Dramatists

Methuen Modern Plays

include work by

Jean Anouilh
John Arden
Margaretta D'Arcy
Peter Barnes
Sebastian Barry
Brendan Behan
Edward Bond
Bertolt Brecht
Howard Brenton
Simon Burke
Jim Cartwright
Caryl Churchill
Noël Coward
Sarah Daniels
Nick Dear
Shelagh Delaney
David Edgar
Dario Fo
Michael Frayn
John Godber
Paul Godfrey
John Guare
Peter Handke
Jonathan Harvey
Iain Heggie
Declan Hughes
Terry Johnson
Barrie Keeffe
Stephen Lowe
Doug Lucie

John McGrath
David Mamet
Patrick Marber
Arthur Miller
Mtwa, Ngema & Simon
Tom Murphy
Phyllis Nagy
Peter Nichols
Joseph O'Connor
Joe Orton
Louise Page
Joe Penhall
Luigi Pirandello
Stephen Poliakoff
Franca Rame
Philip Ridley
Reginald Rose
David Rudkin
Willy Russell
Jean-Paul Sartre
Sam Shepard
Wole Soyinka
C. P. Taylor
Theatre de Complicite
Theatre Workshop
Sue Townsend
Judy Upton
Timberlake Wertenbaker
Victoria Wood

For a Complete Catalogue of Methuen Drama titles
write to:

Methuen Drama
215 Vauxhall Bridge Road
London SW1V 1EJ

or you can visit our website at:

www.methuen.co.uk